REMEMBER WHEN

A Boy's Tribute to His Lower-Middle-Class Family

By Stephen McKinley Simpson

ARGYLE FOX
PUBLISHING

TABLE OF CONTENTS

I dedicate this book to Mom, Dad,
my nephew, Ricky, and my daughter, Stephanie.

I also dedicate this book to daydreamers everywhere
who are still hanging on to a few of those dreams.

PROLOGUE

It was early in the summer of 2006 when I first became a boat owner. It wasn't your typical case of boat fever that made me the captain of a 1965 Larson Runabout. I wasn't even looking for a boat. My close and extended family nudged me into the helm, and I took the wheel.

The scene wasn't as gruesome as *The Godfather*, but it was an offer I couldn't refuse. The price was manageable: a simple trade. An uncle—one of the nudging family members—sold me his KZ 1000 Z1R years earlier. He wanted it back.

That motorcycle was a true classic. But it wasn't a very practical toy. When he mentioned the trade possibility, I'd been married four years. I hardly rode the bike, and it didn't bring much to the family table.

The swap seemed the right thing to do.

I told my wife, Heather, about my uncle's toy-swapping proposition. She was super motivated to move forward with the transaction. In her mind, boat equals family fun. Bike equals bachelor holding onto his single days.

My Kawasaki was capable of speeds in excess of 125 mph—or so I was told. The Larson Runabout's 50-horsepower Johnson outboard could reach 25 knots. With the wind at your back. In calm waters. With two or fewer people onboard. The boat was geared toward the lifestyle of a young family. The KZ was geared for death-hastening speed.

We enjoyed the boat immediately, and my decision brought some great family memories. We took it out almost every other weekend—if it was running. During our third boating excursion, I had a mental breakthrough, a moment of clarity.

We anchored in a quiet, sun-filled cove near our home. My wife relaxed, dangling a fishing line in one hand and a cold drink in the other. Our daughter, exhausted from hours of floating in a tube and playing in the water, napped peacefully under the Bimini shade.

I'm a true family man, I thought, my chest swelling. Then—Bam! Inspiration hit me like a strike of lightning.

I looked up at my wife. "I know what I want to become," I said. "I want to be a writer."

It felt like the clearest thought I'd ever had. I repeated it with conviction. It felt good to say it out loud. For the first time, I knew what I wanted to do with my life.

That was almost two decades ago. What's taken so long? To quote Luther in *48 Hours*, "I've been busy!" Busy raising a daughter, being a better-than-average husband, learning new disciplines, and navigating my way around this thing called life. I've also been paying half the bills and maintaining a home with my wife. So, give me a break! Chasing a dream while working a full-time job is not easy. Especially when that job sometimes takes me away from home.

If I'm being honest, being busy isn't the only reason I've put off writing. I was afraid. Scared of success. Fearful of failure. Frightened of putting myself and my creation out there for the world to see. Could I handle criticism? Could I handle the haters? Could I deal with seeing all my work and effort turned into a coaster at a coffee shop or an afterthought in the greater literary world?

But I eventually faced the fears and stopped using busyness as an excuse.

That day, I internally shouted those three words creators sometimes scream when they have a vision: "What the F%#K!" And with that, I began. Borrowing some writings from my mother and a few short stories I wrote years earlier, I began this book.

Once I started, I realized this may not just be my first book. It may be my last. As it turns out this writing stuff is worse than hard. It's the hardest thing I've ever done. Every time I thought of quitting, I thought of my parents and my siblings and all we lived through and endured. I didn't want to let them down by killing the story. The same goes for my wife and daughter. Having spent countless Saturdays writing in the basement, away from them both, the project would have been a useless sacrifice.

So yes, I wrote this book. Rather, I let it evolve over the decades. My family and I tell stories. I just put it all on paper.

The impetus for this book came shortly after Mother's death on September 2, 2014. However, the idea came during the fall of 2008. As my daughter grew from a toddler to a little girl, I looked back and thought about how different the world was thirty years before she was born.

Spoiler Alert: The above paragraph starts chapter four. Why? I'm a lazy writer. Sue me!

Anyway, very early in the twenty-first century I started getting after my mother. I hassled her about all she had seen and done for three quarters of the previous century. I often whined that those "Remember When" stories don't get told enough anymore.

Keeping It All in the Family

Mom was born in 1935. From afar, she witnessed wars, assassinations, the launch of the space age, the dawn of television, and the height and climax of the Cold War. Mom's generation galloped through the exorbitant good times of the '50s that led to the chaos and uncertainty of the '60s.

Some of the history Mom experienced hit close to home. Very close. The 1967 Detroit riots transpired a few miles from our front door. Mom seldom recalled the infamous riots. When she did, it unsettled her. Like Edith Bunker from TV's *All in the Family*, Mom would lean in close and recall sorrow and tragedy in a slow, loud whisper.

In the summer of 1967, Mom's fear simmered, as she cared for four young ones under her roof while civil unrest tore apart the once-great city of Detroit. Televised for the whole country to see, Detroit's bleakest hour started a downfall from which the downtown area never fully recovered.

To backtrack a bit, I need to give homage to one of the greatest sit-coms ever, *All in the Family*. The acting was good, the writing was better, and the plotlines were fearless. It was a real, era-accurate depiction of lower-middle-class life in the '70s. How do I know? Because we were the Midwest version of the Bunkers—just add four sons and take away one meathead. My mom was Edith and my father a younger, real-life Archie. Dad even had a sacred living room chair that was to be occupied only by him. Fuzzy, soft, and durable, that hospital-green chair had enormous arms like miniature jungle gyms. We climbed all over that chair . . . when Dad wasn't home.

On special occasions such as Christmas or when nothing good was on TV, those furry chair arms transformed into seats—even with Dad in the chair. One brave soul would ease a butt cheek onto the angled, green fuzzy arm. Peeking through his bifocals, Dad would slant his eyes up at the brave little Simpson and stare for a long, silent moment, as if to say, "You can sit there, for now."

That was the signal. We were safe. Victory was ours!

Looking back, I suspect he thought, "You can get close to your dad, but don't get too comfortable and don't make a habit of it." If I wanted his fatherly attention or to feel close to him, I had to seize the moment when presented. Squeezing onto the green chair with him was about as good as it got. My brothers Tom and Vic attempted the chair arm maneuver often and failed more than they succeeded.

Dad was so much like Archie Bunker, it's no surprise *All in the Family* was one of his favorite shows. Archie despised and distrusted most minorities. So did Dad. My dad, like Archie, hated change and longed for bygone eras. Both men were world-class get-off-my-lawn, everyone-is-out-to-get-me cynics. The most glaring similarity was how both men regarded their wives. Edith and Elaine were very good women that neither man appreciated or deserved.

Setting Expectations

This is no history book. The objective is to share family stories and spawn memories that carry us back to a simpler time. Compiled on the following pages are several short stories that tell how one lower-middle-class family made it through to the other side.

A Boy's Tribute to His Lower-Middle-Class Family

I want to illustrate how it was back in the not-so good-old days while highlighting bright spots along the way. As meager as things were, it could have been far worse. We never missed a meal. We always had clothes to wear and a roof over our heads. While our struggles were typical for our era, these tales should be repeated to appreciate what we now take for granted. I think each new generation should take a tour of how things used to be. Open the memory catalog from time to time and pluck out a story to share with some young people. Maybe they'll listen. They may even grow to appreciate where we came from and where they now reside.

In my early twenties I attended a motivational seminar featuring the captivating Jim Rohn. During his opening he said, "The best thing about sharing these great ideas and stories over and over is that I get to listen again too." Or he said something like that. I don't remember his exact words. Forgive me, but the message is what matters. Good ideas and good stories always stand the test of time.

My daughter and my nephew yawn and sigh when my siblings and I rehash memories from decades past. To their credit, both youngsters listen most of the time. They raise questions that cause my siblings and I to hesitate and appreciate the lives we lived.

In recent interactions with people a decade younger or older than me—I'm a spry fifty-two—I find I'm not alone. A majority of Gen-Xers feel as I do. We carry a constant desire to tell current and recent generations, "It wasn't always like this!"

We couldn't always access the entire planet in our hands. Instead, we connected to the world through TVs with thick glass and a picture tube. The list of channels could be counted on one glove and a mitten. The big, heavy box emitted a snowy, dull picture. Voices, sound effects, and music crackled through a single four-inch speaker. The programs ranged from tolerable to unwatchable. Information and news came from only a few sources.*

I think that may have been a good thing. Remember newspapers? Remember the weekday nightly network news programs? Does anyone under age sixty-five still sit down and watch the six-thirty news?

Once any generation gets four or five decades under their belt, the tune is the same. It seems every Gen-Xer makes frequent use of the worn-out cliché: "It was a simpler time."

We used a key to open the car door. We actually stuck the key into the door or trunk. There was no magic button to pop up the locks from outside. Once the gas needle on the old Chrysler stopped moving, we made off-the-cuff calculations in our head. It was a way of life to guess how far an eighth of a tank would carry us. Travel plans changed with every turn. We eagerly watched the analog fuel gauge sway with every bump and fall to E around every sharp left turn. "Oh, now it's half a tank—wait, no, it's empty!"

Finicky carburetors had to be prodded to come to life on cold days. If the car started, it took fifteen minutes of gas-pedal feathering to reach our destination. Put the pedal down too aggressively or too many times, and the car wouldn't start. The carb was flooded. After waiting twenty minutes, we'd try again, fingers crossed that the battery would cooperate.

January in Michigan was cruel to clunkers. With older car battery technology and our subpar family fleet, turning the ignition key was akin to playing the slots. Three or four good cranks, then the throttle finessing would fail or the battery would die.

Static on the car radio was expected and a traveling challenge. Lose a station during a good song and it might be days before you got another chance to hear that tune again. Eight-track tapes and cassettes were no better. After thirty or forty playbacks, the tape stretched, pulling the sound quality down. Leave an audio or video tape in a hot car for a few hours, and the polyester type plastic film would almost liquify, leaving a misshapen, unusable pile of plastic that would never be enjoyed again.

Digital music and movie formats were decades away. The only digital things we had were two thirteen-inch computer screens in the school library and the display on our Casio calculators.

Hot water was so scarce we rationed it. We kept showers to three minutes and hoped only the last two people showered with cold water. When Mom was a teenager in the '50s, she only showered once a week. To get hot water, she had to stoke a furnace and wait twenty minutes as

14

the water chugged up from the basement to the second floor. The water went from cold to lukewarm to scalding hot in just under a half an hour. What convenience!

Challenging the Next Generation

The mid- and late-twentieth century was a different time, a tougher time. To confirm another cliché, it built character. We were stronger for living through the '60s, '70s, and '80s, just as The Greatest Generation was made great by surviving the Great Depression and winning World War II.

What will give the current generation strength, courage, and fortitude? Fending off social-media bullies? Surviving a two-hour wi-fi outage? Deciding what to binge-watch on Netflix this weekend?

I worry this life of convenience and instant gratification is making our future leaders soft and unappreciative. I'm not alone in this fear. Fellow get-off-my-lawn members share the same concerns. Granted, today's kids are smarter than any previous generation, but will big brains be enough?

What if the big one hits? What if a major war or worldwide epidemic sideswipes this generation?

What if a weird, unknown virus from China breaks out and no one knows what to do? Will the current generation make reasonable, data-based decisions after considering multiple options based on various age groups and vulnerabilities? Will they remain calm and listen to all opinions or will they silence different opinions and create mandates that hurt children and cripple businesses?

Will they ask questions or will they comply, do as they're told and follow Big Brother down the rabbit hole of deceit? Will they accept leadership responsibilities and take accountability when things don't go as planned? Or will they make rash decisions based not on science but on fear and paranoia?

Will the majority look for a phone app to get us out of harm's way? ("Send for an Uber, I don't know where the spare tire is or what to do with it!") Or will most of them order food from the comfort and safety of their parents' basement?

Okay, you get the idea. This is a book that looks backward. I'll save my angst and conspiracy theories for future books. Perhaps a fictional thriller or a dystopian day-after scenario. Until then, thanks for taking a chance and picking up this book. I hope you enjoy it thoroughly.

I wrote these words for my family and to clear my head. I also did it for everyone out there who feels like I do. This is for anyone and everyone who occasionally pauses, lets out a deep sigh, and ruminates over those two words:

Remember When.

Part One

MEET MY PARENTS

Chapter One

DAD

My father, William Loring, was born in 1931 and raised in a holler just outside of Charleston, West Virginia, in a place called South Park. His parents were resourceful, and their occupations varied. If memory serves me, my grandpa fixed watches and did other repair work. He also worked at the railroad for a season. Dad used to help him collect scrap metal for money. Grandma cooked, cleaned, and made clothes. She ran a boarding house at one point, but I think that was during one of her frequent separations from Grandpa.

Dad's parents didn't follow career paths or have a normal relationship. Grandma was only fourteen when she got hitched to Grandpa. That brought her formal education to an end after seventh grade. She became a mother one short year later.

Money was always very tight, and anything other than food and basic shelter was a luxury. No surprise there. It was a holler in Depression-era West Virginia. Early in the twentieth century, the Simpsons' life was emblematic of the era and their locale.

Dad didn't have a good relationship with his father. According to Dad, Grandpa had two moods: mean and meaner. Starting at age fourteen, Grandpa went to work in a coal mine. Perhaps his cheerful disposition got its roots there. When Dad once spilled some paint in the workshop, Grandpa spanked him with a belt immediately afterward. To make sure the little guy got the message, Grandpa spanked him again before bed.

Dad's relationship with his mother was better. In fact, he spent most of his time as a young boy steering clear of his father, often hiding in Grandma's shadow.

Dad rarely discussed his childhood. His few fond memories were buried under dozens of bad ones. He did love sharing one wintertime story though.

As a young boy, Dad was proud of his steel-and-wood runner sled. In all likelihood, it was probably made of scrap metal or started as a junked sled that Dad and Grandpa refurbished. That didn't matter. According to Dad, it was the fastest in the holler.

He and his friends often walked their sleds up the roadside hill to race down. They went so fast that stopping or maintaining control was almost impossible. Once the hill was so icy and slick that—unable to slow down—he slid under a stopped school bus at the bottom of the holler.

At this point in the story, my mother always chimed in. "Why weren't you on the bus, Bill?" she asked.

Dad had a few precious childhood recollections that involved his two sisters, whom he loved dearly. I remember a picture of my father, approximately four years old, on a pony. His sister Lois stands on his right, her arm around his back to ensure he doesn't fall. That photo was one of Dad's prized possessions.

Bright spots in my father's adolescence involved playing and running in the school yard. Dad was small, but he got picked for recess activities because he could run like the wind. During football or baseball games the kids would call out, "Look at little Willy Run!" Dad's legs held up for years. When I was a kid, the fifty-year-old, two-pack-a-day smoker beat me in a sprint.

When Dad alluded to his upbringing, it typically involved money. Dad often sounded like a bitter old man. "You kids don't know how good you have it," he said. "When I was a kid we were lucky to get some used shoes about every two years. Would you look at these prices?" He frequently reminded us that every stitch of clothing he wore as a child was either handmade by Grandma or handed down from another family member or neighbor.

With so many strikes against him as a young boy, it's remarkable that Dad accomplished anything as an adult. Exhibit A: Staying married longer than Mom should have allowed. My parents' union was survival of the most unfit. It lasted more than twenty-five years with help from hopes, dreams, and an unhealthy dose of alcohol. Dad even helped Mom raise five kids. Well, sort of.

He did another significant thing that surprised me. Dad made it to my wedding. An angel named Cloise, one of my father's few friends, escorted Dad to New York and kept him in line the whole time. Cloise was bigger than Dad. They respected one another, but Cloise called the shots. Cloise made sure "nasty" Bill Simpson didn't show up to the party.

Dad was happy I met someone, and he liked my wife, although he struggled to recall her name. After six years of this uncomfortable confusion, Dad stopped trying to address Heather by her name. Instead, he nodded, said "Hey," then spit out a few syllables of mumbled gibberish.

If it's not obvious yet, let me say it plainly: Dad had flaws. It's impossible to pinpoint the one that led to his unfulfilled, somewhat regretful life. He was the middle child and the runt of the litter, the oldest boy who struggled mightily to please his old man. I suspect many of Dad's issues were generated by a lack of fatherly love and other bad childhood experiences.

One of Dad's biggest flaws was occasionally his best characteristic. Dad was a dreamer. Dropping out of school after ninth grade, his options were limited. There in the coal capital, he could drive a truck in and out of the coal mines or transport the black-ash cargo on the railroad. Neither option compelled my father. Though not the brightest kid around, Dad knew enough to dream of escaping West Virginia.

The Adventure Begins

Bill Simpson liked cars, boats, speed, and action. He had ambition and aspired to be his own boss. Fulfilling those dreams near his childhood home was impossible, so he set his sights on the Motor Capital of the World.

In early 1947, my father and his friend Dave set out to reach Detroit,

Michigan, making their way north to the Great Lake State in hoboing, hitchhiking style. As Dad's story of the journey changed with each telling, I suspect several laws were broken along the way. The first months in Detroit, however, were always cited as a brave and sobering reminder of how tough life was back then.

Dave and my father spent their evenings scouting park benches or sneaking into junkyards for old cars to slumber in. During the day they labored as the lowest member of the restaurant hierarchy: dishwashers— or "pearl divers," as they were called. The job paid a few bucks a day for a twelve-hour shift and guaranteed at least one free meal. Dad admitted to perusing trays that came back to the kitchen, eyeballing unfinished dinners for snack opportunities. When he saw something tasty, he jammed the morsels into his pocket for later consumption. It was a glamorous life. When not washing dishes, Dad sought more gainful employment.

The hunt for better pay led Dad to a few more restaurant jobs. He also sold cars and worked at the DeSoto automobile factory for a short time. With more money, Dad and Dave entered the exotic boarding-house lifestyle.

In the late '40s and early '50s, Detroit was one of the most prosperous cities in the world. Opportunities in the auto industry were endless. Dad fantasized of owning a car dealership and was full of dreams and determination; however, he also had challenges. Some challenges were a product of his shoddy upbringing. Others came from a lack of discipline and an insatiable desire to have a good time. Then, there was his draft card.

Chapter Two

MOM

My mother, Elaine Elizabeth, was born in Detroit in 1935. She grew up in the Highland Park area in a four-family flat that provided cramped but adequate accommodations.

Sometimes, the walls of her flat closed in as extended family or "houseguests" made the flat their home for weeks or months at a time. Census data confirmed the tiny domicile housed numerous adults through the years. When these guests stayed over, Mom stayed on the couch. She didn't mind—at least not for certain family members. Her younger brother had an almost permanent daybed in the dining room until he was thirteen.

Mom's parents were simple, quiet people. Grandpa was a school custodian for the Detroit Board of Education and a man of very few words. As kids, we listened well when Grandpa spoke, because conversation with him was limited. He kept up with local sports and enjoyed gardening. I believe he even won some awards in Detroit for his horticulture prowess. That gene passed directly to my mother. Her ability to grow anything anywhere is legendary.

I never knew my grandma, who died before my second birthday. She was one-hundred percent Finish and represents the only ethnicity I know for certain runs through my blood.

Mom was proud of her Finnish heritage and gloated about things Finland is known for. While making nissua bread every December, she would repeatedly call out, "Sisu!", a word meant to describe a Finn's stoic determination. Mom loosely translated it to mean "Finn Power." She would then state proudly, "Finland is the only country that paid war reparations from World War II. Finns always pay their debts." After a few drinks, she would also remind us that "Finland has one of the best education systems in the world and is also the country of origin for the heart-rate monitor and the sauna."

Mom's parents were typical. They didn't want Mom to marry the guy she was stubbornly going to marry. Mom's parents wanted the best for their two children but were never going to fill their heads with unrealistic dreams or aspirations. Go to school then go to work or go after a sensible career.

One time as a teenager I went to my grandparents' house to cut the grass. It should have been an easy task. But Grandpa complicated things. He was very set in his ways and specific about how things should be done. There were seventeen steps Grandpa laid out for me to follow before I got the lawnmower out of the garage. If I didn't follow all the maintenance tips and procedures before firing up the mower, Grandpa didn't want me mowing his lawn.

Mom told me that Grandma loved sweets and always had a pastry or two stuffed into her purse or coat pocket. Most Saturday evenings my grandparents stopped by so Mom could set Grandma's hair for church in the morning. They would stay for a few hours to drink coffee and enjoy cookies, crackers, or other treats. After Grandma and Grandpa's late-night departure, Mom often found goodies and maybe some food in a bag left behind. My grandma's attempt at being sly and generous.

In contrast to my father's upbringing, Mom had a wealth of happy childhood memories. As a young girl, she spent large portions of her summers at the farm where her mother was raised near Kaleva. A small community in northwestern Michigan, Kaleva was a refuge for Finnish settlers in the early 1900s. In time, it became home to a creamery and other agricultural endeavors. The soil was sufficient for most crops, but cucumbers and pole beans thrived there. Salted cucumbers left Kaleva by the trainload destined for pickle factories.

Kaleva is also known for the John J. Makinen Bottle House and

Museum. To be honest, that's all there is to know about Kaleva, which is likely why the Finns adored the quaint, secluded town. "That is just how the Finnish people like it," my mother told us on more than one occasion.

My great grandparent's farmhouse was on the outskirts of town, but they later moved to a house in town. Both houses lacked running water and had outhouses. However, the house in town did have electricity.

Like most childhood memories from that uncomplicated time, stories about food were front and center. Mom smiled as she explained how her mother and aunts picked blueberries. The berries grew like crazy behind the farmhouse on the edge of the swamp. The aroma from blueberry pies baking on the wood stove was heaven to my mother. The wild onions— or "smelly plants" as Mom called them—had a less pleasant smell, but Grandma picked them to go with her chicken dinners.

Mom's rehashed tales often included the best, freshest chicken dinners during her farmhouse visits. Her Grandma Maria would kill chickens by wringing their necks behind the barn. While the kids knew about this fowl—pardon the pun—end-of-life ceremony, they weren't permitted to watch.

For meals, adults dined around a big, tall table. Children ate quietly to the side or in another room around a small, low table. My great grandmother, however, ate alone, sitting on the second or third step of the stairs inside. She also drank coffee from a saucer rather than a cup. According to one of Mom's aunts, that's how Great Grandma cooled her coffee before drinking it.

My mom had a good relationship with her grandparents. Unlike her grandma, Mom's grandpa spoke and understood English, so Mom talked with him more than her grandmother. Mom remembered laughing with and being teased by her grandfather. A tall, thin man, he would pick Mom up and raise her high in the air until she laughed and sometimes got dizzy.

Farm to Town

My mother's pre-teen and adolescent years, though more pleasant than my father's, were peppered with sad and scary events.

In those years, Mom's grandfather became very ill with cancer. He was brought to a Detroit hospital for surgery. Unfortunately, the cancer spread so aggressively that the surgeon took one look and then sewed him back up. Mom's grandfather died shortly thereafter. His death brought the end of Mom's summers at the Kaleva farm. She still visited her grandma, but the visits took place in town and were not the same.

Soon after becoming a widow, Mom's grandma lost her ability to handle the harsh mid-Michigan winters. So, she came to the Detroit area and spent three weeks at each sibling's house. Each spring, she returned to Kaleva. During the winter visits, Mom's mother and grandmother fought—a lot. When simple matters such as Great Grandma's infrequent bathing, lack of appetite, and increasing memory lapses turned into major arguments, the family decided she needed full-time nursing care.

"Grandma was a dear, sweet woman," my mother said years later. "She was simply lost without her husband and her home."

Mom only visited her grandma once at the nursing home. Mom felt ashamed to see her in "that place." It's no wonder Mom was adamant we never submit her to such a fate. "You will not," she said, "under any circumstances put me into a nursing home to rot and die." She didn't have to worry. A nursing home would not be her final destination.

Making a Way

During the Second World War, Mom's parents bought a bunch of war bonds to save for a house. As my mother attested, there was no such thing as "No money down" in those days. Funds were limited, but Mom was promised a two-wheeler for her eleventh birthday. Sadly, her mom was in the hospital at the time. The birthday bike Mom wanted so badly was no longer a financial priority.

Mom later learned that her mother was hospitalized for a nervous breakdown. Before the hospital stay, Mom recalls a vague, scary recollection of her mom threatening to kill herself with a knife. To protect her, Grandpa took Grandma to the "special hospital" on East Grand Boulevard.

As years passed, Mom realized the war bonds were used to pay the hospital bill. Without the bonds as a down payment on a house, Mom's family remained in that small flat until 1961. The two-week hospital stay involved seven or eight shock treatments, which weren't cheap. Grandpa advised young Elaine she would not be getting her bike that year. He also explained that when Grandma returned home, she would require help remembering things because of how the treatments affected her memory.

The following year, Mom got her two-wheeler for her twelfth birthday. Sixty-seven years later, when asked to recall her favorite birthday story, getting that bike was at the top of Mom's memory podium.

As a young girl whose family lived a meager life, Mom's days were scheduled and routine. Summers meant traveling north to the country to visit friends and family. School years were spent at Longfellow Elementary, where Miss Allen, Mr. Reid, and Miss Treager provided a thorough education. Miss Allen, Mom's fifth-grade teacher, was the toughest. She was also Mom's favorite. At that time, Mom was a self-proclaimed "Miss Goody Two Shoes." This fact was affirmed by Miss Allen, and Mom quickly became her favorite. Mr. Reid was an oddity, Mom's first male teacher. Miss Treager taught sixth grade. She sat on her desk while teaching. For that, she was dubbed strange by the students.

Mom's grade-school and intermediate-school experience was mostly uneventful. She was excessively shy and embarrassed easily. She was terrified of getting called on in class and never raised her hand, even if she knew the answer.

At an elementary school program, Mom was one of the bills in the Bill of Rights, but she couldn't remember which one. She got her lines out without making a total fool of herself, but she was certain everyone was looking at her and laughing.

In sixth grade, coaxed by her father and her cousin Don, Mom started violin lessons. Oh, how she hated dragging that violin around! She didn't hate the violin. She just hated practicing when everyone else was playing outside.

After school every Friday, Mom got on a city bus to go downtown to the Wurlitzer Building. "No one in their right mind would let a kid do that today," Mom told me when I was in middle school. "But back then it was safe!"

Her weekly lessons were with Pasquale Briglia, one-time concert master of the Detroit Symphony Orchestra. During the bus ride home from practice, Mom always hoped her dad would be waiting for her, especially during winter. Mom feared walking alone at night and swore that the three blocks from the bus stop to her home stretched on for miles.

With three choices of where to attend high school, Mom made the easy choice: Cass Tech. Her friends Connie and Phyllis signed up for the pre-nursing curriculum there, and another friend enrolled for the school's outstanding music department. The school had an excellent reputation, and all the smart kids went there. Students had to choose a curriculum, so Mom—with no career goals or reasoning—chose science.

This proved a major scholastic mistake. In her second year, Mom failed a class for the first time, Chemistry 2. Her low self-esteem took another blow. Mom negotiated with her counselor to transfer into the poly-tech curriculum. This was essentially a standard high school course of study, though more credits were required for graduation.

A high school student with no particular aspirations, Mom broadened her circle of friends. She even stuck her toe into the sea of boys and began dating. First was Ron Jones. He lived on the east side but rode Mom's bus after school and worked at the grocery store in her neighborhood. Ron was a very nice boy with a slight stutter. This gave Mom secondhand embarrassment. Their dating life included football games and movies, getting to both by taxicab.

After Ron came Al Lewellen. He was tall, thin, and gangly. Mom's self-esteem perked up when she snagged Al. Mom's best friend, Phyllis, had a crush on Al, but Mom reeled him in. Al came with the added benefit of access to his family's car. At just fifteen years young my mother went on her first car date with a boy!

Now Mom's social circle really filled in. Nancy Reasons, Delores Culp, and Ginny Corby all lived in Mom's neighborhood. By dating a boy who could drive, Mom's status among them elevated a notch or two.

Delores's parents had a campsite and a tent at a place Mom called Homestead. Homestead featured a lake for swimming and fishing, and the group of friends—usually driven by Al—often went there on the weekend to do what teenagers at that time did.

Memorial Day weekend at the lake in 1951 was unforgettable for young Elaine. Bob Connors, an older guy with a convertible, drove a group to Homestead. Bob brought a housemate who was going steady with Ginny Corby. By the end of that weekend, Ginny was in this man's rearview mirror. As Mom recalled the story, when this "short but cute" man climbed out of the convertible, "ZAP! I was hit." Hit with what? Who knows. But that was the weekend she met my father, Bill Simpson.

Chapter Three

ABANDON COURTSHIP

In typical teenage fashion, Mom wound up in a short-lived, yet very uncomfortable love triangle. She was smitten with my father the moment she laid her big hazel eyes on him. This was a problem because Dad was going steady with Mom's friend Ginny. Further complicating things, Mom's steady boyfriend, Al, was coming to the lake. When Al arrived, she ended their relationship quickly and decisively. She was already bored of Al after just a few months, and Bill was the shiny new thing. Granted, she didn't say these exact words to Al, but that was the message.

Dad paid her the attention she sought and made her laugh. By the end of the weekend, Mom was swept off her feet by five-foot-five, 140-pound Bill Simpson. His smooth-talking southern charm and advanced age added to his mystique. Mom fell hard. So did Dad.

As far as I know, Ginny and my mother remained friends. In a strange twist, Dad and Al became good friends later. The two men even roomed together for a time. Perpetually self-conscious, Mom feared Al and man-child Bill were swapping stories about her behind her back.

Soon after my parents got together, an unofficial sixsome of friends was set. The three couples—Delores and Bob, Nancy and Ray, and Elaine and Bill—spent that summer and the next few years hanging out together. Weekends were whiled away at soda shops and diners, where the couples sipped coffee and sucked down Vernors. Lake excursions and trips to the drive-in filled their evenings. However, movies were rarely viewed with all the back-seat necking and other teenage tomfoolery.

Even then, Mom noticed the two other couples got along better than she and my father. My parents fought early and often. The good news is that habit only continued for another four decades.

Early signs of a rocky road were in plain sight, but Mom ignored them. She was in love—somewhat with Bill, but mostly with the idea of being in love. The few times Mom's parents let her stay the weekend at Homestead, the girls would pass out in Nancy's tent while the guys got "roaring drunk," according to Mom.

Somehow, my parents made it through their first tumultuous year relatively unscathed. Mom was a junior in high school, and Dad was a twenty-year-old boy. He was indifferent to most of my mom's wishes and commitments she'd made to herself, uninterested in anything important to my mother. Her commitment to my aloof father underwent its first test in the summer of 1952 when the Army came calling.

Introducing Uncle Sam

Dad and Ray Kangas, Nancy's boyfriend, got drafted when school let out for the summer. Bonded by having their boys borrowed by Uncle Sam, Nancy and Mom were inseparable. The two girls sat together on weekends, writing letters to their homesick boys. Although neither of the young men died in the army, Mom and Nancy dubbed themselves The War Widows. Knowing Mom, I'd guess they thought it made them sound more grown up.

Dad was stationed in Kentucky at Fort Knox and often returned to Michigan on weekend passes. Sometimes the weekends were good for the young couple, sometimes not so much.

While Dad and Ray were stuck in the Army, Delores and Bob tied the knot. Ray's brother filled in for Ray as the best man. Mom served as Delores's maid of honor. At the time, Mom's insecurity caused her to think Delores only chose her because she was Protestant. The other candidates, Ginny and Nancy, were Catholic. As such, both were prohibited from standing in a non-Catholic wedding.

Early in the fall of 1952, Dad's platoon prepared to go to Korea. In a lucky-son-of-a-bitch twist of fate, my father suffered a hernia during boot camp. While his platoon headed overseas, Dad was left behind in Kentucky awaiting surgery.*

Before the procedure, Dad slipped away to Michigan for a few days. He went to Al's apartment and called Mom with an elaborate plan for Mom to skip school and spend the morning with her soldier boy. Mom thought it odd. Dad's past trips were on Fridays. This was a Wednesday.

The next day, Mom and her friend, Connie, rode the city bus to school. Then Mom hopped on another city bus to Delores and Bob's apartment. Dad showed up in Al's car. After a few niceties with Bob and Delores, my parents went for a ride.

Mom, still too young and naïve to possess a fully functioning woman's intuition, had good reason to feel odd about Bill's midweek visit. Mom wasn't sure what happened first—the fighting or Dad's declaration. Either way, he insisted that after he recovered from his impending hernia surgery he was getting shipped overseas. With that certainty in his future, Dad wanted more freedom as he traveled the globe. Being tied to a girl back in the States wasn't part of the plan. Oh, they could keep in touch, and he begged her to keep the letters coming, but Dad suggested they both start seeing other people, or whatever assholes said back then when they wanted to start screwing around.

Knowing Dad, I imagine his declaration was an ultimatum: "If we don't start doing this, I'm gonna start doing that." Whatever the exact words were, they devastated a young, fragile Elaine. But hey, if the guy was going to shit all over Mom's heart, at least he did it in person.

As the joy-ride-turned-break-up journey around Detroit heated up, Dad sped up. The conversation turned into an all-out scream fest. To make a point during the debate, Mom leaned against the passenger door to face my father. She was attempting to gauge his level of emotion as he tiptoed around her interrogation.

Dad, who struggled with words and emotional expression, countered

---

Apparently, hernias run in my family. I recently got my hernia ticket stamped. Just another bump (literally) on the road of life.

in his own special way. Attempting to scare her and show off his driving expertise, he took a sharp curve way too fast. As he navigated the car around the left turn, the passenger door launched open, and Mom was ejected from the car.

Though battered and bruised, Mom was still in one piece. Both were so scared they contemplated going to the hospital as if discussing a trip to the dry cleaners or the corner market. The day's rap sheet was growing, and Mom didn't want to face any of it. She'd lied to her parents, skipped school, and now this! Covering up this crime proved impossible. Mom's bloody chin and heavily bruised arms forced Dad to do the right thing.

Because of Mom's age and the suspicious circumstances surrounding her injuries, the hospital declined to treat her without parental consent.

As an aside, this wasn't the only car accident Mom had no business walking away from. She later survived a spectacular end-over-end roll-over crash that killed my sister's dog Kobe. My mom, however, age sixty-six, was up and walking, albeit gingerly, only a few hours later.

Mom was—to put it crassly—a tough broad. She washed floors on her hands and knees for hours seemingly without pain. For decades she picked weeds and cultivated her gardens in a thirty-degree, bent-over position that would make an occupational therapist wince.

All that toughness showed itself after Dad wrecked the car while trying to wreck his relationship with Mom. Speaking of . . .

With Elaine's mom working part-time on the sales floor at Hudson's, Bill and Elaine had only one option. It was a call my father dreaded like no other. He called Elaine's father at work. The stern, quiet man granted permission for the hospital to treat his daughter. There was just one condition. After Mom got treated, Dad was to bring her straight home, where they would both wait for Grandpa to finish his workday.

Grandpa, realizing the day had scared Mom severely, must have gone easy on her. Her punishment wasn't serious enough for Mom to remember, and she was allowed to see Dad that weekend. The whole ordeal also scared Dad. He stayed in Detroit another two days to ensure his estranged girlfriend was all right. As a kind of ceremonious wind down to the relationship, they went to the movies with Delores and Bob.

REMEMBER WHEN

Mom was eager to put the incident behind her. She wanted to forget about her concrete faceplant and involuntary exit from Al's car. This proved difficult when she returned to class on Monday with two huge black eyes and scars on her face and arms. In a feeble attempt to avoid teenage ridicule, Mother donned a pair of sunglasses. Rumors that Mom was abused, recovering from a fight, or got involved in some other socially unacceptable activity spread like wildfire through the halls of Cass Tech.

Grandpa sent Elaine to the school counselor with a note detailing her three days of truancy. I've always imagined she was forced to pin a large sheet of paper to her shirt the entire day. The paper contained a single four-letter word in bold letters: "LIAR."

The counselor read the note from Mom's father, and Mom gave every mortifying detail of the ordeal. Looking at her, the counselor came to the same conclusion as Mom's parents: She had suffered enough. Elaine was dismissed without punishment.

Afterward, Dad returned to Fort Knox where the term AWOL was explained to him in short order. One day passed and my mother received her first telegram. She was instructed to call the Red Cross in Kentucky. She obeyed and was asked to verify Dad's whereabouts and the circumstances that led to him being away "too long" without permission.

While Dad's platoon shipped off to Korea, Dad underwent hernia surgery. He eventually got sent overseas, but not to Korea. In the meantime, he recovered from his procedure and got sent to truck-driving school. Nine months after the break-up, Dad's truck-driving qualification punched his ticket to Germany. There, he drove buses and moved large equipment all over Europe in cargo trucks.

The time away from Dad was a blessing for Mother. She regarded it as one of the best times of her life.

With Bill out of the picture, Mom dated other guys, but never for too long, and no relationship ever turned serious. She went to dances and parties and her senior prom with Ron Seldon. Mom wanted to have a ball her senior year, and she did. The result was a general aloofness toward Ron and anything else that threatened her new carefree, one-day-at-a-time attitude.

34

At this time, Mom partied and did "wild and crazy things." In the mornings before class, she and her friends drank coffee and smoked their silly heads off at Sherwood's restaurant close to school. Mom had such a good time with her friends that she began leaving school early to meet up with them. She got caught and almost didn't graduate as a result. Fortunately, she was given an opportunity to make up for missed time by her combination home economics/woodworking teacher. Mom jumped at the chance to hide the indiscretion from her parents and get her diploma.

The Big Apple, the Bigger Choice

The highlight of Mom's senior year was the class trip to New York City. These trips were much rarer than they are today. It was not a cheap trip. Between working part-time and getting some help from her parents, Elaine gathered enough money to make it to NYC. Grandpa even splurged and gave mom a new set of luggage.

In New York, Mom felt she was a world away from Highland Park and the halls of Cass Tech. Her class went to Radio City and saw the Rockettes live. They stayed at the Henry Hudson Hotel, four to a room with a single adult chaperone responsible for three rooms.

One night they went to a movie. Another night they skipped out on a telecast they were supposed to attend. Their curfew was one in the morning. The teenagers had a grown-up sense of freedom being so far from home. Seven couples hung out looking for trouble and Mom paired up with her future prom date, Ron Seldon. Billy Eckstine was playing at the Band Box on 52nd, and all seven couples wanted to go. They pooled together their remaining money and had enough to get in and order a bottle of scotch. Mom did not enjoy the scotch.*

Another day in New York was spent with just her roommates. The girls went shopping between scheduled tours. All four girls bought big

---

Around age fifty, Mom was diagnosed with type 2 diabetes. For health reasons the cheap wine and high-sugar Schnapps she favored was no longer an option. The lower caloric content of scotch and water with a twist was re-introduced to mom, and a new beverage bond formed.

hats and identical sweaters. Mom cherished a photo of the four of them in their sweaters on top of Rockefeller Center.

The conclusion of high school brought sadness, shock, and surprise. As if on cue, Bill Simpson showed up again practically as the final bell rang. He was back in Detroit and wanted to see Elaine. Knowing her mother would have a fit seeing the two together again, Mom agreed to meet him at the corner. They talked and agreed to meet at Al's house the next day.

I'm not sure how many lines of B.S. Dad laid on her, but it was thick and overwhelming. He got Mom to promise to write to him often and convinced her to wait for him to return. Dad was leaving for Europe, but he still wanted his ace in the hole back home.

Dad had a grand time overseas. He visited France, Spain, and Germany. He went to a bull fight and saw things no boy from a holler in West Virginia could hope to see. He got loads of letters from Mom. And while he only wrote her occasionally, the letters must have been golden, because whatever he was selling, she was buying.

By the time Dad returned from Germany in August of 1954, nineteen-year-old Elaine was getting a little diamond-ring crazy. Girls at work came in with rings and wedding dates. Mom wondered when her ring would arrive. She felt if she weren't married by twenty-one, she could die alone.

One Sunday afternoon, her ticket out of potential old-maid status arrived. Dad came by with a ring. Against her better judgment, Mom accepted the shiny token. Following more fights and disagreements, Mom returned the ring in defiance of her hormones and mortal fear of dying alone and childless.

The following summer, the relationship was back in full swing. Mom had grown weary from the on-again, off-again nature of their relationship, and Dad didn't even need a ring. Mom suspected Dad hocked the original or gave it to another girl. No matter. Mom's old-maid clock was ticking, and she threw in the towel. By November of that year, they visited a pastor and began planning a spring wedding.

Grandma was not happy. She openly hoped for another off-again scenario. Both parents warned Elaine that a man's faults couldn't be changed by a woman and to carefully consider what she was getting into. Mom didn't dream of a white picket fence and a station wagon in the driveway for weekend trips to the lake. She pictured herself at the Available Man Store. The sign in the window read, "Closing Soon." To avoid missing out, she stifled her looming fears and insecurities and jumped in with two feet and a prayer.

Part Two

ADDITION LEADS TO TRANSITION: SUCCUMBING TO SUBURBIA

Chapter Four

THE DARK YEARS

Allow me a few lines to share how this book became a reality. I didn't exactly write the book. Rather, I let it evolve over the decades. My family and I tell stories. I just put it all on paper.

The impetus for this book came shortly after Mother's death on September 2, 2014. However, the idea came during the fall of 2008. As my daughter grew from a toddler to a little girl, I looked back and thought about how different the world was thirty years before she was born.

And what about the '40s and '50s? Those were ancient times. A World War? What's that, and how do we prevent one? Don't forget the toothpaste containers. Why were they rolled as tight as a steel coil spring? People gladly turned in the aluminum scrap for a new tube of paste. Every ounce of every product was used and consumed. Everything that could be reused or recycled got poured back into the war effort.

The years before my birth seem like ancient history, especially to my siblings. So much time has passed, and their recollections diminish with each passing year.

Mom and Dad married in April of 1956. And for the first couple of years had a care free, newly wed type of lifestyle. They likely celebrated their second anniversary by conceiving their first of five kids. Soon after Rick was born they rented a flat in Detroit on Tuller Street.

If you read carefully, you'll notice the title of this chapter has a double meaning. The stories in this chapter occurred during a time of struggle and uncertainty for my parents' flailing marriage. This is also a time with the smallest amount of recorded family history. It went a little dark, without much footprint. Times were notably dim between 1963 and 1972. The number of happy childhood memories my siblings share barely reach double digits.

While I was doing research for this book, my sister enlightened me. She pulled out the family album. You know the one. In big, gold letters on the front cover, it called out: "Our Family." The oversized, tattered catalog seems incomplete, with dozens of baby pictures missing.

The album starts strong with pictures of Rick from his newborn days. When Denise comes along four years later, the frequency of pictures slows. It's surprising, as Denise was my parents' first and only girl.

After that, the twins came along. There are a handful of pictures that document their first eighteen months, every picture featuring the twins together. By the time the twins turn four, the candid photos get replaced with a standard, free-of-charge church-directory photo that features all six Simpsons.

In 1962, Mom had a miscarriage. A few weeks later, she was pregnant with Denise. The emotional ride of losing a baby and getting pregnant immediately afterward twisted her up inside. Mom knew a second child would almost certainly bring an end to her career at Ma Bell.

A year after Denise was born, Dad did one very important, considerate thing for Mom. In the most adult move of Bill Simpson's life to that point, he got the family out of Detroit. They just didn't move very far.

Dad wanted to move to Utica, more than twenty miles north. That would have put them nearly thirty miles from Mom's parents. Yes, Dad had an agenda. It involved his friend Dave, with whom he first came to Detroit as a teenager and now lived in Utica. Mom and Dad visited Dave earlier that spring. While there, they visited Lake St. Clair and Anchor Bay. Dad loved the water, and visions of weekends on the lake swam in his head.

Mom won out though. The house in Utica cost too much. A house at 8 ½ Mile Road in Southfield was more affordable and—most importantly—less than three miles from the security of Grandpa and

Grandma. This was essential, because at that time in 1964, my mother was still a decade from possessing her driver's license.

Bye-Bye, City Life

The Simpsons were now in the suburbs, but just barely. Like our pets' names through the years, our street name was obvious and simple. 8 ½ Mile Road is a half-mile long and just as far from the border of Detroit, Eight Mile Road. When the Simpsons moved in, the road wasn't yet paved in front of the spacious half-acre lot.

With a fresh new start, a new house, and two young children, Mom began making a home. My parents were eager for their slice of the American dream, and here it was: new neighbors who would become longtime friends, our own mailbox, driveway, and tree-filled yard. And

Dad (minus a wedding ring) holding Victor, the pair displaying self-satisfying grins like they just stole a car or knocked off a liquor store. The other twin, Tommy, and my sister, Denise, wear forced smiles that suggest a bit of fear. Oldest offspring, Rick, about ten years old, standing tall in the rear. He looks so good you would think he's with the wrong family. Then at left, holding Tommy, is my mother. She has a pretty smile that appears sincere to anyone unacquainted with her. I see a woman sitting as far from my dad as possible while remaining in the frame. Her head tilts to her right and her too-wide smile has an unstable Joker-esque quality.

most importantly, it wasn't Detroit. Bill and Elaine were warned for years by friends and family: "Keep your kids out of the city schools." The move gave Rick access to the Southfield Public School District, where he began his scholastic journey.

Thanks to Dad's draft-forced tour of duty for Uncle Sam—his second-longest stint doing anything—he secured a G.I. Bill-backed, low-interest mortgage. At a purchase price of $13,500, the house's monthly note was an inconceivable $93. That was important since the bread Dad brought home maxed out at $100 per week. But they were thankful. My parents had a home, and Dad had topped his military tenure working for a legendary wheel and automotive parts manufacturer.

For decades, Kelsey-Hayes was the predominant wheel maker for many cars manufactured in Detroit. They also produced hydraulic brakes, brake drums, aircraft parts, and—during World War II—machine guns. President Richard Nixon was fond of saying, "Deader than Kelsey's nuts!" The saying refers to the secure attachment Kelsey's nuts guaranteed. In the public's view, nothing could be fixed more tightly.

Dad worked at Kelsey-Hayes two times for a total of nearly five years. An educated guess at his likely salary breaks down to between $2.50 and $3.25 per hour. It was a job, but not quite a living.

Dad could have stuck it out and risen through the ranks, but ass-kissing and being subordinate wasn't my old man's mug of beer. He felt like a prisoner every time he punched the clock. He longed to escape, but a surprise in the fall of 1964 added to Dad's sentence.

Two More Bundles of Joy?

Denise was just over a year old, and I'm sure this pregnancy was not scheduled at all. Unless, of course, it was a devious plan of Mother's to propel Dad into full adulthood by adding a third little mouth to feed. If that was the case, I would bet alcohol played a part.

Broadcasting the news resulted in an awkward sister-in-law moment. Mom confided with one of my aunts while they were both using the facilities in a community bathroom. Mom felt obliged to share her news after my aunt said she was with child as well, swapping the *Stork*

Digest between adjacent stalls. Another footnote to add to the lore of the women's restroom.

I don't know how far into the pregnancy Mom was before they learned the blessing was plural: twin boys. Dad saw their impending arrival as less than ideal. This attitude spilled into his care for the twins, but I'm getting ahead of myself.

With two kids, a new mortgage, and a pregnant wife, Dad was strapped for cash. He had to start selling his other babies. A boat, two motorcycles, and a newer car all left the nest. Dad was more than mildly distraught to sell his toys.

The instant doubling of little mouths meant our family was beyond complete. However, the blessing of twins wasn't paved in sunshine and songbirds. It was 1965, and my two-pack-a-day mother was not a beacon of healthy living.

Mom's morning routine was constant for almost three decades. For breakfast, coffee and a few cigarettes. Lunch was the same unless someone else was buying. Between meals, more cigarettes. The evening meal ended with more cigarettes and on the weekends, a glass or two of cheap wine.

Mom's diet and lack of exercise eventually caught up with her in 1985. She started complaining about feeling sluggish and dehydrated. She was drinking gallons of generic, high-fructose juice each day, but the dehydration didn't improve. Two or three weeks of pounding high-fructose combined with the stress of the Christmas season created the perfect health storm. In the first week of January 1986, Mom fell ill at work and had to be rushed to the hospital. She passed out on the way into the emergency room, where her medical team wondered how Mom was still breathing and not comatose.

Two Small Doses of Difficulty

The twins were challenging. Fortunately, they weren't dangerously premature, even by 1965 standards. Tom and Vic made it to about week thirty-six before making their grand arrival. Upon their birth, it became evident which twin hogged most of the food and space in Mom's womb.

Victor was small, weighing between five and six pounds. His breathing was fine, and he got cleared to go to the newborn nursery hours after being born.

Tommy was a different story. He was tiny and sickly looking. Dad later said, "They should have put him back in because he wasn't done!" The smaller twin was a miniscule three pounds. He spent his first two weeks in an incubator, a devastating blow to a couple with so many insecurities. Instead of being excited about bringing home twin boys, Mom and Dad feared for tiny Tommy's future. Fortunately, time did the trick. Three weeks after being born, Thomas James joined his twin brother and the rest of his family at home.

It wasn't an optimal beginning for Tommy, and it predictably led to other childhood health complications. For the first few years of Tommy's life, Mom struggled to help him gain and keep weight. By age five he was diagnosed with a lazy eye and prescribed the ugliest glasses in the history of children's optometry. He also had a learning disorder.

Learning was easy for Victor, but he was lazy. Since both struggled early in school, they both got a second chance at first grade.

Victor's school adversity was always attributed to effort. As early as third or fourth grade, it was evident he didn't want to work. If he was interested, he would pay attention. If not, he mentally checked out.

Tommy liked school and could read and comprehend at a pretty good pace, despite the fact that writing and spelling gave him fits. He likely had some type of dyslexia. But a few teachers worked with him, and he made great strides. Mom cherished those teachers who took extra time for Tommy, and he always responded well to their efforts.

The extra attention, however, wasn't as consistent as it should have been, leaving Mom bitter and angry with the school system. Tommy was smart. He just had trouble getting the information from his brain to a piece of paper. Mom and other family members insisted if Tommy received consistent special attention throughout middle school, his education experience would have been much different.

Maybe if my parents had better resources or more money and education, it would have been a different story. If they could have afforded private tutoring or private school, someone could have caught Tommy's learning disorders early enough to correct.

But there wasn't spare money, and other resources were scarce. So Vic and Tommy got pulled through grade after grade. Teachers had one goal: keep the twints' butts in the seats and get them on to the next level.

For over six years, six Simpsons lived in our modest Southfield home. The two oldest got along well. Denise was a seemingly normal elementary student in the Brownies (a.k.a. young Girl Scouts). Mom, boosted by doctor-prescribed amphetamines, was a troop leader. I don't know how many years she was moderately hooked on the pep pills, but it started shortly after the twins' birth. Mom once admitted to using them on and off until 1971. At that point, amphetamines were upgraded to a schedule II substance due to the potential for abuse and addiction. Who knew?

Ballgames and Another Birth

Rick was a good student and in love with baseball. He loved playing baseball, collecting baseball cards, listening to games on the radio, watching the Tigers on TV, and going to games with his older friend Jerry. Rick often recalls how the 1968 World Series was one of the most unbelievable fall classics of all time.

It sounds crazy now but as early as age twelve, Rick and Jerry headed to Downtown Detroit to enjoy America's Pastime. In 1971, Rick, Mom, Dad, and Grandpa took in a game at Tiger Stadium. They had box seats down the third baseline, a few rows from the field. That was more than half a century ago, and Rick remembers it like it was yesterday. Growing up Simpson wasn't all bad.

While Tom and Vic struggled with school, Dad struggled with everything else. He struggled with not having much to show for his labor. He struggled at being a supportive husband, a good father, and a decent person. To put it simply, life was a daily challenge for Dad.

A few things came easily for him. He could drive anything on wheels. If something broke, he could either fix it or smooth talk someone into helping him fix it. And he was exceptionally skilled, almost expert-level, at making babies.

When Mom learned I was on the way, she heard it all. Family and friends called my impending arrival a joke, mistake, accident, and medical miracle. They referred to me as a bonus bottle of milk delivered by the milkman, an extra package in the mail carrier's bag, and a few other things I don't wish to be addressed as.

Before I was born, I was a joke, a funny tale for summertime backyard parties. Friends and family laughed and pointed at Mom's baby bump. Mom took it all in stride. "Yep," she would say, pushing her belly out, "Bill knocked me up again. Can you believe it?"

It had an unexpected effect on Dad. He beamed with pride at his baby-making ability. Six months shy of forty years old, and the salmon were still swimming upstream. He didn't completely redefine himself or become a born-again Christian, but my conception and birth made Dad a little more tolerable—for a while. My brothers and sister all agree he lost some of his nastiness when I arrived on the scene.

I was born pudgy and healthy. At over seven pounds, I was Mom's heaviest baby, which allowed Mom to be discharged from the hospital faster than with any previous pregnancy. We were sent home less than seventy-two hours after I was born. As a parting gift, the nurses gave Mom a warm beer to help milk production.*

On our way home, we took a detour to Grandma and Grandpa's house. Mom held me up to the front window. Denise and Victor pushed their faces against the glass and looked out with chicken pox-riddled faces, eager to regain their health and hold their newest sibling.

The Simpson household now boasted seven people. Over the years, I've wondered what precautions my parents took to make sure it didn't become eight. My initial conclusion was that they never slept in the same bed again. The real answer? Mom probably talked to Dad. With five kids, it was an easy sell. His "quality" parenting skills were already spread too thin. So, he did the honorable thing. *Snip, snip!*

I tolerated breast milk fine, but I was allergic to certain dairy items, especially milk, in my first few years. I would break out in hives and turn red when I consumed it. Fortunately, I outgrew my intolerance by age five. I spent the next few years making up for lost time by making milk and cereal a staple of my diet until I was in high school.

Chapter Five

SNOWED OUT

My first childhood memory features a snowy, congested highway and a top speed of ten miles per hour. To be truthful, it's more of a vision than a memory. I was only two-and-a-half, but the tale has been retold so many times it's burned into my subconscious.

On what's commonly referred to as the busiest travel day of the year—the Sunday after Thanksgiving, snow began to fall. The storm was later called a "Super Snowstorm," and news headlines read, "Worst Snows of Century Hit Michigan." The storm of 1974 still ranks as the second-heaviest recorded snowfall in Detroit history.

Major holidays in our family usually mean one thing. Some part of some family is going to have to travel. Calls were made, travel plans coordinated, and through the magic of adults, *VOILA!*—a family holiday get-together was born.

Complete with food, beverages, home movies, storytelling, and singing around the piano or fireplace, the holidays were a glorious event. Sometimes the night before a holiday gathering, I would get so nervous with excitement that I would make myself nauseous and sick.

In the fall of 1974, it was our turn to travel. Uncle Bill (my mother's brother) and his family were temporarily living in a Chicago suburb, while Uncle Bill was in dental school to become an orthodontist. So, we traveled to Chicago. (I haven't been back since.)

This pulled my father out of his comfort zone. He protected his precious leisure time and long holiday weekends. There were, however, two or three times a year when my mother could sway him into doing what she wanted to do. It usually involved family, and Dad somehow managed to keep his opinion to himself.

Mom was smart. She knew if she only asked Dad a few times a year to leave his comfort zone, he would look like an ass if he failed to comply. Whatever trickery she employed, we made the trip to Chicago. But this story isn't about the trip there or the time spent with family. This story is about the ride home.

A Ride to Remember

We left the Chicago area on December 1, 1974, around eight on Sunday morning. We were in no rush when we set out on what Dad anticipated would be a simple five-hour drive home.

The snow started as we approached the Michigan state line. According to Tommy, "It was the biggest flakes I'd ever seen." That's saying something, because big flakes aren't uncommon so close to Lake Michigan. After all, large snowflakes are just several snowflakes stuck together. With so much annual snow, big snowflakes were normal. Tommy recalls the huge flakes coming down for hours and hours, coating the surface of the interstate.

Our family car was a 1968 Mercury Monterey with a 390-cubic-inch motor. Dad was a Mercury man who didn't feel it necessary to upgrade the sedan to a larger vehicle when my 1972 arrival put our head count at seven. Since Mom was an unlicensed passenger, Dad didn't request or notice her input on the car situation. All decisions made regarding family transportation were made by Dad. Mercury made a wagon, but my father, still in his early forties, wouldn't be caught dead in one. He had a reputation to protect, a reputation he'd spent years building up in his own mind. He would never let a thing like safety or family comfort damage his impression of who he thought he was.

Despite the Monterey's lack of space, we all have fond memories of the car. Its main shortcoming was a lack of temperature control. Mom cranked the heat, but the car never got beyond lukewarm. The heater's abilities were put to the test on our trip to Chicago, the Merc's longest journey to that point.

A Boy's Tribute to His Lower-Middle-Class Family

Back then family transportation, being so dramatically different than today, made things like seatbelts and child seats optional devices. They were never used by our family.* My seat always fell in one of two places in the car. If I was crying, I would be positioned on my mother's lap sucking on a bottle. There I would sit with nothing between me and the windshield except my mother's left arm. Most of the time I was wedged between Mom and Dad, all three of us sitting on our seatbelts.

As Dad guided the Mercury through drifting snow, my mother began to worry. Visibility grew worse. Mom worried more. Six hours into a five-hour trip, we were only halfway home. Mom looked out the window as Dad drove past Battle Creek, the last big town before Ann Arbor. Dad showed no hesitation, no inclination to stop.

An hour beyond the Cereal City, the Mercury and all other highway traffic came to a crawl. I sat on my mother's lap. There was no need to sit in my usual "safe" position on the big bench seat. With the Mercury creeping forward at eight miles per hour, I began to cry.

Dad navigated the snowy highway, passing an increasing number of cars pulled off to the side of the road. Some roadside travelers were without gas, some stopped to save gas and wait it out, and some couldn't carry on through the foot of snow. It was getting harder to see and keep the car on the road. Though a persistent man, Dad knew it was time to stop and evaluate the situation.

Leaving the interstate wasn't an option. The exit ramps were closed due to the extreme weather. It wouldn't have helped to get off the interstate anyway. It was a Sunday evening. Nothing was open in the smaller towns east of Battle Creek. None of that mattered, because my dad was Bill Simpson. Paying anyone an exorbitant amount of money for luxuries such as food and lodging was out of the question.

Besides, our old man probably didn't have more than twenty or thirty bucks on him. Even in the best circumstances, there was no reason for

---

Sometimes laws are good things. Seatbelt and child seat laws are a necessary nuisance to protect us from ourselves. I don't even know what a child seat from the '70s looks like. I just know I was never in one.

anyone in the car to consider the improbable, impossible idea that Dad would stop for the night. With the off ramps closed, we were stuck in the Mercury.

Before leaving Chicago that morning, Aunt Sandy packed us enough turkey sandwiches for a five-hour car ride. A few hours into our journey, they were gone. Our only remaining food source was a crumbled-up pack of graham crackers at the bottom of Mom's purse. We had no water, and our miserable heat source, the 1968 Mercury, couldn't run forever.

Dad nervously watched the fuel gauge fall to under half. While it was still light outside, a small roadside community began to form. A father of multiple girls stretched three large blankets outside the family van. His girls had to go to the bathroom, and he had a plan.

Other kids played outside, throwing snowballs and laughing. People on snowmobiles periodically cruised the median, stopping if they sensed a dire need. Occasionally, state police cruisers lumbered by, equipped with tire chains to cut through the snow.

Inside the Mercury, Mom and Dad were silent. Once or twice an hour, Mom reiterated her concern over my hydration situation, and then the car would grow silent again. Their lack of conversation concerned my older siblings. No talking or fighting? That brought fear.

Dad allowed Tommy, Vic, and Rick out to relieve themselves behind a tree—but they weren't to linger long. Scurrying back, Tommy ate as much snow as possible. My sister never used the outdoor facilities. Mom held it also.

At midnight, a plow truck cleared a path on the interstate. A couple four-wheel drive vehicles followed, and Dad geared up to do the same. Soon, he eased us onto the interstate, trailing a small caravan of vehicles. We never reached full highway speed, but Dad put miles behind us, and progress was made.

Fewer than ten miles from Ann Arbor, the fuel gauge indicated we had a quarter tank. It was very early on Monday morning. Finding a gas station was going to be difficult. Twenty-four-hour gas stations were fifteen years from reality. The closer we got to home, the closer the gauge got to that big E.

Dad made a judgment call and drove south, into Detroit, thinking his chances of finding an open gas station were better there. Dad was wrong.

The car sputtered into a station just in time. The owner was there, gassing up his car and loading up on supplies. Like other business owners in the area, he had no intention of opening. My father used his sweet-talking skills and convinced the guy to sell us three bucks worth of gas.

Simpsons: 1, Snow: 0

It was eerily quiet as we pulled down our little street, the calm after the storm. After reaching our house it was another two hours before Dad maneuvered the car into the driveway. That's how long it took Rick and him to get all the white stuff out of the way. They hurled the heavy, wet, snow into the air as Tommy and Victor looked on. Then the twins began to play. Like kids at a carnival, they jumped and climbed on the snow mountains formed by the Simpson men's work. Inside, Denise helped get me into warm, dry pajamas and began rehydrating me. Mother made a larger-than-usual breakfast. My siblings chattered happily about how many school days they hoped to miss.

The day before the storm, no meteorologist predicted more than three inches of snow in Detroit. Some forecast models predicted as little as an inch of accumulation. In an article about the missed estimates, Bill Deedler wrote:

> The models in 1974 failed in forecasting the weakening trend of the Ohio Valley system. The five hundred millibar low and the surface low not only failed to weaken they actually intensified and became vertically stacked in the atmosphere. Generally, when this happens the system tends to hold on to its intensity longer and slow down in movement, both of which proved detrimental to the computer forecast.

Detroit's final snow tally was 19.2 inches over a twenty-four-hour period. From the *Detroit News*:

The 1974 storm claimed at least twenty-seven persons, twenty-two from heart attacks while shoveling snow. Roseville canceled a safety course for snowmobiles. Schools everywhere were closed. Workers were snowed in too. Pontiac Motors, Fisher Body, and General Motors Truck & Coach all closed due to a lack of workers. The Sheriff's office in Oakland County averaged ten calls per minute and Deputies used snowmobiles to deliver three women in labor to area hospitals.

This family tale is a story of victory. Every time it's repeated our family's low self-esteem bumps up a notch. It was the classic little guy winning the big game, my dad's Al Bundy moment. The odds and the snow were against us, my dad poor and unprepared, but the Simpsons made it home.

Chapter Six

PLAYING IN THE PRETTY WATER

My dad was the original do-it-yourself guy. This kept him outside and away from Mom. Granted, he did things in the house, but he and Mom didn't collaborate on many projects. Mom generally stayed in the house, where she baked, cleaned, and made dinner. Dad hung out in the garage and yard, fixing electric pumps, appliances, and cars and maintaining the lawn.

Yard work was the first skill Dad taught us boys as our ages neared double digits. Lawn upkeep was Dad's least favorite task, so he passed it on to us as soon as possible. I pushed my first lawn mower at age eight and was picking up leaves and fallen limbs by age seven. Dad viewed manual, outside labor as grunt work. With four boys, he figured, "Why the hell am I behind this mower when I could be tinkering with a motor or fixing something to sell?"

Many of these DIY undertakings spawned from Dad being the cheapest man to walk the earth. Actually, that's an exaggeration. Dad's father was even cheaper. However, I never met or had to live with Grandpa. His cheapness, combined with a negative attitude about everything and poor health, led to his demise before I was born. I never heard anything good about him except that he worked hard and could stretch a dollar further than anyone.

Aside: I began my adult life that involved house-upkeep and child-rearing, I learned on the fly. There are certain things men are required and expected to do. That isn't sexist. It's just how my wife and I were raised. I'm required to hang light fixtures and pictures, install shelving, and try to fix anything broken or not working at an optimal level. My wife organizes and keeps our home fresh. She handles seasonal decoration and makes our home look great in spite of our restrictive budget.*

I like to imagine my father's thought process toward home projects. I have theories on his math, because I've run the same numbers. "There is no way I'm paying anyone that much money if I can do it myself."

My dad would shell out up to fifty dollars. Any more than that and he would do it himself. My financial DIY scale comes with project-based variables. How much experience do I have at plumbing? Do I have the necessary tools to install flooring or ceiling tile? I ask these questions before launching into a project or sliding into another six months of procrastination. When anything costs over a couple hundred bucks, I'm going to at least try to do it myself. Just because everyone wants a slice of my money is no reason to give up the whole pie.

Dune-Buggy Dreams and Oil Slicks

At my childhood home in Southfield, we had a rickety, unattached garage where Dad engaged in the art of tinker. He dug electric motors out of dumpsters. Sometimes, he fixed them. Other times, he removed the motor's pulleys and fans and sold the rest for scrap. He also worked on old cars outside of the garage.

Sometimes Dad worked on cars for some under-the-table cash. On more than one occasion he surprised Mom with a hunk-o'-crap car from the junkyard with big plans. "I'm gonna fix that clunker up and make a few dollars." That plan failed more than it succeeded, but I admit I suffer the same affliction.

----

*Weekend projects have offered some of the best times my wife and I have spent together, as we share our time, our minds, and our love for all things DIY. However, there is an exception: major painting projects. I'll never again paint the exterior of my home. That endeavor is dangerous, boring, tedious, and never-ending. Some home projects are done out of necessity, not desire. When you live smack dab in the lower-middle class, options are few, home improvement dollars are thin, and paint labor is too expensive.

During an eighteen-month period in the early '80s, we had no fewer than five Volkswagen Bugs in our driveway. My dad developed his own blueprint to build a dune buggy. We just never understood why it took four or five Bugs to build it!

Unlike many of Dad's ideas, the dune-buggy plan came to fruition. Being deathly afraid of anything fast, fun, and dangerous, Mom was not pleased. Dad never finished making the buggy street legal, but that didn't stop the Simpsons. We drove that thing everywhere that lacked pavement and police. For a few joyous months, we were a dune-buggy family.

When tinkering on cars, Dad never bothered with environmental concerns. Used motor oil got dumped on the ground beside the driveway. The same rule applied to antifreeze disposal. Dad figured if you put it in the ground, it would never be seen again. Gasoline, oil, antifreeze—you name it, if it was liquid or could be buried without detection, Dad poured it into the ground, trusting Mother Nature to consume and conceal.

In a weird character oddity, Dad absolutely hated seeing litter of any kind. When he saw trash on the ground or roadside, he would point it out and make an irritated sound with his tongue.

This taught us the art of contradictory living. If it sank, seeped, or could be buried, it got returned to the earth. Roadside litter, on the other hand, was deplorable, and an oil-stained driveway was a sign of laziness and inability to care for a vehicle. "Would you look at that?" Dad would say. "Poor bastards can't even keep up with changing oil."

One Saturday afternoon, Dad changed the oil on a couple cars and did a brake job on another. After disposing of the oil in his special way, Dad headed inside as rain arrived. It rained all night. When Sunday morning came, it was still sprinkling. Mom took us kids to church, leaving Dad to whatever he did on Sunday mornings alone.

Sometimes he would listen to his music loud on our Craig eight track stereo. Usually something in the Johnny Cash or Willie Nelson genre. If he was in the mood or if he had pissed Mom off the night before, he would have breakfast waiting for us after church. This particular Sunday we got the full buffet: runny eggs, burnt toast, crunchy bacon, and leather textured, shriveled up sausage. He added about a half cup of milk for every two eggs. Yummy! The sun came out during breakfast. That meant as soon as we survived Dad's cooking, it was play time.

The Rainbow of Horror

I am the youngest of five by quite a bit. Six years and ten months separate me from twin brothers Tom and Vic. Play time for the rest of my siblings was "get lost" and don't even consider coming home until dinner. For me at age four, my play time was restricted to our yard and our lack of cool toys. But I had my bag of Hot Wheels and Matchbox cars that went with me everywhere.

Mom gave me a new paper lunch sack every couple weeks to carry them. I held onto my cars so tight the brown paper sacks didn't last long.*

The sun shone bright and warm. The drainage ditch in front of our house flowed strong from the rain the night before. It was too soggy for the older kids to use as a bike ramp, so I ventured out with my paper bag of Hot Wheels and Matchbox cars. I split my cars up on either side of the ditch and commenced a series of jumping competitions between racers from rival gangs. At four, I had an odd imagination.

After a few magnificent competitions, I noticed something. The cars that landed in the water and dried off in the sun had a shimmer to them. That was cool, so I dropped all the cars in the ditch. Before long I was waist deep with my cars, playing and splashing.

The sun was warm on my face. All was well as my imaginary racing gang members crashed and jumped through unseen explosions. Then the ditch water caught my attention. It had all the colors of the rainbow. When I splashed the water, the colors separated and then reconnected in the water. Wow!

After an hour in the ditch, my skin warmed. I felt sick to my stomach. When I stepped out of the ditch, I froze. My clothing didn't look like a color-filled rainbow. My shirt and pants looked like old, wet shop rags.

---

*When I was seven, some kid brought the Hot Wheels Rally Case to school. It held over twenty cars, was shaped like a mag wheel, and had its own stand. All I could do is stare at it and wonder how much it cost, knowing I would never have one.

I picked up my cars and dropped them in my beloved paper bag. I started toward our front door as my wet cars soaked through their paper confinement and fell out, one after another.

By the time I reached the front door, tears ran down my cheeks and rolled off my oil-stained clothes. Holding the top half of my empty lunch bag, I gathered the courage to knock on the door and call for my mother.

"Stephen McKinley!" Mother screeched in horror and agitation. "Where have you been and what have you been doing? Has your father seen you? He was supposed to be keeping an eye on you. Bill! Bill!"

A minute later, Dad came around the corner—not quite running, but moving at a better pace than a call from Mom normally generated. The pitch of Mom's scream made it clear: This could be an emergency, and it was most likely Dad's fault.

"Jesus, boy!" Dad exclaimed. "What happened to you? Where have you been and why are your clothes all black and oily? Answer me!"

Along with everything else currently wrong in my world, Dad was mad. As the youngest, I was rarely the focus of his anger. After a few moments of crying while Mom and Dad went at each other, I caught my breath. Between sniffles, I muttered the truth.

"I was just playing down in the ditch with my cars," I said. "I was playing in the pretty water!"

In our family, group bathing among younger brothers was the norm, since Dad considered hot water liquid gold. The twins normally bathed together, but sometimes I bathed with one of them. That Sunday evening, I got a hot bath all to myself. The cars my brown sack littered all over the yard were now safe inside. A few favorites even joined me in the bathroom, lined up on the edge of the tub with a faint coat of oil glistening over their die-cast metal.

That bath wasn't just hot. It also involved extra soap and sponge detail from Mom. To remove the oily residue from my hair, she used adult shampoo instead of the "No more tears" brand. Wash, rinse, repeat. Wash, rinse, repeat. Mom followed directions to a letter. That said, there was no call to 911. No visit to the emergency room, no expensive, unnecessary trip to the family doctor. Just some extra attention and a long, hot bath to detox my motor oil-soaked body. This was the lower-middle-class solution: Handle it in-house whenever possible. Lessons were learned, catastrophes avoided, and obviously, I lived.

Chapter Seven

BONDING AT THE LAUNDROMAT

For a small window of time, it seemed life was just me and Mom. Many memories from when I was four and five only involve my mother. A few scraps involve my siblings and father, but those memories aren't as vivid. I attribute this to one fact: Mom gaining independence in the form of her driver's license.

As mentioned throughout this book, Mom was led by fears and worry. Afraid as she was of driving, she was more scared of having something bad happen and not being able to get to a hospital. So, she learned to drive.

Her driving instructors, Dad and Grandpa, soon learned that Mom lacked skills needed to become a good driver. Her coordination, confidence, and peripheral vision all needed improvement. On top of that, she drove automatics with two feet. Operating a third pedal was out of the question. Fortunately, our 1968 Mercury was an automatic.

No one knows exactly how many times Grandpa and Dad attempted to teach Mom to drive. All we know is many, many failures eventually led to success. At the tender age of forty, Mom got her license and was free to travel. For the first few years, she restricted herself to a five-mile radius around our home. The store, bank, church, and her parent's house were all in Mom's safe zone.

She had a safe speed, too—forty miles per hour. I was learning numbers when Mom started driving. The speedometer on the big Merc seemed three feet long. I frequently peered over Mom's shoulder and confirmed our pace. No matter the surface, weather, or traffic congestion, our top speed never eclipsed forty miles per hour.

With Dad at work and my siblings at school, I became Mom's back-seat copilot. Everywhere she went and everything she did, we went and did together.

Trips to the bank were dull, but Mom often went there first. Comerica Bank featured old stanchion post dividers to herd bank patrons toward the tellers. As a fidgety toddler, I couldn't help but hang and play on the post dividers. But the best thing about the bank was the penny gum dispenser. Everyone has a penny, even the Simpsons. Mom usually gave me two or three and let me put the money in by myself.

Once or twice a week, we bought groceries at A&P or Farmer Jack. Nothing about the grocery store was fun for four-year-old me. Mom was at her best when looking for sales and finding bargains to stretch every dollar. But that meant giving me almost no attention. Bored, I walked behind her, careful to avoid touching anything, knowing if I acted up too much I would have to sit in that damn cramped cart. (Those shopping cart seats were not made for husky little boys.)

If vegetables were in season, we stopped at a nearby farm on the way home. Dad loved fresh produce. Green beans, ripe tomatoes, and corn on the cob were his favorites. After we got home from the farm, Mom let me help shuck corn. It made me feel so good, like I was really helping with dinner. She would position two chairs around an old bucket, and we would sit and shuck every ear of corn purchased.

Some days, especially when the weather was nice, Mom visited people before we started our errands. Family friends Bobby Sue and Tommy Williams lived less than a mile away, and Mom sat and drank coffee with them some mornings. Bobby Sue was the only woman that could outsmoke mom. She and Tommy were Detroit-era friends. Their house was weird, with wall-to-wall shag carpeting. I believe even a few walls had carpet on them. If my memory serves me, Tommy Williams, not Dad, took Rick to his first Tigers game in the Summer of '69.

About once a week we visited Grandpa and Grandma. After

1976, *Grandma* was actually Grandpa's second wife, Grandma Ethel. Mom never smoked there, but those three put away the coffee. I don't remember much about my real grandma who died before I turned three, but Grandma Ethel doted on me and always gave me something sweet to eat.

One errand was like no other. Going to the laundromat should have been a bore fest, but Mom made it special. Just how special it was on any given visit depended on how long we would be there. If we didn't have enough money to replace or fix our washer or it wasn't a warm spring or summer day, we stayed longer. Mom hung clothes to dry for at least thirty years of her life. But in the dead of winter or when there were too many clothes to hang, we went to the laundromat.

Soon as Mom dropped the first few loads in, we headed next door to the Red Barn restaurant for a snack. We got the same thing every time—a large fry and a large Pepsi. We took the snack back to the laundromat, and she gave me most of the fries and Pepsi.

While waiting for the clothes to wash, I raced the wheeled laundry carts. If I remembered my cars, I played with them on the floor and folding tables. When the clothes finished washing, I followed Mom and picked up any items that slipped out of her hands. Then she boosted me up to put the quarters in and start the dryer.

While Mom folded clothes, I sat on the table and listened to stories of Mom's childhood. She also prepared me for kindergarten by quizzing me on numbers, letters, colors, and small words like *stop, walk, run,* and *park.* If we were going to be there for hours, Mom read children's books to me and taught me about animals, trees, and flowers.

For Mom, the laundromat was an escape where she always seemed calm. She couldn't be bothered or preoccupied with anything else at the laundromat. She couldn't hurry or rush the clothes clean. She simply waited through the cycles. While she did, we enjoyed each other's company.

Our time at the laundromat speaks to a very simple parenting cliché: Spend time with your kids. Decades later, while traveling around eight southeastern states as a truck driver, I passed countless billboards that read, "Take time to be a dad today!" Every time I spotted one, especially if I was away for a few days, I would let out a somber sigh. It's hard to be a dad from four hundred miles away. We can give our kids every material thing they ask for, but things can't equal the value of sharing time with them.

When Elaine and I went to the laundromat, she took time to be a mom.

Chapter Eight

FAMILY ENTERTAINMENT

I wouldn't describe my parents as fun. We had good times with Mom, but it was seldom a knee-slapping, laugh-out-loud chuckle fest. And getting her to be fun when Dad was around was a chore.

Dad was rarely in a good mood, but when he wanted to make you laugh, he could usually get the job done. Dad had a better sense of humor and was more fun around a crowd. It was easy to tell if Mom or Dad were having a good time, which only happened a few times a year. Mom's face would light up with a sincere, yet not-too-wide smile. She would belly laugh so hard that her tar-tainted throat and lungs would send her into coughing fits. Thanks again, big tobacco.

Dad only had fun when he was where he wanted to be, doing what he wanted to do. His face would darken like a shadow of a person was emerging. The hat on his head would tilt off center. In those moments, he would be a man in his environment. Camping, grilling out, watching us fish, going up north, being around old cars, or captaining a boat—doing any one of these put my father into his happy zone. Funny enough, my mom hated every activity with the potential for turning Dad into good-time Willy.

Another clue Dad was enjoying life was his speech. I hate to break this to the Mountaineer community, because I love your state, but West Virginia isn't really in the South. It's in the eastern middle of the US. That said, everyone I've ever known from West Virginia has a southern accent.

My dad, having spent more than half his life in Michigan, only sounded southern when he was having a good time. His tone softened, his southern(ish) accent became more pronounced, and his words came slower than usual—not quite the speed of molasses, but deliberate enough to appreciate. And it always came out more around his family.

Neither of my parents were good at faking fun. When unhappy, they were tight lipped with little to say. Bill and Elaine were equally unskilled at initiating a good time. Lemons rarely turned into lemonade through their efforts.

Society tends to deny common ground with previous generations. As decades go by, however, a few similarities rise to the surface. Then in our mid-forties, all adults wake from a deep sleep. In a cold sweat we cry out, "I am my father!"

Bill and Elaine were no different—a product of how they were raised. Therefore, I can't over-criticize them for raising us like they did. I can't fully opine on all four grandparents, because I only knew two. But I heard stories and saw pictures of them all. Improv actors and comedians they were not.

Out of all four grandparents, there was a slight exception: Mamaw Dickey, a.k.a. "Dixie," my dad's mom. Mamaw took us fishing and hiking, baked sweet treats for us, and delivered life sermons like a big-tent southern preacher. Mamaw was fun. She was even more fun after her old man was out of the picture.

My mom enjoyed baking. Whether making bread or cookies or holiday pies, her favorite ingredient was stories. All baking involved Mom unloading stories of her life while we chopped nuts or sprinkled flour on the wax paper.

While Mom wasn't one for laughs, she had a soft spot for solo entertainment. Dictionary at her side, she worked on crossword puzzles for hours. She also loved big jigsaw puzzles and would piece them together on the kitchen table. If you were quiet, you could help. As a younger, less skilled puzzle-builder, my job was finding the flat side pieces that form the puzzle's perimeter.

Solitaire was the one card game Mom taught me as a child. All you need is fifty-two cards and yourself. It doesn't get any more exciting than that. We were, for the most part, expected to entertain ourselves. Sometimes, that wasn't a bad thing.

TV, Fortified Sugar, and Family Game Night

Saturday morning cartoons were a tradition. The key was waking up first to gain control of the TV and get the first go at the one box of sugar cereal in the house. If we were sneaky, Saturday morning was the one occasion we could eat in the living room by the light of the television. If Dad caught us, he would have a fit, but Mom let it slide.

Normally, Mom bought the basics—Corn Flakes, Rice Krispies, and Cheerios. Once or twice a month, she splurged on Golden Grahams, Cap'n Crunch, or Honeycomb. We didn't need three spoonfuls of sugar to make these special cereals taste good. Bought on Friday, a.k.a. payday, these cereals were typically gone by Monday morning.

Saturday morning cartoons offered three solid hours of pastel animation full of comedy and violence. Hanna-Barbera gave us *Scooby Doo*, *Laff-A-Lympics*, *The Flintstones*, *Tom and Jerry*, and *Superfriends*. Warner Bros produced my favorite show, *Looney Tunes*, which featured Bugs Bunny, Daffy Duck, Elmer Fudd, the Road Runner, and all the rest. It was funny and action-packed.

Victor always woke up after Tommy and me. When he stumbled into the living room, he'd walk up to the TV and change the channel. The boring crap Vic liked often drove me outside to play. *Jonny Quest*, *Thundarr the Barbarian*, and *He-Man and the Masters of the Universe* never held my attention.

When Dad came in from working in the garage, our preferences didn't matter. Whether it was morning or night, he overruled our control of the TV. On Saturdays and Sundays, Dad watched boxing and auto racing. At night, *Hee Haw*, *60 Minutes*, and anything about nature or animals. The only show my parents enjoyed together was *Dallas*. It was a true guilty pleasure for both of them. Dad rooted for J.R. Mom felt bad for Sue Ellen and thought Miss Ellie was the perfect family matriarch.

Of course, the idiot box wasn't our only entertainment. If it was nice out, Dad hit balls to the oldest three boys. Denise and I watched as Dad kept all three of them busy, hitting sharp ground balls from both sides of an imaginary home plate. On rare occasions, Dad joined us in a game of Monopoly. It was never fun for anyone. Dad was a terrible cheat, and if he was losing, he would lose interest and walk away.

Dad's Dangerous Creation

My father did create one fun thing—a legendary game that was thoroughly enjoyed by six of us and tolerated by Mom. Walking a fine line between playful laughter and child endangerment, Dad birthed slipper fighting on one dark, cold winter evening.

At the start, we all took strategic positions in the dimly lit living room. Denise and I got the best foxholes because we were most vulnerable. Dad sat in his chair, armed with a rolled-up newspaper and two slippers. One of us would initiate the war by stealing one of Dad's slippers, while another brave soldier, usually Tom or me, occupied Dad by jumping on his back while he read *TV Guide*.

Just before the slipper theft went down, Dad would attempt to thwart the crime by defending his chair and launching artillery at us. First, he would grab the little chair climber and throw him on top of the slipper scrounger below. And that was it—the battle was on! Quicker than you can say "blunt force trauma," Dad would kick off his slippers and began launching them at us repeatedly.

Once I was old enough to play, Rick was too old to play. The dejected frontline soldier's role was reduced to platoon leader. As such, he handed us slippers and pillows to throw at Dad and tell us what flank to attack next. If you made it all the way to Dad's chair, he would use a slipper like a rubber-soled baton, striking gently until you retreated. If Tom or Vic cowered behind furniture on the other side of the living room, they took the old man's best shots, as Dad threw at them as hard as he could.

The whole event filled the room with laughter—and a bit of crying. As slippers bounced off walls and furniture, we would secure the weapon and unload it back at Dad. That's when his rolled-up newspaper came in handy. He used it like a bat to defend himself from attack.

This family activity produced quite the conundrum for my poor mother. It involved several things she despised: throwing things inside, violence, and destroying a room in her home. A broken lamp or damaged table was a strong possibility. And if one of her kids ended up permanently damaged by a slipper to the retina, Mom would seriously regret her casual spectator status. "How would I ever tell the rest of the family? Victor got a concussion or Tommy is now blind in one eye because I watched as Bill threw slippers at them!"

Even to a stick in the mud like Elaine Elizabeth, this pickle was undeniable. The time we spent violently hurling slippers in her living room was true family bonding. The fun we had while slipper fighting was genuine. Her husband shared quality time with the children, and everyone had a blast. So, she stood just outside the dining room leaning against the doorway, flinching with every throw. She chastised my father through a smile if she thought he was being too rough and let out a muffled laugh if Dad took a slipper to the head or midsection.

Every battle concluded with all of us facing our fear of flying slippers and overtaking Dad in his chair. The victory trophy was a three-ounce ration of milkshake for every soldier. Dad drank his much larger portion straight from the stainless-steel tumbler. I guess he felt he earned it. For giving us that fond memory, I suppose he did.

Chapter Nine

SOUTHFIELD OR NORTHWEST DETROIT?

Big cities always outgrow their limits. When they do, people go hunting for a more suburban or rural way of life. As young families climb up the socioeconomic ladder, they trade in weekends at the city park for cutting grass on their own third of an acre.

While not a politically correct term, the Great White Flight brought a real population shift. Over the last sixty years my family fled several times. It's not just us. Most people, not just white people, want to raise their families in a suburban community rather than the middle of a big urban setting.

The boom phenomenon happened in Detroit at the beginning of the twentieth century. The same happened in Atlanta when I lived there in my early twenties. By the time the '90s were upon us, the ATL was the place to be in the south. The same thing started a few years ago in Nashville. There's no state income tax, plenty of opportunities, and a decent climate. No wonder people are sprinting to the Volunteer State.

The flight still exists this century. If you doubt me, Google "How many people are leaving Chicago every day?" Illinois's population has fallen for six straight years, with an estimated one-fifth of those former residents now calling Tennessee home. This doesn't bother me. But please, Bears fans, leave your big-city politics in the Land of Lincoln.

As the suburbs sprawl fifty or more miles from big cities, people begin to see the light. Houses are cheaper and come with a front yard and—

Wait, what's that?—a backyard, too! Criminal activity is minimal, and people don't fear going out after a certain time. The biggest evening news story is that the local high school football team ended their thirteen-game losing streak. Go Mustangs!

All these factors attract growing families to the suburbs or the country. My parents felt the pull as well. While they didn't have the means to move out of Southfield, they constantly looked for the opportunity. In the late '70s, Southfield was considered the 'burbs, but just barely. It bordered Detroit, and the plight of the big city was closing in fast.

Denise was a freshman at Southfield High during the 1977–78 school year. The area and the schools were already in decline. Traffic, people, litter, and crime were invading our neighborhood. Southfield was becoming another tentacle of the Motor City.

At this time, Denise got into an altercation during Spanish class. My sister, never one to back down from a verbal discussion, was surprised when it became physical. A large female student launched a desk that almost hit Denise. My sister claims she's never been more scared. Whether it was a warning shot or just a bad furniture toss, it was not a good beginning to what could've been a very long four years of so-called education.

To the Woods!

About this time, my parents learned of an unusual opportunity. Our church in Redford, St. Johns Lutheran, owned a church camp and apple orchard in rural Livingston County. There were also several buildings and a small farmhouse. The house on the property was vacant, and the camp—Camp Luther Vista—needed a young family of caretakers.

This blessing, combined with the Spanish-class clash, was all the motivation Mom and Dad needed. Dad was unemployed again, and the Brighton farmhouse's free rent sealed the deal. Without a second thought, we kissed goodbye to Southfield, Michigan. For my father and his rural roots, it was time to go.

Because our church was involved, Mother had work to do. To get the job and the free rent, she had to sell Dad and herself to the Luther Vista

Steering Committee (LVSC). It was up to the members of the LVSC to ensure the camp was taken care of, and they took their job seriously. The main requirement of rent-free living rested on the Simpson's ability to be good caretakers. Mother used a fastball and a deceiving slow curve to pitch herself and Bill Simpson to said committee.

Buildings had to be kept clean. The campground had to be cared for and equipment had to be maintained and repaired. Other responsibilities included helping during the apple harvest in the fall and tending to camp guests' needs and concerns.

With the help of five kids, Bill and Elaine could easily handle the role of camp caretaker. No problem. However, they also had to finish raising those kids, put food on the table, and somehow not kill each other along the way.

It's hard to understand why, but the LVSC approved us as the new caretakers. Maybe there was a short line of people excited about life in the country. Or maybe Mom was so desperate to leave Southfield that she pulled off the best sales job of her life. Whatever the reason, we were moving on and moving out.

Remember, this was a different time. The kids were never brought into the decision-making process. There was no "little Jimmy has bad hay fever so we can't live there." "Oh, Suzy would be leaving her friends and won't have her own bathroom." Nope, none of that shit was even considered in the '70s. Mom and Dad didn't even run it by my oldest brother, who was nineteen at the time and partially living under their roof.

"Have you seen the house? Can we go see the house?" Those words were never uttered. It was spring of 1978, and my parents told us, "Start packing and start cleaning. We're leaving the first week of April." That's all we knew.

My family was familiar with Camp Luther Vista. My siblings and Mom visited the camp a couple of times each year. Our church held a weeklong summer camp there for kids every July. Rick and Denise belonged to church youth groups that held regular retreats at the property. I tagged along with Mom when she volunteered to help during youth events. But this was different. Now we were going to live at church camp all year long. Though we were familiar with most of the property, our new home was a scary-looking mystery.

It sat in front of the property, shielded by enormous trees on three sides. It had a separate driveway that was off limits during camp and other church events. A hedge row served as a boundary crossed only by the church's pastor. A big detached garage included a private room with its own entry door. This room served as the pastor's quarters.

Relocating led to a better life for us kids. Denise could have survived three more years at Southfield High, but is surviving high school what parents want for their only daughter? As for the twins and me, staying in Southfield would have meant a direct trip to juvie.

On the Run

Looking back at the move, one of my brothers commented that Mom and Dad weren't headed toward a great new life with a fresh start. "They were kind of just running away," he said.

Q: Running away from what?

A: Southfield schools and the community inevitably morphing into northwest Detroit. Dad's disreputable acquaintances in the valley, Dad's zealous drinking, Dad's unemployed status, and Mom and Dad's marriage that offered more convenience than love. Have your pick. Whatever the answer, a change of zip code probably wasn't going to fix it. This was my parents' version of checking the pasta. They threw a move to the country against the wall and hoped it would stick.

What could go wrong?

Part Three

SMALLER HOUSE, BIGGER YARD

Chapter Ten

SLEEPING ON THE FRONT PORCH

A ccentuate the positive and minimize the negative. It was another tactic our lower-middle-class parents lived by. The day we moved to Camp Luther Vista in Brighton, I don't remember one thing about the house. I didn't even spend a night in my bedroom for the first week, thanks to my parents' plan to distract me. With the help of my sister, they allowed me to discover all our new home had to offer on the outside.

The first thing I remember about the property was getting out of the car and walking away from the house, as Denise escorted me to my new playground. It was as if she were a tour guide and the "house attraction" were closed for repair. "The tour starts over here at the playground," my sister said. Or she would have if she were a paid employee. Monkey bars, swings, a slide, and a really fast merry-go-round were all there for my enjoyment.

After that we went to the beach and the swimming pond, then the tour concluded with a viewing of the fishing lake. It was like a dream. Besides, what six-year-old kid cares about an old farmhouse anyway? With Mom, Dad, and the boys moving stuff in, I would just get in the way.

My brothers Tom and Vic were almost teenagers. So, they were busy carrying boxes and furniture into our new home. As they did, they noticed something—or rather, a lack of something.

Standing in the living room, Dad opened a large, thick door, heavy as our old Mercury and sturdy enough to stop a bull. The door had windows at the very top that looked outside. Behind the door was the new bedroom all Simpson boys would share. Even Rick, when he was home from college for the summer to help around camp, would sleep in the dank cave.

It was smaller than the room we shared in Southfield, and it lacked a closet. It did, however, have plenty of windows. In fact, it had more windows than walls. As most front porches did on houses built in the '50s, this room had windows on all four sides. There was enough room for two bunk beds and two dressers. Our porch bedroom had one overhead light and one electrical outlet. Being just a porch, it was constructed for drinking lemonade and wintertime storage. It was never fitted with luxuries such as insulation and climate control.

Icy Hot

I could tell stories for hours about that front porch, which became known as the back room. It faced the road but to disguise it as a bedroom, it was never referred to as the front of our house. One benefit was that it had a door to the outside. My brothers really appreciated the "escape hatch" during their high school years. Strangely enough, no one ever entered the house through our bedroom. Guests entered through our kitchen door, which faced the camp.

The windowed interior wall of our room separated us from the living room. Painted plywood covered the windows for our privacy. Inside the living room, a large, hideous, 60's-style curtain remained permanently shut over our boarded-up windows. The heavy curtain served triple duty. It hid the plywood-covered windows and acted as a sound barrier and insulation for anyone enjoying the heated interior of the home.

The first winter we spent on the porch was an anxious time for Mom. When the temps got below freezing outside, she came to the back room and acted like she was tucking me in or putting away laundry. She would set an ugly, ancient green thermometer on one of the windows and make small talk as the needle dropped to the left. If the temperature dropped below forty, she insisted we be allowed inside to sleep on the living room floor. It never happened, but a few times it hovered around the forty-five mark. I heard her plea with Dad, while I carved my name in the window frost using my thumbnail.

"Bill, Bill!" she shouted. "Those boys are going to freeze out there! And what about Stephen? He's too little to be out there."

"They're boys 'Lain, they'll be fine," Dad replied. "If it's not below freezing how are they gonna freeze? And Stephen—have you ever sat next to that boy? It's like he's his own furnace. I start sweating when he sits next to me on the chair!"

As a show of generosity, Dad put some crappy plastic on the outside of the windows before that first winter to make life a bit more comfortable on the ice porch. But he didn't use plastic made for window winter insulation. That stuff fit well and was too expensive. The light-gray stuff he used made it impossible to see outside and looked like he "borrowed" it from a construction site. When the wind blew off the lake, the plastic whipped around like tent flaps in a hurricane.

All those windows didn't make us more comfortable in the summer either. Our backroom sat on the west side of the house, and there was no cool summertime breeze there. During the last half of every hot summer day, the sun beat through those windows, lighting the room up like a greenhouse. At bedtime, we literally lay in our own sweat until the room cooled at two or three in the morning. The windows stayed open all night. In the morning we woke up wet and shivering to cool, fifty-degree summer mornings. Who says being poor doesn't make you stronger?

After two years the Simpsons proved adequate camp caretakers. It appeared we were staying a few more years, so the Luther Vista Steering Committee upgraded our accommodations. With volunteer help from two retired contractors, some help from my dad, and several cases of cheap American lager, the back room got a facelift. Still no closet or climate control, but we went from eighteen windows to three. Insulation was installed and exterior walls erected. It was a cheap solution to our uncomfortable situation, but it helped. After the improvements, our front porch was twenty degrees warmer in the winter and ten degrees cooler in the summer.

The rest of the house really wasn't bad. It had plenty of storage, which Mom liked. The kitchen had an open layout and a large window facing the fishing lake. The living room had a great fireplace with working vents that warmed the entire room if you could build a big enough fire. The two real bedrooms were big enough and both had closets. My sister's closet held the home's electrical panel that had extra fuses in a can to swap out everytime we asked too much of the knob-and-tube wiring system. The one and only bathroom was tiny, but no smaller than the one

The chimney at the Luther Vista house.

in our Southfield home. If it was warm enough and we had to pee, we boys just went outside.

The house didn't matter much though. That's not why we moved. We wanted out of the Detroit area. New schools, new friends, no rent or mortgage, and a new way of life with new responsibilities. The dwelling was never the highlight of our new address. Our gigantic new yard was.

The Real Jewel

There were eighty acres of woods and fields and two apple orchards to explore. The property included a swimming pond, fishing lake, playground, baseball field, volleyball net, and shuffleboard court, along with all sorts of farm equipment. We couldn't have imagined so many ways to be entertained. The one downside: Everyone's chore list tripled overnight. At age six I had chores. I became pick-up-tree-limbs boy.

Nearly every waking moment was spent cleaning camp buildings, cutting grass, trimming hedge rows, picking up apples, and burning garbage. Anytime Dad spotted Tom, Vic, or me slacking off, he would yell his go-to command: "Pick up limbs!" We heard that phrase at least ten thousand times during our childhood.

We groaned, complained, and avoided Mom and Dad on the vast property. But not always. Sometimes, we just took our time enjoying the more enjoyable chores. For the older boys, nothing beat trash duty. They got to light stuff on fire. Once the burn barrels cooled, they were rounded up and taken back to the back of the property. This involved driving the tractor, scrounging around the dump, and breaking bottles. Good times indeed.

My favorite chore was cutting grass. I pushed my first mower before I was ten. Granted, cutting grass wasn't nearly as awesome or exciting as burning trash and crushing glass, but it was better than picking up limbs. Even at a very young age I loved the smell and look of a fresh-cut lawn. I was responsible for the three yards closest to the house and trimming around all camp buildings.

When I started cutting grass, I felt I was truly helping Dad and was part of the team. I sometimes cut our side yard two or three times in a crisscross pattern. I tried to emulate the outfield at Tiger Stadium, while evading chores I considered less fun that involved more manual labor.

While we all griped about cleaning bathrooms, sweeping dorms, and helping Mom mop and wipe down the cafeteria-sized kitchen, it was a pretty good deal. We learned the value of a hard day's work. We were training to be adults.

The reward for growing up was a backyard to get lost in, large fields for sports, ponds for swimming and fishing, and fresh apples ready to be picked off the tree. Near the barn a concord vine produced juice-bursting, shirt-staining grapes that were so purple they looked fake. We even had a couple of plum trees.

Here, there were four seasons of nature, fresh air, and freedom (when we weren't doing chores). When my siblings and I started developing friendships, we rarely ran out of things to do. We played sports and games almost every weekend.

In Detroit and Southfield, my father grew to despise city and suburban living. Most of all, he hated the noise. The Simpsons were now free from litter, pollution, traffic, and noise. The only kids around were the ones we invited over, and that was fine by me. There was so much to do at Camp Luther Vista, somedays I just liked being by myself.

Nothing Gold Can Stay

I recently returned to the camp. It wasn't the same. Nothing ever is. You can never go home again. Enough remained, however, that it instantly took me back. Our house was radically different, but the chimney still stood in place. That made me smile. Seeing the baseball diamond, the fields we played in, and the camp buildings—most of which are still standing—made me laugh. Seeing the overgrowth, the uncut grass, and the neglected apple trees made me angry.

I walked by the pond, fishing lake, and canal where we enjoyed skating, fishing, and swimming through the years. They were no longer pristine bodies of water. Instead, they resembled swamps. Seeing the two useless water holes in overgrown, unkempt condition caused me to bow my head and cry.

Chapter Eleven

DAD PLOWS, GETS PLOWED, AND THEN . . .

Michigan winters during my childhood were rougher than they seem now. Full disclosure: I have not been a resident of the Mitten since January 1996. Friends and family up there give me the details though. If three or four winters in a row are unbearable, I hear the stories. I can tell how bad it is by the tone on the other end of the phone. "Yay, we got through January. Only three more months of this shit to go!" Lately, there's been very little cursing about the weather.

I love Michigan. I will always call it my home, but the year-round climate lies somewhere between stinks and unpredictable. When Michiganders enjoy eleven weeks of better-than-average weather each summer, they turn it into one long party. Who can blame them?

As I write this in late March from my Tennessee home, it's eighty-two degrees with a sky full of blue. Livingston County, where I grew up, is experiencing a fifty-four-degree, cloudy, windy day. We planted a Victory Garden and did yard work here in Tennessee yesterday. My wife and daughter are both outside painting today.

I must say though, when I go home, the weather is great. Mostly because my wife put her foot down a decade ago. "No more trips to Michigan," she said, "from mid-September to the end of May—ever!" Granted, Michigan doesn't always connect summer months with warm weather. One freaky late July weekend in 2015 was plain cold. "The calendar says July 29, but I guess that doesn't matter here. The thermometer reads fifty-six, and it feels like forty."

Coincidently a similar, mid-July cold blast in 1992 spurred my move south.

My brother Victor and I lay on chaise lounges at a lakeside park, goose bumps running up our arms and legs. We shivered our way through several twenty-two-ounce Icehouse beers. Our hands shook over the pages of car magazines and lottery tickets. After scratching off another unlucky lottery ticket, I looked at Vic. "This weather sucks," I said. He nodded and said, "Gotta be a better way to spend summer." Two weeks later, we moved to Georgia. Climate matters.

Winter Wonderland

Winter fun was abundant at camp. Hiking in the snow and looking at nature was good for killing a couple of hours. We thoroughly enjoyed building snow forts, snowball fights, skating, sledding, and driving beater cars around the property.

We didn't have expensive toys or ATVs to add to our good time. Oh, how I would have loved a four-wheeler or a snowmobile to ride around the camp! Friends came over with their toys and we had fun, but it wasn't the same as having our own.

When Tom and Vic were seventeen, they pooled their money and bought an old Ski-Doo snowmobile. I only rode three times and never got to drive it before its track broke, rendering the machine useless. They couldn't afford to get it fixed. Life lesson learned: Impoverished people have no business buying toys.

Our dad did have a sort-of wintertime toy. The camp had three slightly different old Ford tractors for maintaining the property. They were all variations of the classic Ford N series tractor. The newest featured a front loader bucket and spotlights for nighttime operation. Like a kid with a new Tonka truck, Dad looked for reasons to drive that thing. He worked on it the most and used it for dredging seaweed out of the pond, moving large amounts of dirt, and—in the wintertime—plowing snow.

Anytime snowfall began, Dad headed to the barn to charge the battery on Ole Gray. Soon, he began artfully plowing the driveway and the camp roads, rarely bringing the tractor to a complete stop.

Fifteen minutes into Dad's plowing efforts, I had a brand-new playground. Snow piled ten feet tall, sending my imagination to the peak of every white mound. Sometimes I carved out a snow fort topped with a roof of scrap wood. I built snowball-fight bunkers and premade snowballs for that night's inevitable battle and turned really high snow piles into slides or sled runs.

One January morning, Dad's plowing routine changed. I looked outside where my white pile playground awaited me. But there was no tractor cleaning roads and no Dad to wave at as I carved out my snow fort. I blew it off like any eight-year-old boy would. "Oh well," I thought, "he must have had to go to work or something." I had my piles of snow. It was time to play with my new toy.

After playing in my snow mound city for most of the morning, I joined my brothers for some ice skating. When their friends showed up, they started playing hockey. I was too young to play, so I was left on the sidelines watching. Soon, I got bored, so I grabbed a shovel and skated down the canal.

Slowly, I shoveled piles of snow all over the canal. Then I skated as fast as I could and jumped over the piles. After each jump, I checked the snow piles for skate marks, ensuring I cleared the obstacle cleanly. Eventually, the day disappeared into darkness. We all went inside for the evening meal. Strangely, Dad wasn't home yet.

Dad Returns the Hero

My father rarely missed dinner. If he did, it was because he was trucking out of state or just had a larger-than-usual fight with Mom. Those battles never had a winner and always ended the same way. "Bill, get out, stay out, and don't come back." "You're kicking me out 'Lain, out of my own damn house?* Don't bother, I'm leaving!" Door slammed,

---

*We always found it funny that Dad called the house at the camp "his." The house in Southfield was his. The farmhouse in Brighton belonged to Dad as much as the Ambassador Bridge belongs to me. That home was the property of St. John's Lutheran Church. We were one notch above squatters.

Dad exited through the back door. Another door slammed, Dad revved the engine and peeled out of driveway.

That evening, Mom was quiet. We talked about our day, and she remained disinterested. We cleaned up after dinner as the snow started falling again. This was warmer, wetter snow, the greatest enemy of any outdoor skating surface. If not dealt with, the snow falling on top of our rink of smooth, glassy ice would turn into choppy, frozen slush snow. Impossible to remove and no fun to skate on.

By the time my brothers layered up to clear the ice, almost two inches of slush had fallen onto our precious rink. As they shuffled toward the lake, shovels in hand, Dad's car pulled up the driveway. He parked the car and sat in it for a few minutes.

In the distance, Tom, Rick, and Victor made the first few passes with shovels, digging at the slushy frozen water, while I sat on my ass and ate snow. A few minutes went by and we heard an engine fire up. When the loader's spotlights bounced off trees near our driveway, we knew Dad was plowing the driveway again.

Where had he been all day? Why was he avoiding Mom? It was weird, and if anyone knew what was going on with Dad, they never told me.

Dad finished plowing the driveway and a good stretch of our road. He drove to the lake, killed the motor, and watched my brothers work. "How you boys doin'?" he asked with a cocky smirk and half grin. "That snow looks pretty heavy." Then, for a brief moment, we thought Dad was going to climb off the tractor and help. It would have been out of character for him to help us do grunt labor, especially on something like the ice rink, a non essential part of the camp's day-to-day operations.

Several years later I heard Dad tell a story to a family friend. Dad told the friend, "Me and 'Lain looked on the lake, all five of our good, healthy kids skating at night. I don't know, I think we did alright. The kids were having fun. I know when I was their age, I would have been tickled pink to have all that these kids have!"

And there it is, my dad was not a complicated person. He was just bitter and angry and lacked the perseverance to turn his dreams into reality. But he got us to the camp, and that was big for him. Dad enjoyed watching us skate at night. But it was more than that. As he looked on from the kitchen window, his pride got an enormous boost. For Dad, this was a big bump up the ladder from the West Virginia holler. Skating at night under flood lights? That could only be imagined by the wealthiest of kids back home. Now, his kids were doing it right in front of him.

One of the twins started to hand Dad a shovel. Dad chuckled and fired up the tractor. Tom went back to shoveling, and Vic gave Dad a dirty look. Before Victor could mumble profanity in Dad's direction, Dad made a decision that went down in Simpson family lore. My father, Bill Simpson, raised the plow and drove the tractor onto our ice rink. Then, he began plowing.

Now, any readers out there who are unfamiliar with the Ford N series tractor, let me provide a few details. They are slow, two-wheel drive tractors not built to maneuver on ice. They are also heavy, weighing an average of 2,500 pounds. A front-end loader and a short, cocky guy behind the wheel easily put it over 3,000 pounds.

Dad smiled and smirked as he plowed. Water bubbled up through cracks. The cracking grew louder, but Dad couldn't hear it over the tractor. My brothers and I watched, speechless. The heaviest thing anyone ever dared driving on our ice was the neighbor's Arctic Cat snowmobile, which was maybe 500 pounds. This weighed six times as much.

In the house, Mom was beyond nervous, so she employed her classic self-defense mechanism: She pretended it wasn't happening. After confirming through the kitchen window that we were off the ice, she sat down and resumed her crossword puzzle. She knew if Dad broke through the ice, none of us would be dumb enough to try to save him. The water was only ten or twelve feet deep, and we knew Dad could swim.

We often talk of the stupid stuff men do to impress women. We rarely talk about the dumb-ass things fathers do to impress their kids. Dad liked being the man, and he loved showing off. He also liked to make everyone think he was fearless.

Dad clearing the snow saved the rink from the dreaded slush snow freeze. It was his Super Dad moment.

Years afterward, I overheard the rest of the story. When he decided to plow the driveway upon his return, he was avoiding Mom and didn't want to start a fight. When he took the tractor on the ice and started plowing? He was drunk as shit, the real reason he was avoiding Mother.

I never learned why Dad was gone for so long that day. None of us knew where he went. Was it a failed job interview, a successful one? Dad was always trying to start a business. Perhaps he was excited about a budding new opportunity? Wherever that day started, it ended at Sammy's Sail Inn, The Cozy Inn, or the Log Cabin. Maybe all three.

Eight-year-old me didn't know or couldn't comprehend that my father was drunk. I just thought he was happy and acting a little strange. He was doing something nice for us. I didn't understand or care why.

That night, our little lake could have become a grave, and the grill of a Ford tractor could have transformed into a tombstone. But Dad survived. He may have staved off death that night at the camp, and he definitely scared Mom, even if she wouldn't admit it. If Dad fell through the ice, it would have changed a few things for the Simpsons. Selfishly speaking, our days of living at Camp Luther Vista would have ended immediately and way too soon. Also, I don't think I would ever want to go skating again.

As it is, he survived, our rink was salvaged, and we all lived to skate another day.

No Southern Skating

I miss skating on lakes and ponds. Do people still do it? There's something about skating over water—knowing you could fall through, wondering how deep the water is below—that adds to the experience.

Even though I live in the south, I take my daughter ice skating a couple times each year. I'm happy to do it and am grateful to still be physically able. But there's no pond skating in Tennessee or Georgia. Someday soon I want to skate on a real lake or pond one more time, while I still can.

Chapter Twelve

TOMMY

We all have memories—childhood memories that fade over time but remain with us until our dying days. Everyone has them. No matter how bleak or well-off a family is, during any given childhood, some specific memories live forever. Most of us have at least a few personal events, images, or visions that reside deep down inside. Sometimes they're so powerful they produce a smile or a tear on any given day. One such memory involves my elementary school, Birkenstock Elementary, and my older brother Tommy.

My twin brothers got their first real part-time jobs at the ripe age of fifteen. Like my oldest brother and my sister, the twins finally started contributing to the family bottom line.

This was out of duty, not choice.

Our family was dirt poor, and in the early '80s, Dad found it difficult to stick with any source of income for much more than a year. It wasn't for lack of opportunities. He got jobs, good and bad. Then a layoff would set him back for a few months. He also had endless business ideas— some good, some bad. Dad just had trouble seeing things through to completion. He wasn't lazy. He lacked perseverance and the ability to look into a mirror. I'd say those were my father's biggest flaws. With Dad stuck in neutral, Mom had to do something quick and radical to save the family mis-fortune.

As a consequence of being on welfare and food stamps, Mother applied for and was accepted into a government-sponsored program that paved the way for her to return to school. Soon, Mom began her freshman year of college at the seasoned age of forty-five.

One of the conditions of Mom's free tuition/welfare gift was that all able-bodied people in the home ages fifteen and older owed Uncle Sam. I'm not too sure on all the facts, but the way my sister tells it, the three Simpson high schoolers were "encouraged" to go to work. The bill to Uncle Sam came to about fifteen hours a week of unskilled labor.

On December 28, 1973, President Richard Nixon signed the Comprehensive Employment and Training Act, or CETA as it came to be known. The program offered work to low-income and long-term unemployed individuals. It also procured summer and part-time jobs for high school students who came from low-income families. Denise went to work at the Salvation Army and raked in a little less than three dollars per hour. Tom and Vic got jobs as after-school custodians at local elementary schools.

The whole thing was a win-win for Mother. She didn't have to worry about three kids' pocket money, and they could contribute to their clothing and other household costs.

The after-school employment also kept Tom and Vic out of trouble while Mom went to school and later got two part-time jobs of her own. Or at least the jobs reduced the number of hours the twins spent on the trouble train. They were no choir boys.

School Daze

After school, Victor went to work down the road at Latson Road Elementary. A couple of bus transfers later, Tommy would show up at my school, Birkenstock Elementary. It was a very small school by today's standards, but I loved it there and it was my learning home for just over four years.

There was one class for every grade, two portable buildings, and an all-purpose room that served as the gym, lunchroom, art room, music room, and assembly hall. Some years there would be a few too many students and classes had to combine. I was a third grader in Ms. Snider's third/fourth grade split classroom. Everyone knew everyone, from the teachers to the principal, Mr. Clay. They all provided a very friendly atmosphere to learn and play.

The school's best attribute was its vast playground. We had a flat field for soccer and baseball, a black top for running that we also played football on after a deep snowfall. We needed the extra frozen layer to cushion the pain and terror of being tackled on the rough tar/gravel surface. After four or five inches of snow, it was the perfect gridiron.

In the winter we also had a hill for sledding and building snowmen. The playground had swings, slides, monkey bars and giant tractor tires for climbing on and hiding from girls. Most of the girls were afraid of the large, old dirty tires and for the most part would stay clear of them. It was late spring of my third-grade year on that playground that I have a few of my best childhood memories.

As luck and public-school transportation would have it, some days, Tommy arrived at my school for work in time for my class's last recess. Mr. Clay was really laid back. He didn't mind if Tommy took a detour to spend some time with his little brother and the other third-grade children. Anytime Tommy arrived at recess, I became an instant star.

His antics always began with an imitation of being trapped in a tornado. He'd head to a swing set, grab hold of its nearest pole, and suspend himself in midair. As a teenager, Tommy had almost no body fat and could perform this feat for an eternity. My face glowed in pride as my friends gasped in awe. "How is that even possible?" one would ask another. The next day, away from Tommy's heroic view, my fellow third graders would give it a try. My friend Jason was the only one who ever came close.

Down, Set, Race!

If we were lucky enough to have an aired-up football, we played Football 500. Just like the baseball version, you got more points for catching the ball in the air and fewer points if it hit the ground first. When a real football was unavailable, a Nerf ball served the purpose. Tommy was the official thrower. Most of the boys in my third-grade class stood on one side of the blacktop. Tommy launched the ball from the other side, a hundred feet or more, and cheer as we tried to catch the bombs falling from the sky.

Often, recess ended with races on the blacktop. Jason, who was a year older than the rest of us, usually won. His legs were longer than my body. Steven, another friend, and I usually tied for second. He was faster out of the gate, but I usually caught him by the end. The rest of the third-grade class came in a distant third.

The days Tommy joined us in our final dash were extra special. When he lined up for the final sprint, half the kids on the playground joined us. With all of us lined up on the surface and Tommy at the far end, Tommy yelled "Go!" We all jumped off the starting line and barreled down the rough, black surface. Meanwhile, Tommy stood still. After giving us a twenty-yard head start, Tommy would take off, bolting past us like we were standing still. Jason, Steven, and I put up the best fight and were always the last he passed. Sometimes, Tommy toyed with us, staying by our side for ten or twenty feet, only to hit another gear and sail by. The race always ended with my brother at the finish eight or ten strides ahead of the fastest three elementary racers.

On those days, I ran a little faster and dug a little deeper. I did my absolute best. Couldn't let my big brother down.

Those afternoons Tommy spent with me at recess were the best show-and-tell a third grader could have. Those are memories I've cherished for over forty years, a true lifelong treasure. Thank you, Tommy. You gave me something that can never be taken away.

Chapter Thirteen

THE NINTH LIFE AND OTHER PET STORIES

Like everything in our household, family pets came with a set of Bill Simpson rules. These rules weren't written down or posted, but they were memorized and understood. It's hard to forget something when it's preached at you several times a year. Dad reiterated the pet rules anytime an innocent child seeking additional companionship—*cough, cough, Denise*—wanted to give an animal a loving home.

The first rule: Pets are animals and therefore belong outside. This rule only had a few exceptions. Dying or very sick dogs were allowed access to the basement if Dad liked them. If the dog was new to the family or Dad disliked it for any reason, that canine took its last breath in the garage. Cats always expired in the great outdoors. Dad had a tolerate/hate relationship with cats. He tolerated cats that did their job and understood that Dad hated them most of the time.

The only thing on four legs that my dad hated more than cats were varmints. Skunks, squirrels, chipmunks, opossums, rats, and mice were all high on Dad's hit list. The top of the list never changed though. The dreaded raccoon was rodent enemy number one to my father. In Dad's opinion there was no need for a trial. It was straight to execution for those despised critters. Raccoons not only did the most damage, but every single mask-wearing one had rabies and contracted it the day they were born. Or that's what Dad said.

I never knew why Dad's hatred for the raccoon ran so deep, but it was unmistakable. "Damn coons" is all he said when he saw one or inspected damage left by one.

Once while driving down an old dirt road, Dad spotted a raccoon on the shoulder near a stop sign. The car swerved a little, and I feared my dad seriously considered wrapping the front of our Plymouth Fury around a stop sign to kill a raccoon.

Dad wasn't the only one who hated raccoons. So did Scooter, the one cat Dad tolerated more than he hated. This big Russian blue gained inside access to the basement and back porch, a seemingly impossible feat. All because mice, rats, and squirrels were mere appetizers for this furry southpaw. When Dad witnessed firsthand that Scooter did her job well, Scooter found a place in our family.

The Legend of Scooter

Legendary stories involved Scooter (with possibly one assault charge still pending), but none topped Scooter's run-in with Mrs. Zurcher.

Mrs. Zurcher lived four houses down and had a little dog that liked to go after cats. Scooter didn't like little annoying dogs. The result was Mrs. Zurcher at our front door, threatening a court battle. "Your cat attacked my dog!" she yelled on our front porch holding her pirate-patch-eyed pooch. "She tore his eye out!" I'm not sure how Dad responded, but I suspect he just laughed and shut the door in her face.

Like Mrs. Zurcher's annoying dog post-attack, raccoons seldom stopped by. When they did, Scooter didn't back down. Screeching and hissing in the night sounded through the upstairs window. Quick as it started, it ended. In the morning, we'd find proud Scooter sitting by the back door. No Championship belt, no trophy, just a few drops of blood and shreds of coarse raccoon hair on the back steps.

Scooter did have one enemy she could not defeat. The automobile. Early one morning, Dad eyed a greasy spot on the road. "Rick," Dad said, "get that cat off the road before it gets hit again." Rick placed Scooter in the bed of an old pick-up in the driveway. Labored breathing, possible internal bleeding, a broken leg, and a nose of blood and puss filled poor Scooter's medical chart.

There was no trip to the vet though, and everyone knew better than to ask. Scooter's condition was grim. Dad was firm. "None of you kids go near that damn cat!" he told his children. "It's either gonna die right there or it'll hobble off and die in the woods later tonight. Nothing you think you're going to do will help save it!"

Denise spent the rest of the day looking down at Scooter from her bedroom window and crying. Later that night, Denise and the rest of the family missed part one of a small miracle. Dad showed empathy toward Scooter, a cat.

The next day when Denise ran down to see if Scooter survived the night, Scooter was gone. Before she could ask, my father gruffly filled her in. "I didn't want the neighborhood dogs or other varmints to pick at her all night," he said, "so I put her in the Dodge. You can check on her but don't touch her!"

Denise ran to the teal blue Mopar and found Scooter in the back seat. She was still breathing, licking slowly at her drying blood. Wrapped in an old shop blanket, she lay in front of the food and water Dad left her the night before.

Then, three days later (no intended comparison to Christ), Scooter the cat stood up and limped out of the car. She was alive and—well, almost—well. With her bad-ass varmint-fighting and dog-bullying days in the rearview mirror, Scooter still had a purpose. She stayed around as a companion to Denise for several more months. Her ultimate demise came as it did with most of our family pets. One day beloved Scooter went missing without a trace.

Dad's Favorite Animal

A few years before Dad passed, I asked about his favorite pet. I knew the answer. I just wanted to hear him tell an old story or two. His simple answer: "The Beagle." As with most of our family pets, The Beagle's name was less than dynamic.

Traditionally, the first thing families do with a new pet is name it. They hold a family meeting in the den or kitchen while observing the fuzzy, clumsy puppy, brainstorming aloud until someone creatively nails it. A consensus forms and most, if not all, members agree on the new name. Then training begins, and the first trick is teaching the name to the confused, scared puppy that just peed on the kitchen rug.

The Simpsons did things differently. When we got a new pet, it was usually six months to two years old. We rarely got a fresh new puppy or kitten. Our pets usually came to us, strays that never learned their original names and refused to stay put.

These animals sauntered up our driveway or crawled under a fence. Their pathetic, downtrodden look always said the same thing: "Can I stay for a few weeks, you know, until I get back on my feet?" We didn't bother spending much time on the naming process, because we never knew how long those stray pets would stick around.

The oldest trick in the shabby pet-owner manual gave us most of our pets. Someone would have an unwanted dog and head to the country, where dirt roads with farms, big yards, and fields smelled of opportunity. Afraid of being spotted, the pet owner would slow down—but not stop, and chuck the unwanted puppy or kitten out the car window. After all, that apple orchard, farm, or trailer park can use a cat like this one, right?

Some of our pets first traveled down canine or feline skid row. Animals on their third or fourth stop in life glanced up at our humble home and figured, "What the hell? This might be as good as it gets."

Beagle and then later his sidekick, Collie, were prime examples. The Beagle was two or three years old when he wandered into our lives. Dad swore the dog was bred purely for hunting and routinely stated it as fact. We all wondered if it was true. After centuries of breeding and years of training, did The Beagle just lose his way during a hunt and end up in our driveway? More likely, the small hare hunter didn't meet the previous owner's expectations and got released for his last hunt in our vicinity.

Collie, on the other hand, was no purebred animal. He was half-baked. This scruffy, smelly, hairy mess was covered in burrs and plagued by a severe breathing issue. Dad allowed Collie to stay. The mangy mutt was Robin to The Beagle's Batman, a package deal.

Those two dogs followed Dad everywhere around camp. When Dad was on the tractor, The Beagle and Collie flanked out to both sides like security detail. If Dad was in the barn working on equipment, they sat at attention the entire time. Dad didn't train them to do this. The one trick he taught them was to "Sit pretty." Armed with table scraps, Dad would say, "Sit pretty!" The duo then sat on their hind legs and begged with their front paws curled in the air.

Beagle and Collie sitting pretty for Dad.

The Beagle was loyal to my father and friendly with the rest of us, but he was a loner, often taking off for days on end. Dad and the rest of us never worried about it. And after a day or two, we would hear Beagle's loud howling and yodeling, a sign that he picked up the scent of a rabbit in the orchard or the woods. We could all feel his excitement from half a mile away, knowing he'd be home soon.

The first time I heard Beagle hot on the trail of a rabbit, I thought something was eating my poor dog. Dad walked me to the apple orchard and told me to keep quiet. In the distance, The Beagle ran in and out of brush piles and around trees, chasing a terrified hare. Beagle bayed and yodeled, quiet only when he lost track of the rabbit. Soon as he regained the scent, the yodeling commenced.

The hunt was glorious, holding a circle-of-life feel, and I loved it. Dad loved watching all animals in action. Decades before the animated *Lion King*, there was Mutual of Omaha's *Wild Kingdom*. The whole family enjoyed watching it, but it was one of Dad's favorite programs.

Sadly, the conclusions of Beagle's hunts weren't glorious. They ended with a tired bunny cutting left when she should have veered right. Beagle would pounce. Then, a brief struggle and a broken back leg. Finally, The Beagle would drag the poor hare to the house seeking praise and—hopefully—a reward.

The reward came just before Dad put a single .22 bullet into the head of the not-quite-lifeless bunny. Like our cats, family dogs had jobs. We had a huge garden, and rabbits weren't welcome. Mom hated bunnies almost as much as Dad hated raccoons. Mom and Dad both spent too much time working that garden to let some stupid family of bunnies mess the whole thing up. Beagle protected our green beans and carrots, but his most important job was being Dad's best friend.

When Dad wasn't around, Beagle followed us around the property. One early Saturday in January, Mom sent Tommy to the camp kitchen with two bags of meat. The camp kitchen had two large chest freezers Mom used to store extra meat when she stumbled on a big sale. Tommy walked the surplus to the kitchen with Beagle trailing behind. After placing the meat in the freezer, Tommy left the kitchen. He locked the door of the unheated building and returned to the house.

Five days later, Mom asked, "Has anyone seen Beagle lately?"

We all started to worry.

Dad wouldn't admit to being concerned for his friend. To keep us from worrying he most likely just said something like, "He'll turn up somewhere. Always does." Considering the low temperatures that week hit the single digits, this was pretty sketchy optimism, even for Dad. "There's a blanket and some hay in the garage," he said. "The Beagle knows his way home."

Two more days passed and still no sign of Beagle. Saturday brought slightly warmer temperatures. I played outside in a snowbank as Rick and Tommy headed to the camp kitchen to retrieve meat and produce for the weekend's meals.

Moments later, I heard loud, excited talking and laughing. I looked up to see Rick and Tommy taking turns holding and petting Beagle. Rick placed the pooch on the ground, and I ran over to pet him. I stroked Beagle's back so hard I almost knocked him to the ground.

He was so weak he could barely stand. I could see and count each of his ribs. Our reunion with Beagle was a warm and happy gift on an otherwise dreary January day. Rick and Tommy guided The Beagle to the basement and warmed him up with some old blankets. Tommy fetched water and Rick brought down the big, cheap bag of dog food with some table scraps mixed in. According to Rick's estimate, Beagle ate almost five pounds of dog kibble that day.

Who could blame him? He'd just spent a week alone in the camp kitchen with every bit of food locked away, out of reach.

But he didn't give up. Every time Beagle heard or saw one of us nearby, he likely howled and clawed at the window desperately. Shredded curtains lay at the bottom of several windows, evidence of his attempts.

The frost that normally coated the old windows during winter was patterned out with tongue and claw marks. Every window Beagle could reach by standing on a nearby table had the same dog saliva stains. Our beloved dog licked his way to hydration. His search for nourishment was almost his doom.

Several nearly empty boxes of rat poison were scattered in the kitchen area. Nearby were frozen pools of dog vomit. Thankfully, the poison wasn't enough to kill Beagle and whatever filler it contained was enough to keep him alive.

Two beds near the kitchen were reserved for ladies who cooked during camp weeks. One bed was beaten down pretty good and featured clumps of Beagle's hair near the pillow.

Forty years later, Tommy still feels bad about what happened to Beagle. He blames himself and thinks how horrible those seven days were for our family dog. Beagle didn't die that day, but he was never the same. Tommy insists Beagle was less trusting and never went near the camp kitchen again.

A couple years later, Beagle was gone. Like so many of our pets, we never knew the end of his story, though Dad assured us he was picked up by a hunter.

Everyone was so relieved that Beagle survived those seven days of doggy hell. If Tom and Rick had opened that kitchen door to find a dead Beagle, out of respect for our dog and my father, this story would have died there too.

My Kitty Two

Another less-than-original pet name was coined when our black-and-white short-haired cat birthed kittens in the attic—the garage attic to be precise. Mama's name was My Kitty, and she chose the hottest month of the hottest summer ever to become a mom. As expected, Dad instructed us, "Stay away and let it take its course!"

After a few days we went up to check on the litter. Three kittens crawled all over their new mother. One was alone in the corner, the victim of the heat. We removed the deceased kitten and brought down an alive male to show our neighbor. That kitten left us for his new home a few weeks later. That was fine with me. We still had two kittens to play with.

The next few weeks, My Kitty adventured beyond the attic. Sometimes her kittens followed her downstairs, but they never got far before turning back in fear. Sometimes My Kitty snuck away while her babies slept. On a late summer afternoon, one kitten took its final journey outside of the attic.

I was in the backyard washing my bike. Mom was hanging clothes in the side yard. Tommy was nearby practicing walking on his hands. Rick was in the garage fumigating a large wasp hive. Something woke the kittens—perhaps it was the noise below or maybe a few wasps made it into the attic. Regardless, something stirred the kittens. One of them approached the attic window, which was missing a lower glass pane.

The tiny female feline cried furiously for her mother. Her ear-piercing call sounded like she was being strangled. But her mom didn't reply. My Kitty was likely wandering the neighborhood, enjoying some needed "me" time. The crying continued. It became so loud that Mom, Tommy, Rick, and I gathered to see what the problem was.

Overhead, the little kitten looked fine. To be sure, Tommy decided to go upstairs to invesgitate. He took two steps toward the garage, and that little furball, still shrieking at full volume, poked her head through the hole in the window. "No Kitty!" we shouted in unison. But we may as well have screamed, "Go for it, you can make it!" Because that little kitten jumped out of the window and—THUD!—died on the spot.

Before we could react, that kitten's brother poked his head out of the window, taking up the cry his sister abandoned. As if unwilling to live without his sister, the young male cat followed his sister right through the window.

There was no thud this time. He landed with a bonk and a little kitty grunt. As if someone painted a bullseye on the back of kitty one, kitty two landed right on his sister. It was not a soft landing, but the kitty survived with no broken limbs and no bleeding. My Kitty Two lay next to his dead sister in seemingly perfect health.

All cats are born with an innate ability to orient themselves and always land on their feet. It's called the cat righting reflex. While all cats are born with this ability it takes six to seven weeks after birth to master. Falls or pounces greater than a few feet also require a more developed backbone, which neither of our two kittens had.

Both kittens tried to land on their legs. But at just four or five weeks old, their righting reflexes weren't perfected, so what did they land on? Kitten number two survived. A few days after the accident, he gave us a clue regarding what he landed on.

The (Temporary) Sound of Silence

Something didn't sound quite right.

Kitten number two soon became My Kitty Two, named after his mom. Kitty Two was odd and oddly quiet. His mouth was open a lot, but no sound came out. It looked like someone was perpetually stepping on his tail in a soundproof room. As he aged, My Kitty Two developed a barely audible chicken-like clucking and scratching noise that sounded nothing like a meow.

We concluded that My Kitty Two's little neck absorbed the attic fall, permanently damaging one or both vocal producers. I suspect My Kitty Two ran through three or four of his nine lives that hot summer day.

You hear jokes about people or animals who are "not long for this world." My wife and I have always been of the same opinion. Stereotypes and clichés stand the test of time because there is some level of truth behind them. Sometimes you can just look at a dumb puppy or spunky wide-eyed kitten and be confident in predicting, "This one won't be around long."

My Kitty Two was never destined to be one of those legendary generational pets that reaches legal drinking age. He was never going to be like an aging congressperson who sees three decades tick by and sticks around beyond their prime.[*]

To be honest, we had our doubts that My Kitty Two would survive Reagan's first term. He just didn't pass the eyeball test of longevity.

There were plenty of opportunities for him to die. He faced a dark autumn night fight with a skunk and later fell through an inch of early-winter ice. One cold night he got his tail slammed shut in the screen door. A week afterward, part of his tail was gone. It either fell off or My Kitty Two chewed off the wounded portion. He had multiple close calls with moving tractors, and he made a habit of sleeping under cars to avoid the hot, afternoon sun.

It would have made an exciting, albeit brief, Discovery Channel documentary. "Follow us around Camp Luther Vista as we present *The Nine Lives of My Kitty Two*." Each episode would have concluded in similar fashion. Another life would get exhausted, the number of remaining lives displayed in the final scene.

Michigan winters in the early '80s seemed colder than usual. It was

---

We really need to pursue term limits for congress in this country. Three for the senate and five for the house. Hopefully I get to write more books and can take up that issue in the future.

102

good for ice skating but not much else. As stated previously, when it got real cold, Dad graciously opened the basement to our pets.

On one such occasion, my siblings and I called out for My Kitty Two to come inside. After at least ninety seconds—sorry, it was too cold to stay out longer—we gave up. Frustrated with our inability to get the cat inside, Dad threw on his overalls and went outside with a light and some food. The temperature outside dipped down to seven or so. After a few minutes, Dad came back inside and delivered one of his classic lines, a line I use to this day: "He's a cat, he'll be fine."

Morning came, and the house came to life. One of my brother's friends who stayed the night went outside to warm up his car against the harsh winter air—standard operating procedure in Michigan.

That day, the morning ritual forced two amazing results. 1. My Kitty Two got his voice back for a brief moment, sending out a piercing screech that was followed by a long, harsh growl. 2. My Kitty Two joined an elite group of cats that somehow jump through the moving fan blade of a small block V8 and live to screech about it.

Cat hair flew out of the grill and all sides of the hood. My brother's friend killed the motor as My Kitty Two tore off into the woods, presumably never to be seen again.

A week went by with no sign of My Kitty Two. Considering the frigid temperatures, not even Dad could confidently assert that, "He's a cat, he'll be fine."

It was a Saturday morning when the legend returned home. It had warmed up outside, and an eerie fog hung over our snow-covered lawn. Tommy and I shoveled snow and slush off our makeshift hockey rink when Tommy spotted My Kitty Two emerging from the fog—a mystical, tragic sight.

My Kitty Two hobbled on four frostbitten paws and a broken leg. All his white fur was gone. He was now black and gray, a zigzag mohawk of frostbitten skin and fan blade-shaven hair striping his body. His little face was covered in cuts and gashes, and his shriveled-up ears were green.

Tommy went to get Dad. I just stared at My Kitty Two. He hunched over himself, a picture of death. He sat at the lower corner of our side yard, on the first square of sidewalk. When Dad got a look at My Kitty Two, he immediately, yet slowly, turned around and went back inside.

Tommy and I looked at each other, dumbfounded. Tommy shrugged. "Is he going to get Mom?" I asked. Tommy didn't answer.

When Dad returned, he came bearing his Remington model 341. If any critter smaller than a dog needed to be taken care of, this bolt action .22 was Dad's weapon of choice.

Every kid wants to tell stories about how deadly accurate their father is with a gun. Every boy fantasizes about their old man being Atticus Finch, and I'm no exception. At fifty yards, he could hit every bulb on a strand of Christmas lights. He could take off a turtle's head from one side of the fishing pond to the other.

Dad picked up My Kitty Two with gloved hands. He placed the worn-out cat on an old stump near the garden, dropped some table scraps at his feet, and pat My Kitty Two on the head. My Kitty Two sniffed at the scraps, took a bite, then looked up, as if giving thanks before slumping his head.

Dad counted out twenty-five paces and faced My Kitty Two. He chambered a round and brought the rear sight to his right eye. Dad could shoot with either hand/eye, but he was slightly better with his right. He let out a breath and pulled the trigger. A split second before the shot rang out, that damn cat twitched and moved his head two inches down and to the right. The bullet hit a tree, and My Kitty Two's left ear fell to the ground.

Dad grimaced. Then, faster than you could say "dead cat," Dad chambered another round and hit My Kitty Two right between the eyes. My Kitty Two's ninth and final life only lasted a second, but what a second it was. Surviving a speeding bullet! As pet stories go, It doesn't get more legendary than that.

Chapter Fourteen

VICTOR

Throughout my childhood, my brothers and sister took on various roles helping to raise me. My older siblings took turns guiding me through life and showing me the ropes. Most importantly they did their best to keep me out of harm's way.

As I write this chapter, I've not had contact with my brother Victor in several years. I don't know where he is, how he's doing, or if he's even alive. I anguish about him, have eerie dreams about his current situation, and question how I should feel about his absence in my life.

My siblings have similar feelings. Our level of concern varies, but we all think and worry about Victor in our own way. As the months and years go by, I feel less and less emotion for my lost brother. The emotion that exists has transformed to anger—anger over decisions Victor made, bridges he burned, and the path he chose.

We all offered and gave Victor assistance, but his life only worsened. Our handouts and good intentions led nowhere. We all reached a point with Victor that, although we still loved and missed him, we had to move on. For the sake of our own families and lives, we could no longer allow him to cause "detriment to the team."

Lately, my memories of Victor have grown foggier. It's less painful not to think of him than to ponder what has happened to him and what his life could have been.

If all five siblings' lives were intertwined, would each be richer? Maybe. Our connection could have made the years easier after our parents passed away. But it was not to be. Adulthood, as it turns out, is a bitch. And for Victor, the sacrifices and challenges were often too much to overcome.

While many are fading, some childhood memories of Victor are crystal clear. For years, he looked after and protected me like a big brother, serving as one of my guardian angels. He once looked after and protected me like it was his duty. Now that angel is a distant memory from a previous life. He is missing, but he is not forgotten.

Luther Vista, my childhood home for over seven years, was a magical place to grow up. One of my favorite wintertime activities growing up at the camp was sledding, but not just any sledding.

The landscape at the camp was true lower-middle Michigan. It was mostly flat with just a handful of gently rolling hills. So, unless you found yourself on a golf course with a toboggan or at Birkenstock Elementary with a roll-up or saucer sled, good sledding hills were hard to find. At Luther Vista we had to make our sledding hill.

Before the first apple orchard and just above the swimming pond was the Land of the Pine Trees. It was just another odd mystery of the camp property. In the middle of fields, ponds, swamps, and willow trees and just in front of a good 100 or so apple trees were three hundred or more closely planted, sixty-foot-tall pine trees. These trees occupied one of the few hills on the property. Right down the middle of this hill was a path about six feet wide. The path was our sled hill, and it led directly into the swimming pond through our so-called beach.

The Beach at Camp Luther Vista

I shouldn't berate the beach. It was more than adequate by summer church camp standards, and having it in my backyard was more than I could have imagined. But to call it a beach is misleading. It consisted of hard black and brown clay covered in a paltry four inches of a sand-like substance. During summer camp, the Buddy Board resided there.

Everyone who wanted to swim had a buddy and a corresponding number on the Buddy Board. Lifeguard Lori used the board to wield her power over the young campers. When that woman yelled "Buddy check!", you better find your buddy—right now! God forbid you left the swimming area without moving your token to the "out" side of the board. Lori would find you and verbally destroy you.

Of course, there was more to the beach than the Buddy Board.

Building a sandcastle there was more work than fun. Set on a thirty-degree pitch, the beach was impossible to sit on in one spot for long. The clay was hard and black. Any castle over a foot tall required a small earth mover and the touch of a skilled potter. There was, however, one benefit to the beach substance. Any pond or moat surrounding a sandcastle estate held water significantly longer than those fancy sand beaches allowed.

Cold, Hard Fun

The beach also served a special purpose in the wintertime. Situated at the bottom of the pine tree hill, it doubled as a fun descent and the deceleration exit to our sledding adventures. Why did we need a deceleration lane? Being impoverished and having few entertainment options brought out our creativity. Bored children and adolescents were forced to use more brain power to have a good time.

The pine trees' height and density only allowed a fraction of snow found elsewhere. So, while we had a hill and cold winter air, we had only an inch or two of snow under those trees. But my brother Victor developed a plan. This plan was executed over several winters at the camp, but I will always remember the first.

He decided our hill would be faster than snow, because our hill would be ice! The pond below was spring fed. As a result, the two sides near the shore never completely froze over. With some buckets from the barn, Tommy and I carted bucket after bucket of water from the pond to the hill. Victor supervised and told us where to place the murky water. He then went to work, using a snow shovel and saucer sled to sculpt his vision. Slowly, our ice trail took shape.

The final step in Victor's plan came courtesy of nightfall. Despite our protests, Victor forbade sledding until the next day. We had to let Victor's predicted January deep freeze put the final touches on the slope.

Every year, the deep freeze came, just as Victor predicted. The first year, the temperature got down to single digits. When I woke up, it was only eighteen degrees. I know because I asked my mother. Her response stuck with me. "Stephen McKinley," she said, "why do you need to know so many details about the temperature? What difference does it make how cold it got last night?"

Ready as I was to see how Old Man Winter complimented our efforts, Victor never wanted to be disturbed until the little hand crept past ten or eleven. But Mom never let anyone sleep past noon. Not even Victor.

With Tommy gone to a friend's house, I had two choices. 1. Get dressed, go to the hill, and risk a beating by Victor for going without him. 2. Wait for Victor to awaken and have the first run on our hill together. As impatient as I was to test the finished product, I chose to wait. It was the safest and most brotherly thing to do.

As Victor came out of his hibernation, I got dressed and prepared the sleds. I rubbed so much candle wax on the roll-up and saucer sleds that the orange and red plastic was barely visible. When Victor stepped out into the noontime air, he sneered at my sleds. "What are you doing with those?" he asked. With the excitement of Beagle chasing his first rabbit, I replied that I had them waxed up and ready to go.

Victor rolled his eyes. "Do you like hitting pine trees with your face?" he asked as if talking to a blunt object instead of his little brother. "We can't use those sleds. They have no control, no steering," he continued. "We have to use the other sleds."

Other sleds? What other sleds?

Victor led me to the garage and ascended to the forbidden area, the attic. It was an area of which I was both terrified and banned from without supervision. Victor instructed me to wait on the stairway. Moments later he lowered the first sled down.

To that point, I only knew plastic sleds and big, long wooden toboggans. This was something altogether different. As I received the first runner sled on the stairway, I beheld it with curious awe.

In my hands was a Flexible Flyer with red painted steel runners. It featured an image of an eagle soaring through an American flag. A rope passed through the handle that, as my older brother explained, turned the sled "almost like a steering wheel."

I took the sled outside, leaned it against the garage, and ran back to the stairway. As Victor lowered a second sled, he told me it was mine. The second one lacked the charm and beauty of the first. The runners were puke green and rusty. A faded Japanese rising sun was barely visible in the middle of the wooden boards.

Questioning or whining to my brother about my second-class sled would be futile. So, as I watched Victor tow his American Flexible Flyer toward the ice hill, I decided to add some two-wheeled fun to the morning.*

I mounted my metal steed.

Sure, Victor would have the better sled, but I would beat him to the hill. Until that day, I was restricted to riding in circles in our basement or driveway. There was too much snow for a bike ride, according to Mom.

Just after a recent snowstorm, Dad cleared most of the snow from the gravel road leading to the orchard and the pine hill. It was the perfect time to see what that bike would do. Instead of asking Mom's permission, I planned to play dumb and ask for forgiveness later.

I looped the rope of my Jap Flyer around my bike's banana seat and took off after Victor. Soon, I passed him on the gravel path, and he didn't give me a second look. Typical Victor. He rarely showed excitement or any sense of urgency. Besides, he knew there was no way I would take the inaugural run down his creation.

I parked my bike at the edge of the pines and ran the rest of the way, dragging my sled behind me. Victor arrived soon enough, and we trekked up the side of the icy run together. The whole time, he instructed me to never walk on the run.

At the top of the hill, Victor continued his instruction. "You can sit

---

A few weeks earlier, Santa bestowed me my first bike at the age of eight. It was, without a doubt, the cheapest twenty-inch two-wheeler K-mart sold. But it was mine, and I was proud of that bike. Early Christmas morning my dad sent me to fetch his slippers at the bottom of the stairs. I opened the door that led to the landing and there it was on full display. "Santa left it there because it was far too big to put under the tree," mother would later chime in. It was bright orange with a full banana seat, shiny chrome fenders, and a chrome chain guard. When I saw it on Christmas morning, I cried. Now those tears were all joy.

on these sleds and use your feet to steer," he said, "but you go faster and have more control if you lay on your stomach, steer with your hands, and lean to avoid trees." Convinced that's all I needed to know, Victor laid on his Flyer, folded his legs up behind him, and shoved off.

Ice crystals shot up behind his sled as he rocketed down the hill. The little beach near the pond slowed him down, but not enough. He glided several feet onto the pond where the ice was thick enough to support him. Then he jumped to his feet and motioned me his way. "Stay clear of the trees and lean into your turns!" he yelled.

Scared and excited, I lay down on the rising sun. It was time to fly. I couldn't chicken out and let my big brother down.

I closed my eyes, shoved off, then popped my eyes open as I picked up speed. My sled moved so fast it felt like floating on air. The steel runners glided over the ice, sending me down the hill, through the beach, and onto the pond, two sled lengths past my grinning older brother.

We spent hours that day walking up and sledding down that hill. Eventually, some of the ice chipped away on the hill, and our run slowed down. But Victor wanted more. So, he built a makeshift ramp at the base of the hill. My first time over it, I landed so hard it knocked the wind out of me.

Frozen Through and Through

Like all good things, our day of sledding came to an end. We were both hungry and dinnertime was fast approaching. It was getting dark and the temperature was dropping fast, so I looped the Jap Flyer around my banana seat and tugged it down the trail. I rode over the dirt-covered bridge separating the swimming pond from the canal.

I was pedaling down the trail when it happened. It happened so fast I had no reaction. My bike's front tire caught in a tractor rut left by dad's plowing efforts. The rut, once wet and muddy, was now frozen stiff. With one hand on the handlebars and the other guiding the sled behind me, the frozen dirt rut was now in control. It led me right where my dad had put the first bucket of snow.

The rut guided me, my bike, and my sled into the pond. Water

110

splashed onto my arms and face and froze to me immediately.

The water was only a few feet deep. I was in no danger of drowning, but I was in real danger of freezing—fast. If Victor reacted at his normal pace, I would have died right there. Something threw Victor into hyper speed. He threw his sled in the water to stand on and jerked me out of the pond in a flash. I stood beneath him crying, shaking, and likely wetting myself. He bent down and looked at me. "You have to run right now," he said. "Run as fast as you can to the house."

He grabbed his sled and my hand, and the race began.

The cold water in my snowsuit turned to slush. It wanted to freeze, and 100 feet from the house I could hardly move. Victor threw me on his sled, secured my frozen mittens around the handles, and pulled me the rest of the way to the house. With one arm he picked me up and shuttled me through the door. Then, he took me down the basement steps and placed me on the concrete floor.

I didn't question the basement trip at the time, but I realized the significance years later. If the goal was restoring my core temperature and getting me out of my frozen clothes, why not upstairs? Or the heated back porch where we get our skates on? While my brother was doing the right thing and possibly saved my life, he also had an agenda.

Victor is a classic CYA (cover your ass) guy. He needed to get me dry and out of my clothes, and he needed to keep the entire incident hidden from our mother. If she found out I was sledding on thin ice under Victor's watch and then rode my bike into the pond and nearly froze to death, ol' Vic would be in a lot more trouble than me.

Victor settled me on top of a laundry basket, yanked off my boots, and worked my frozen snowsuit zipper open. Once the zipper was down halfway, I started removing my top layers. Victor tossed me a blanket and a towel. "When you get your bottom layers off, hang them up and then wrap up in that blanket." Victor hung my boots over the workplace vice. "Sit by the furnace and start drying yourself off. I'll be back in ten minutes."

Then, he shot upstairs.

When he lumbered back down the basement stairs, he brought a full change of clothes for me, two piping-hot ham-and-Velveeta sandwiches, and a cup of hot cocoa. I put on warm, dry clothes and ate quietly.

We were both relieved and happy with the day's outcome. I would give anything to know what went through Victor's head after our sledding went from wintertime bliss to near catastrophe. My brother was calm the entire time though. If underneath his cool demeanor he was figuratively shitting his long johns, I couldn't tell.

It may seem a bit dramatic to say Victor saved my life that day, but I'm sticking with my story. We were a good 200 yards away from the house when I took my bike for a polar bear plunge. If I were alone, what would have happened? Well, I don't know. I'd like to think I could have pulled my frozen, full-of-water snowsuit out of the pond and up to the house, but I doubt it.

Once I stopped shivering, we laughed and rehashed the afternoon's events. Then I asked Victor about my bike and sled. He assured me he would recover both. Victor's instructions were clear, "Get warm and keep this between us."

That day Victor escaped the wrath of our worrywart mother and created a special bond with his baby brother. That bond would last a very long time—just not forever.

Chapter Fifteen

OUTDOORS WITH WILLIE

Willie was my father. The name originated from the West Virginia holler where he grew up. He left that name behind when he moved to Michigan, where he became Bill.

As you could guess, William was Dad's legal name. It was also Dad's dad's name too. When some of his friends found out that Dad's childhood moniker was Willie, they gave it new life to mess with him. Dad didn't mind. He liked being known as Ole Willie. Mom never called him that. She either called him Bill or asshole. My siblings and I called him Dad. Not Papa, not Father, not Pops, not Daddy, and definitely not William, Willie, or Bill. When we were kids, calling either parent by their first name was a major sign of disrespect and dealt with accordingly.

I always wondered what would have happened if one of us called Dad by his name. "Hey Bill, how about sticking with a job for more than a year?" Or "Hey, Willie, can you give me a hand fixing this old Pontiac you warned me not to buy?" None of us ever had the courage to try it out, not even Victor. Not even as a joke. Calling Dad by his first name would have resulted in a long pause, a deadly stare, and eventually, a volcanic eruption.

But Bill Simpson isn't with us anymore, and it's my book. So, this chapter is "Outdoors with Willie." It just sounds right. Besides, it lets you know it's not gonna be too serious or life-changing, but you're gonna have a good time.

Outdoor Freedom

My father was not a true outdoorsman. He was just a man who liked being outdoors. He hunted a few times with friends and family but never talked about it much. He fished some but never alone. It was something he did to spend time with us kids.

I think Dad's longing to be outside stemmed from his shitty childhood. Because of Grandpa's demeanor, Ole Willie looked for every possible way to avoid him. The best way to do that was to be outside, where he was free. Free to roam the hills of West Virginia after finishing the day's chores. Out of sight and out of the mind of his old man. Any hour away was a welcome reprieve.

My father treasured several things about the great outdoors. I appreciate some of them, too. I'm not a big rules guy. I'm pretty sure I got that from Dad. Willie always scoffed at restrictions.

Being outside, away from people and society's rules, is true freedom. You can pee anywhere. You can talk to yourself or shout and cuss at the heavens. You can be quiet and listen to your thoughts in peace. You can go a few hours or days without worrying about breaking a social norm or offending anyone. Put simply—you can be you.

When heading outside for freedom, Ole Willie lived by a specific set of rules. A campground, fishing hole, or picnic spot had to be a good distance from any city or major road, and cost mattered. A natural-born tight ass, Dad believed the great outdoors should be free for everyone. He might pay for a few nights at a campground or cabin, but picnic tables and fishing spots were enjoyed at no cost to the Simpson Family.

His cheapness was on full display on family trips to West Virginia. Every time, we stopped near the ass crack of Ohio—Portsmouth, a.k.a. the hottest city on earth. Dad would pull off at his familiar spot. At the store he would pick up smokes and a thing of table salt. At the adjacent roadside stand he would get a watermelon.

Watching him buy a watermelon was a treat. Dad grazed the produce stand like a wise old farmer at auction. Ole Willie would dig out pocket change and pick out the biggest, ripest watermelon there. Minutes later, we dined on that delicious fruit under the shade of a busy bridge. Salt was

114

available for the watermelon, but you had to ask Dad to get any. So, most of us went without. The entire meal was washed down with our own saliva. If you had any complaints about the menu, Dad uttered another famous line: "Eat it or wear it!"

This was all part of Dad's money-saving plans. Ole Willie knew when we rolled into West Virginia, we kids would be treated like angels, fed immediately by Grandma or one of Dad's sisters. He wasn't parting with eight bucks to feed us on the road when free food was coming. Besides, lunch? It's the forgotten meal. We were lucky to get anything.

It was a big discovery if Dad stumbled on a campground or picnic spot with a place to fish. Fourteen bucks for four concrete walls, a bathroom, place to cook, a bed, and a fishing hole right across the road? That was winning the lottery, Dad's idea of a great weekend. This was why we frequented Johnnie's Cabins in Kaleva, Michigan.

Johnnie's Be Not-So Good

I was introduced to Johnnie's outstanding accommodations at the age of eight. It was my first big-boy camping trip with my brothers and Dad. Uncle John and Grandma Dixie came too. It was the middle of October, and we were there for the annual salmon run near Tippy Dam. Snagging season.

Sadly, I was too young for snagging on the river. But I didn't object much. I'd heard what happens when your waders fill up with water. I wasn't interested in getting weighed down by 100 pounds of river and carried downstream, never to be seen again. Despite my fear of a watery grave, the grownups said not to worry.

Right across the dirt road from our concrete castle was a fishing hole. Johnnie's Lake had a dock and row boat for fishing. In the middle of the lake—it was really a large pond—several trees stood tall, surrounded by seaweed, countless turtles, and a handful of fish.

"Don't get your hopes up," Victor mumbled, "we've never caught a thing in that damn lake!"

"Last time we were here," Tommy added, "the turtles and trees stole most of our hooks and all of our bait. We didn't get a nibble."

However, I had something they didn't: the blind optimism of a child. I was an above-average pond fisherman and planned to prove my big brothers wrong. The next day we went out early. I was eager to catch the fish that would make me the star of the weekend.

As my brothers expected, it got boring fast. I never even saw a fish. The turtle-infested pond took our bait and half a dozen hooks. After an hour, we were on shore throwing a football.

Dad exited the cabin with a look of disappointment. "You boys done fishing already?" he asked. We were. Dad always talked about fishing at Johnnie's, but I never saw him throw a line in. The fishing was free at Johnnie's, but it was the ultimate example of getting what you pay for.

Salmon Snagging

After breakfast, the adults shot the shit for an hour before the Simpsons headed out for some real fishing. The big boys and my uncle fished, while I sat on the banks of the Manistee River. But sitting on the sidelines was a great time. I didn't know fishing was a spectator sport. It is. There at Manistee River, it's a damn enjoyable one!

Our salmon-snagging days started mid-morning, giving the perfect mix of October Michigan weather. The early day was overcast and damp, mostly cloudy with temps barely getting to fifty. Close to water, a dense fog rolled through the trees.

A little after lunch, the sun popped out and took the chill out of the air. In the middle of the afternoon when the fish weren't running, the sun was bright and hot. Temperatures peaked in the mid-seventies. Clothing layers got removed as we built up good sweats running around or playing football. Then the sun went down.

We gathered firewood well before dark. On the banks of the Manistee, I've felt the temperature drop thirty degrees in three hours. Once the sun sinks below the trees, the temperature sprints toward the mid-forties. And the moment nightfall hits, you can't see a thing.

On my first snagging weekend, a light rain chased us to the cabin each night. When we left for the river on the second day, a light drizzle in forty-four degree weather reminded us it was October. Despite the rain and clouds, our second day at the river was a hit.

On the first day (sorry to go back in time), Uncle John enthusiastically showed off his new fishing net. Well, it wasn't really new. It had hung in his garage for a decade without touching a single scale.

When someone had a fish on, Uncle John took his net to assist. He dipped the net in the cold river, placing it under the big salmon that was full of eggs. The net disintegrated, and the fish cut through the bottom like hot butter. Lesson: Fishing nets, much like motorcycle helmets and roof repairs, have a limited shelf life.

If Uncle John was the goat on the first day of snagging, he was the hero on day two.

During spawning season, salmon swim upstream to lay their eggs. They essentially dig their own graves in a gravel bed, release their eggs, and die. Snag one about to lay her eggs, and it's easier to wear her out and bring her in. That's what Uncle John did.

After a few minutes of watching Uncle John battle the mighty coho, Dad grabbed the net. Uncle John had the salmon cornered in a little inlet. The two brothers jabbered back and forth in their smart-ass way. My dad and Uncle John constantly traded sarcastic backhanded remarks toward one another. It's how they displayed brotherly love. "Hey Johnny, is this one of those trick nets?" Dad asked, struggling to get the net into the water. "You know, like the one you used yesterday?"

He lowered the net into the river and laughed as the salmon swam between Uncle John's legs and ducked under a nearby log.

"Damn," Uncle John said, "what were you waiting for, Christmas?"

A young man armed with a net climbed into the river to help. As he approached, the salmon spooked and came out from under the log. It swam right into Dad, who got it in the net and threw the big fish onto the bank of the Manistee.

Uncle John cackled like a twelve-year-old boy. The original Simpson boys finally got a big one. Better than a trophy, that fish was dinner.

Lacking the skills and tools to clean and gut the fish, we took Uncle John's catch into town. The cleaning fee was more than acceptable: a simple small-town barter to avoid the tax man. The cleaner kept the treasure buried in her belly, and we got a meal-ready salmon. The fish cleaner hung Uncle John's fish for preparation, placed a large bucket under the fish, and made a single, long incision. The belly exploded with several hundred bright orange eggs.

Once the salmon was cubed and double bagged in ice, we headed back to the river.

Grandma cut up potatoes and other vegetables while Dad and Uncle John got the fire going. My brothers and I ran up and down the riverbanks hoping to see some snagging action. Victor, eager to do instead of watch, put on waders and casted for a luckless hour.

Then as usual, the temperature started dropping. An hour passed. Partly sunny turned into all cloudy. Our salmon boil still wasn't ready when the first few raindrops sizzled on the top of the hot pot.

Between the excitement of snagging a salmon and having a riverside fish boil, we left most of the things needed for a picnic at the cabin. Fortunately, someone rounded up a half dozen foam coffee cups and a few plastic sporks. The picture in my head is one that was never taken. All of us stood on a high part of the riverbank under the same tree where Dad set up camp every time we went to the Manistee.

We stood in a tight circle near the fire, positioned under Dad's tree with the remaining autumn leaves as shelter. By dinnertime, the rain turned into freezing sleet. While we sporked up salmon boil from our foam cups, the only one who sat down was my grandma, Mamaw Dixie.

At eight years old, I liked hot dogs, ham-and-cheese sandwiches, and pizza. A fish boil in the freezing rain was not my go-to meal. But I'll never forget how good it was. There is absolutely nothing like eating fish caught that same day. I can still taste the cubes of fresh salmon swimming in the broth. It was awesome! I'll never forget it.

Sleep came easy that night, nestled inside Johnnie's Cabins.

Too Chicken for Cabins

A couple years before Johnnie had cabins, there was Johnnie's Place. At the back of Johnnie's property were two old chicken coops. No longer in service and decades old, the coops' rotten walls laid in piles of rubbish.

The five-foot roofs had a few holes but kept things fairly dry. Shelves previously used for housing chickens became beds and storage shelves.

From our first weekend there, Johnnie's Place became a family tradition. For a couple bucks per night per chicken coop, Bill Simpson was a happy camper. Grandpa and Grandma had an entire coop to themselves, and Grandma Marie couldn't have been happier. My sister, Denise, recalls waking each morning to the sound of Grandma singing in her native Finnish tongue.

I wasn't born when these trips took place. Suffice it to say my siblings don't remember coop camping as a joyous affair. The old coops had a thick, pungent odor, and it was hot under the long sloping chicken house roof. Any outside breeze never penetrated the sunken dwellings. The coops also had old, dangerous farm equipment that had to be navigated around. A few old tires full of mosquitos and some rusty barbed wire fence completed the scene. It was like camping at a KOA!

More than once during these outings, my selfish Dad drove off with Mom for some alone time. Denise guessed Dad took her to Bear Lake or maybe Lake Michigan in an attempt to rekindle whatever dysfunctional spark they once had.

This left my brothers and sister trapped for hours like rats with Grandpa and Grandma and nothing to do. They might get a few saltines and some warm chicken salad to nimble on. Or if they were lucky, Dad would leave behind hot dogs and buns, while Grandpa and Grandma did their best to entertain and care for the Simpson kids.

Camping in chicken coops is one of many stories my siblings make me feel guilty about. To be honest, I'm jealous. It's a great story. Who camps in a chicken coop at Johnnie's Place? When people hear about that, they want to hear more.

One of those chicken coop camping trips occurred late in the spring of 1971. Perhaps it was Memorial Day. Perhaps that's where my story begins—in the last meaningful spark of my parents' marriage on the banks of Bear Lake or Lake Michigan. If so, way to go, Dad!

Chapter Sixteen

MY FIRST LIONS GAME

Thanksgiving used to be my favorite holiday. It is getting so I don't even like turkey much anymore. When my wife finds out I want salmon and smoked pork next November there will be a discussion, and I will not win.

Two things occurred to me over the last fifteen to twenty Thanksgiving celebrations. As adolescence turned into adulthood (for me it was my late twenties), I began to realize a few things about the November feed frenzy. For starters, that Friday turkey sandwich is never as good as you think it's going to be.

You don't even get to enjoy it until half past four on Black Friday. After you go to bed Thursday night, an F3 tornado disguised as a turkey dinner destroyed your kitchen and most of your living room. I like my house a little less when it's messy. I like organization, everything in its place, and most things at a right angle. Everyone has quirks. Those are a few of mine.

It takes longer to clean up after Turkey Day than watching five bad documentaries or two meaningless football games. And don't forget about all the damn prepping. The female folks in my family start working on the meal Wednesday afternoon. As my wise older brother has said for years, Thanksgiving is an overrated holiday that underdelivers. Now, as soon as I sign these divorce papers, I can start writing about sports.

Speaking of Sports . . .

Thirty-two years before the Cowboys ever played on Thanksgiving, the Detroit Lions began their tradition. Lions fans have endured this game since 1934, minus six years around World War II. Think "endured" is a poor word choice? Well, let's take a look at the tape, the numbers. Because stats don't lie.

The most glaring and obvious number is the Lions' Turkey Day record. Despite hosting every game after a short practice week, the Lions' overall record is 37–45–2. They've had approximately ten nice performances on Thanksgiving. Most of these games, though, are forgettable. Even when they win, it's usually ugly.

Being a Lions fan isn't all bad—if you were born before 1950. The Lions won four NFL Championships from 1935 to 1957, which isn't too shabby. Being a fan of the Detroit Lions in the six decades that followed the '50s? Beyond painful.

I'll throw in some numbers to cement my opinion. Zero Super Bowl appearances. Three division championships in thirty years. And the worst transgression of all: three playoff victories in over sixty years. No, that is not a typo. The Detroit Lions have won three playoff games since 1958! Two of those came in the 2023 season. Thank you, Dan Campbell and Brad Holmes, for restoring the roar and bringing the "Pride" back.

This would be just another sorry sports story if it were just about wins and losses. However, with the Lions, the new and creative ways in which they lose games is almost unbelievable. There is a six-minute YouTube compilation of failure if you have the stomach for it. Players, coaches, and team officials all come and go, and the story remains the same. Are they cursed? Is it just a bad dream? Are the Detroit Lions just a big blue broken toy for the Ford family to play with? Or is it the most complicated tax write-off of all time?

Is it bad Karma or does the Ford family just suck at this ownership thing? It happened on November 22, 1963. On what most people call one of the single darkest days in United States history, William Clay Ford purchased a controlling interest in the Detroit Lions for $4.5 million. Adding to the darkness of that day was the assassination of JFK. I feel as if Bill Engvall would bark out that line right here.

Sometimes in life you have to look in the mirror. I can only guess that the Ford family doesn't believe in mirrors. The one constant thing in sixty years of Lions futility is the ownership. The passion the Ford family has displayed for OUR team sits somewhere between slightly invested to aloof and absent.

That said, I've been one of those long-suffering fans for over forty years. Those years have offered little to cheer about. Yet, I always have hope early in the season. When July turns to August, I evaluate the roster and schedule, consider their chances of winning the division, and research the current coaching staff. I listen to the GM and read about critical decisions he made or plans on making. Then I pause to consider life without Lions football. For some inexplicable reason, I always continue the journey.

As a seasoned fan, my early season hope diminishes faster each year. That initial hope turns to frustration by Halloween and disgust by Thanksgiving. One day I might take my ball and go home. How much more would I enjoy the fall if I could just become Lions-free?

How the Journey Began

Mom's brother, Uncle Bill, is a big sports guy. He's a fan, and he enjoys playing sports as well. To my knowledge, he's the best golfer in our entire family.

We assumed the Detroit Lions were his favorite team. In 1980 his professional practice and family were rooted in Oakland County. This is when he doubled down on his fandom for our gridiron heroes by becoming a member of the Detroit Lions Quarterback Club.

I'm not sure about most of the club details. What I know is that being a member was a notch above being a standard season ticket holder. Members sat near the thirty-yard line in the lower bowl above a huge banner that identified them as "The Detroit Lions Quarterback Club." Pretty sweet seats.

In addition to having two to four tickets for every home game, club members got additional reduced or free tickets to certain games. Yeah, the Lions were that bad.

Despite the horror that was the Detroit Lions, their home field, the Pontiac Silverdome, was huge. One of the biggest NFL venues for a long time. Seating capacity came in at just over 80,000. So, during some seasons, there were plenty of good seats available. Divisional games typically sold out though, and fans of regionally close teams (the Bengals and Browns) trekked north to support their teams.

The divisional exception to the Lions selling out was under the old format. Remember when the Tampa Buccaneers were a divisional foe in the old NFC Central? Those games rarely sold out because for many of their early years, the Bucs were as bad as the Lions. Thanksgiving games sold out most of the time. Especially if the game involved the hated Bears or Packers. Those fans travel well.

It was Thanksgiving morning, and six of seven Simpsons were running late. Rick wasn't with us. He was heading to the game with some friends from work. We were heading to Lake Orion for the annual family get together at Uncle Bill's home.

As the six of us lumbered along in Dad's Oldsmobile, Mom and Dad were speaking in hushed tones, deep in discussion. Rick not in the family truckster meant I sat in the backseat with my other siblings. My sister, Denise, who sat right behind my mother, leaned forward and was included in the secretive conversation. I heard enough of the chatter to know it involved me.

We were on a road that Dad despised as a motorist and truck driver, M-59. When my parents went silent, Denise whispered something to Mom. Without warning, Mom turned around in the big bench seat. She studied me for a few seconds.

"Stephen," she said, "how would you like to go to the football game with Tom and Vic and your Uncle Bill?"

I was a weird kid and somewhat of a martyr. I sat in silence, wrapped in fear of the unknown.

"It's a big boy question," Mom continued, "and I need a big boy answer."

I shook my head. "Don't I need a ticket? Will I miss Thanksgiving? Why doesn't Denise want to go?"

Denise sacrificed her ticket so I could go to the game. I had been out done, out classed by a world-class martyr, my older sister.

Mom assured me, "Thanksgiving will be waiting for all of you after the game."

"It sounds like too much trouble," I contested.

"It is no trouble at all," Mom insisted. "We're meeting Uncle Bill in Pontiac, and he has extra tickets. So do what your brothers tell you to do at the game, listen to your uncle, and have fun."

My imagination scrolled through all the bad things that could and would happen to me. I wouldn't find the bathrooms, and I would wet my pants. I would get lost or we would lose one of my brothers. The possibilities were endless, but it was out of my hands. Mom made the decision for me. I was going to that game.

We met Uncle Bill at a gas station in Pontiac. We were late, but that didn't change his excitement. He wore a smile from ear to ear, happy to treat three of his nephews to the traditional game.

Uncle Bill drove a mid-70's K5 Chevy Blazer with a lift kit and a plow on the front. As we climbed aboard the classic GM utility vehicle, he advised us of the situation.

"Your cousins are already at the game. We're a little late but if we hurry, we'll only miss a few minutes of the first quarter." He handed Victor our three tickets. "Victor, you hold them until we get there. Your cousin Stephanie has her ticket and will be sitting in the upper level with you."

I ran through more doomsday possibilities. What if we're so late they don't let us into the game? What if Victor loses the tickets before we get to the gate? I was—to put it mildly—wound pretty tight as a kid.

Thanks to Uncle Bill's status as a QB Club member, we zoomed around lines of traffic to access his preferred spot in the Silverdome parking lot. In an instant, Uncle Bill jumped out of the big Chevy and bolted without confirming my brothers and I were keeping pace. Victor gave us our tickets and we speedwalked after our uncle. As we approached the Silverdome, I heard a loud windy noise and felt some strong gusts.

Not coincidentally one of the characteristics of the old sports domes of the '70s and '80s is also the main reason they stopped making them. The roof. The roof was at best a sound amplifying smog center (at a time when smoking wasn't considered a felony). At worst it was an 80,000-client class-action lawsuit waiting to happen. These massive structures consisted of hundreds of Teflon-coated fiberglass panels that were essentially held up by air.

The air pressure that helped "support" the roof was generated inside the stadium. Upon entering you kind of got sucked into the doors. Leaving the Silverdome, you would have to brace yourself and power through like a weather reporter on the scene of a hurricane. If you were unlucky enough to enter or exit through a revolving door you would need both speed and strength to slip through the glass structure.

Once inside, Uncle Bill paused and turned to us. "I'm going to my seat," he said. "I'll meet you after the game or maybe at halftime." He gave us a baker's dozen list of steps to get to our seats. I didn't hear a single one of them. I was too busy counting the seconds until we were lost or abducted.

As we left our uncle, the roar of the crowd overwhelmed me. A loud rumble of clapping and cheering filled the building. The concrete and steel trembled overhead, leaving me temporarily paralyzed in wonder and terror.

Ten minutes later we found our seats and Stephanie. Still breathing heavily from scaling Mt. Pontiac, we sat down, but not for long. We could have stood the entire game, because we were in the top row of the stadium. Behind us was a chain-link fence and a very long fall down if that fence gave way.

The Original Letdown

The Lions had the ball and were leading 3–0. At this time I surmised the loud cheer I heard earlier was for the field goal. The field goal? They always cheer loudly for field goals, especially the first one. After all, it could be the only score of the day.

Minutes later, in the second quarter. Gary Danielson tossed a short dump pass to Billy Sims, and the original number twenty did the rest. With a few blockers down field, Sims weaved through the Bears defense, cut back inside at the twenty and got in for the score. The Silverdome erupted! It was loud, crazy, and thrilling. I felt like I was a part of something big. I stood, mouth open, in total awe. This is how great sports could make you feel! Lions led 10-0.

Going into the fourth quarter, the Lions were up 17 to 3. My brothers and everyone else in our entire nosebleed section were confident the Lions would win. But then it happened—slowly. The Silverdome went quiet. The Bears scored a touchdown, and the smoke-filled stadium got even quieter.

Doubt crept in late in the fourth quarter. Everyone, including my brothers, talked less and worried more. As a newcomer to sports fandom, I couldn't understand why hope was slipping away. After all, time was running out and we had the lead.

In comes the Lions Letdown Effect. Soon as it seems the Lions might do something good, as soon as you think they just might win, they flip the script. As the clock ticked to double zero, Bears quarterback Vince Evans found the endzone. The extra point was true, tying the game at 17. Defeated, Tommy declared, "Looks like we're headed to overtime." "Overtime?" I asked. "what's overtime?" Tom explained, "It's not just overtime like basketball or extra innings like baseball. It's sudden death overtime. First team to score wins."

My eight-year-old, optimistic self was thrilled. I got to see more football and the Lions had a chance to win.

Everyone stood. It was hard to see the field, but the crowd's cheers and jeers told the story. Within just a few seconds, the cheers were doused and replaced with another sound. Disbelief. A collective gasp from 75,000 people. I pulled on Tommy's sleeve. "What happened?" I asked. He didn't answer. I stood on my tiptoes and peered between two large shoulders to see Dave Williams streak down the sideline with four Lions feebly chasing after him. Touchdown. Bears win, Lions lose.

In a matter of seconds, my hope was dashed. The Detroit Lions crushed my spirit for the first time. I think the play took seventeen seconds, but everyone watching knew he was gonna score once he crossed the fifty. It remains one of the shortest overtime losses in NFL history.

My brother Rick was on the other side of the Silverdome. He claimed to be walking towards the exit when Williams made it through the first bunch of Lions at the Bears twenty-yard line. He knew it was over.

What happened next is for the most part a big blur to me. The stadium was an emotional melting pot. Some people were mad. Others were sad. Still others didn't know what to feel. They just wanted to get out as quickly as possible.

I clung to my brothers' coat tails and shut my trap. No one was in a mood to talk or rehash the game.

Uncle Bill was silent too. We climbed into the Blazer, and Uncle Bill began the slow process of navigating stadium traffic.

Eventually, we reached Uncle Bill's steep driveway. One by one, we somberly exited the vehicle. As we approached the home's side entrance, I tapped my uncle's elbow. He looked down at me with tired eyes, still bitter from the heartbreaking loss. "Thanks for taking us to the game, Uncle Bill," I said. Uncle Bill smiled wide as he did in Pontiac earlier that day. "Anytime, kiddo," he said gently. "Anytime."

The Lions lost the game in typical, horrific Lions fashion. However, the roller coaster of emotion turned an eight-year-old boy into a decades-long fan that is still going strong after forty-four years of pain and suffering. But with age comes wisdom and experience, and my fandom loses a little steam every year.

There may be an end in sight to the madness. For the first time, I'm beginning to wonder about my future as a Lions fan. How much more can I take? There's a glimmer of hope, but there always is. Will next year be the year I take my ball and go home? Will I throw in the towel and become Lions-free?

Chapter Seventeen

RICK

My parents separated and divorced in the early '80s. For three years after the separation, I joined my father in West Virginia for a short stay every summer. He drove up to get me a few weeks after school let out. While in Michigan, Dad slept in the shack we called a cottage next to the barn. He spent a little time with my brothers and sister, and after a few awkward days we left for the Mountain State.

Back in West Virginia, Dad lived with his mother or his brother Joe or whomever else would tolerate him. His brief stays in Michigan to collect me often ended dramatically. While I waited in his running car, Dad often got in some last second verbal jabs with his favorite sparring partner. Mom always tried to end it or cut it short by ignoring him and keeping busy in the kitchen, their fighting venue of choice.*

One reason for this approach was that Dad didn't trust kids in the kitchen. Kids are clumsy and messy, and they make mistakes. There was another reason he didn't want us near the knives. He didn't want a kid standing near Mom during their battles. Nothing enraged Dad more than someone standing in Mom's corner. This became an even greater problem for Dad once my oldest brother, Rick, was big enough to stand up to him. Once the twins reached their mid-teens and had Rick's back, Dad was severely outmatched and thus reduced to violently storming off

---

*Throughout childhood, my father considered kids mere dining patrons. We were not allowed in the kitchen. If you didn't earn money or weren't preparing food or cleaning up, then "Get out and stay out!"

and slamming doors behind him.

After ten minutes of sucking fumes in the driveway, I would see Dad emerge from the kitchen. He'd wear a nasty scowl on his face, and Mom would be a few paces behind him. She was often crying or scowling, but she always saw me off.

My father always ended the fight. His most frequent final jab was roasting the tires in the driveway and speeding off through a dusty, anger-filled cloud. I liked the speed and excitement of fishtailing out of the driveway, but the joy didn't last. Soon after we sped off, I always felt bad for Mom, realizing Dad used the accelerator to give her the middle finger.

Back to Michigan

In 1983, I returned from my first West Virginia summer with Dad. I walked toward the side yard where Mom was hanging clothes. She dropped the sheet in her hands, spit out a clothespin from between her teeth, and screamed. My sudden, unannounced return produced tears and a sigh of relief.

In classic Bill Simpson fashion, Dad never told my mom when I was coming home. "Lain" he barked into the phone, "it could be a few more days—maybe a week or two. It depends on work and money." As vague as possible through the long-distance line he would declare, "We'll see."

Dad kept me in the dark too. Just before settling in for another night of sweat-drenched, insect-filled sleep, Dad would tell me to get packed. "Heading to Barboursville in the morning," he'd say. "We'll have breakfast with your Grandma, then head back to Michigan." The next day we would abruptly leave Frametown, the hidden gem of Braxton County, and head home.

Returning from that first summer, Rick was the only sibling nearby. I found him standing beside the lawnmower going through some practice swings with his 9 iron.

"Hey," he called out as I got closer to him. "How was West Virginia?" "It was pretty much the same", I replied. "The people there are nice to me but very hard to understand with their southern, mountain accent. It was very hot and sweaty, and they only get two channels on TV," I would add. In Brighton at the camp we had rabbit ears on the TV that stretched to the ceiling. We were forty-five miles from Detroit but could still pull in seven channels. Two of the seven channels we pulled in were out of Lansing, which is about the same distance away.

"How are the Tigers doing?" I asked. "Pretty good, but so are the Orioles," he said, his voice low with a hint of Simpson cynicism. "The Tigers keep winning but they are just keeping pace with Baltimore." He finished the statement with a pessimistic tone. The Tigers finished the '83 season with the third best record in baseball. However, that didn't get it done in 1983. You either won the division or you stayed home for the playoffs. Most of that '83 team stuck around and delivered a World Series trophy to the Motor City the following year.

"What are you doing?" I asked.

"I'm practicing my short game," Rick said. He gestured to the trimmed grass. "I made myself a little par three course."

The course snaked around the camp's shuffleboard court. "I used the push mower to trim down some small greens, and the sticks in the middle are the flags. I have a straight par three with a water hazard near the green over there and a dogleg that goes over the playground and ends near left field.*

"I have a long, almost par four hole that doglegs around the kitchen and ends in front of the pond." He pointed past the flagpole that stood about fifty feet from the kitchen/chapel building. The idea to create his own golf course may have spawned from an episode of *M.A.S.H.* Rick was proud of his creation, but he may have denied the entire thing in the presence of anyone but his little brother.

"Would you like to go for a drive tonight?" he asked. "Maybe catch a movie?"

"Really!" I said, reaching a pitch in my voice that had been dormant for some time. "Sure, what are we going to see?" I asked as if I had some idea what was playing—which I did not.

---

*At the camp there was a baseball field complete with bases, a backstop and a pitcher's mound.

Our parents never took us to the movies. Going to a movie required a ride to the multiplex and money for things like a ticket and popcorn. Sometimes, Mom snuck us a couple bucks if we found a ride.

Needless to say, going to the movies was a rare, special occasion that happened about once a year. When my sister and her boyfriend took me to see *E.T.* in the summer of '82, I was so jacked about being there I forgot to watch the movie. The year before, Tom and Vic snuck me into *Raiders of The Lost Ark.***

After an hour of following Rick around his par three creation, we headed to the house to get ready for the movie. As I came out the back door, Rick loaded two beers and two Towne Club pops into a haggard foam cooler usually reserved for fishing minnows. He covered the beverages with as much ice as he could borrow from the freezer's two aluminum ice trays without Mom noticing.

High-Octane Thrills

It was odd to take a cooler to the theater, but I didn't care. Towne Club pop was childhood heaven, and I had my hopes set on cream soda.

We climbed into Rick's big Ford and he fired it up. My brother's 1972 Ford Galaxy was at the time the jewel of our family fleet. In a previous life the car may have been a police cruiser or part of some other government fleet. Rick's Galaxy was like the sedans used in the Clint Eastwood classic *Magnum Force*, although some cars in that movie were the upscale LTD edition. Rick's had a 351-cubic-inch V-8 motor with thrush exhaust. Damn, did that car rumble!

As we approached Grand River Avenue, Rick rolled down his window and lit a cigarette. When all four tires hit the pavement, my brother put his foot into it. The rear tires spun just a bit as he aimed the white beast towards Brighton.

*** My friend Matt and I—and our mothers—expected to see* Superman *that day. However, my teenage brothers and their friends messed around at the mall too long, and we missed the start of* Superman. *So, for the first time ever, I defied my mother and saw* Raiders. *The decision paid off. The violence and action in* Raiders of the Lost Ark *was every nine-year-old boy's dream. I was on the edge of my seat the entire time.*

Rick and I were now headed into town on a Saturday night, and my wide smile was difficult to contain. We went under I-96. The mall parking lot was on our left. I gazed over Rick's shoulder to observe the motorcade of teenagers that cruised in and out of the mall's main two entrances. Friday and Saturday nights meant cruising the mall parking lot and loitering the fast food joints in both Howell and Brighton. It was a rite of passage for teen drivers in Livingston County.

Young people, high schoolers mostly, cleaned their cars up every Friday and Saturday, waited until dusk, and began cruising the mall. Kids showed up in whatever they had. Cruisers tooled around in beaters, sports cars, family cars, hot rods they owned, or whatever they could sneak out of the driveway.

A slight exhaust odor produced by the cruisers mixed with the smell of mall-fried food filled the Galaxy's interior. The kind of odor that makes you ravenous the minute it reaches your nose. We drove past fast food row and the Brighton Mall. I was so happy to hang with Rick I failed to realize we passed the only theater in town. Rick navigated through Brighton, passing The Canopy restaurant and Cardonna's Pizza. "Almost there," he promised.

Just before we reached Marv's Bakery,* Rick clicked the turn signal arm down. He slowed, then edged the Ford behind a line of traffic in the center lane. I finally knew our destination.

---

*Some Sundays after church we took Grand River Avenue home. A mile or so from the iconic Brighton Bakery, we would begin to chant. It started as a hum and grew to a cheer: "Marv's, Marv's, Marv's the Bakery, Marv's, Marv's, Marv's the Bakery, Marv's, Marv's, Marv's the Bakery!" That after-church treat was the highlight of the entire weekend. The bakery had the biggest, best long johns in the world, melt-in-your-mouth deli ham and dairy-fresh milk sold in two-quart glass bottles and topped off with an inch of cream. Our chant combined with the tempting aroma of the bakery was too much for Mom. Against her better judgment and her pitiful checking account balance she would almost always stop the car. There were Sundays she knew her joint monetary arrangement with my father wouldn't support the delicious detour. Those Sundays she would, without a word or warning, leave church turning right onto Pleasant Valley Road. This maneuver would avoid Grand River, Marv's Bakery, and produce sad, disappointed faces in her rearview mirror. It was a lower-middle-class solution my mom lived by. Decrease expectations by keeping unattainable temptations out of sight and out of mind.

A Boy's Tribute to His Lower-Middle-Class Family

A thick, heavy dew floated above the freshly cut grass. Summer evening dampness was setting in. A massive wall towered over the line of cars waiting to enter. At the time I was only eleven but I remember wanting to see the other side of that wall since kindergarten. Which, in kid years, seemed like two decades of anticipation. Rick paid the attendant at the booth, and we crept along the gravel path. I was now on the other side of the great wall. I was going to see my first movie at the legendary Lakes Drive-In.

Rick grinned at me, as I took it all in. "It's a double feature," he said. "What's that?" I asked.

"They show one movie, then there's a short intermission," he explained. "After that, the second movie begins."

The first film of the double feature was a Bond film. Although it was already two years old, 1981's *For Your Eyes Only*, starring Roger Moore, was very new to me.**

For Your Eyes Only took us from one exotic locale to another: the North Sea, a Spanish villa, Greece, and Italy. The knuckle-biting chase featured James Bond on skis, trailed by bad guys in all black riding dirt bikes equipped with machine guns and snow cleats. There was action, intrigue, villains, evil plots, and an array of Bond girls to ogle over. For an eleven-year-old boy with a budding appreciation for cinema, it had it all.

The second movie of the night's double feature was *Poltergeist*. I didn't know anything about the Spielberg thriller, and it left me wide-eyed and full of fear.

It was a perfectly exciting and frightening evening for an eleven-year-old boy. Nothing could be better than catching a double feature at the drive-in with my big brother. We talked nonstop on the way home about the movies. At one point, Rick scratched his head and gave me a quick look. "Some of those things in *Poltergeist*," he said. "Well, just

---

**By the time I turned thirteen, I'd seen the first half of a dozen Bond movies, courtesy of ABC's Sunday Night Movie. Unfortunately, Sunday was a school night, which meant a ten o'clock bedtime. Ousted from the living room, I lay in bed trying to decipher the movie's conclusion through our bedroom wall. Sadly, the muffled sound that reached my ears was rarely enough to go to sleep satisfied.*

don't tell mom about the face peeling and the maggots in the kitchen."
Our mother hated horror films and could never understand why people
wanted to be scared on purpose.

I agreed and stuck to my guns, despite having a nightmare or two
afterward. But my fear soon became potential. I couldn't wait to share
the maggot scene with my classmates when school restarted in the fall.
Horror movie highlights are near the front of the bragging train amongst
eleven- and twelve-year-old boys. It gave me a great summer-time tale to
tell. Anyone who had not seen the movie was all ears.

That day, Rick gave me a gift—the gift of expanded imagination and
endless possibilities. Before then, I had a colorful imagination. I could
daydream with the best of them. But spending that time with my brother
sent my imagination into overdrive and made me believe anything is
possible.

Chapter Eighteen

FOOD STAMP DAY

There are times when the ends simply don't meet. While those times occurred regularly in the Simpson household, the circumstances differed each time. Job loss, small business failure, new mouths to feed and clothe, or surprise expenditures. My family never experienced great financial times. Our finances were rarely good. Mostly we lived through variances of okay, somewhere between bad and just getting by.

Later in life my father never talked about the bad times. His pride wouldn't let him. He felt responsible for the bleakest economic periods our family endured. He used his guilt as a self-defense mechanism. If he thought about them and talked about the failures, he might have learned from them. Or, this unlucky father could have taught his children about life, risks, taking chances, and self-evaluation.

Mom, on the other hand, talked about the tough times. She was a master of making the most out of a meager budget and wore the survival of poverty as a badge of honor. Like a wounded fighter, she took on the challenge of feeding and caring for a family of seven on fifty bucks a week.

Mom loved coupons. She took advantage of double coupon day, bought in bulk, and froze surplus when possible. She also knew how to work the system. Mom went to multiple stores armed with a single large food stamp to buy one item. The store then gave her cash back, which she used to purchase gas, paper products, cigarettes, and other stuff food stamps couldn't buy.

While she gamed the system with food stamps, her dignity took a hit each time we went on assistance. She avoided stores where neighbors and friends shopped and went shopping in the evening. Dad's dignity was negatively affected as well, but not as much. Mom did the shopping, so Dad avoided the embarrassment of making government-assisted transactions.

When my parents first separated in the early '80s, the ends of their budget were light years apart. Dad headed south to scout work. After a brief stay in Florida, he ended up in West Virginia. He eventually found work but usually only earned enough to support himself. So Mom was forced, once again, to go on government assistance.

This was a particularly dark time in the Simpson household. Dad was out of state making a buck any way he could, while Mom was stressing about how to feed her family like never before.*

Mom's part-time job barely kept the lights on. We were low on everything—food, paper products, clothes. As the eldest brother, Rick helped out with chores and money when he could. The first winter without Dad, we ran out of heating oil. That night, Mom and I stayed home alone.

As the house thermometer dropped to fifty degrees, Mom asked my siblings to make other sleeping arrangements. She was thinking logically and desperately. If we had to impose on a neighbor or relative, receiving a party of two was a smaller ask than a carload of five or six.

Mother closed all the doors in the house. After dinner, she left the oven on and the oven door open—our only source of heat. I watched TV under a blanket as Mom paced in the kitchen.

Like the purchaser of some of my Christmas presents that year I never knew the name of the angel that paid the oil bill. Mom must have reached out to someone. Maybe a church member or maybe a relative, I never knew. She and I stayed home that night, fueled with faith that her

---

*We later learned that Dad sold a few of his kids' birthrights during this time. Pretty shitty. Even shittier: he didn't tell us personally. Instead, we were informed of these transactions via his family grapevine years later.

prayer would be answered. When the fuel truck rumbled up the drive, Mom emerged from her room with a wide smile and watery eyes.

Moving Up for a Season

A few months later, Mom's nerves were at a breaking point again. She applied for assistance, but approval was taking weeks. In the meantime, Mom awaited the day she could go grocery shopping and put gas in the car. Her anxiety reached such levels that she began sending me to check the mail. On the first really warm Saturday of spring, like a bright new blossom, it arrived: our lifesaving welfare check and an enormous book of food stamps.

I trudged up the steps to the kitchen, set the mail on the kitchen table, and asked Mom to make some Kool-Aid—preferably my favorite, tropical punch. Mom was doing the dishes. While looking out the window, seemingly in another place, she just muttered, "I think all we have is orange." "No thanks," I replied. Water was better than orange Kool-Aid. It was the same with popsicles. No kid in his right mind ever wanted orange.

Just then, Mom saw the stack of mail. She set down the pan she was cleaning and approached the pile of postal treasure. She thumbed through the stack and tore open the two long-awaited envelopes. The stress and burden visibly left my mother's body. "Let's go do some shopping!" she declared. "We'll get any flavor of Kool-Aid you want and maybe an eight pack of Pepsi too! How does cheeseburgers for dinner sound?"

Elated, Mom deposited the welfare check and headed to the mall. Mom got a Coney dog. I got a hotdog with mustard and—surprise of surprises—a frozen Cherry Coke.

With her mom-sized purse bursting with welfare money and an extra-large book of food stamps, she was thinking about trying something new, something different. To know my mother was to be familiar with the words *routine* and *predictable*. She rarely liked anything new. That is, until she had a tiny bit more money in her early fifties and realized she liked driving newer cars and rediscovered her love affair with shoes.

But on this day Mom was considering something bold, something completely unfamiliar. Spending much of her life in the depths of poverty, she suddenly had more money and purchasing power under her arm than she'd had in years. She'd heard the stories. The neighbor ladies down the road went on and on. "Oh, the prices, Elaine, and the selection. You just won't believe it!"

It was less than a month old and the idea, the concept, was brand spanking new to residents of Livingston County. Anyone and everyone from as far away as thirty miles or more came to shop there. Even as a kid I heard rumblings about how great it was, how enormous the parking lot and the store were, all which took up more than five city blocks. Now, we were going to see it for ourselves. Mom was ready to try a dynamic new way to shop. So, we abandoned the familiar faces and setting of our hometown A&P and traveled to the other side of Grand River to embrace the Thrifty Acres of Meijer.

The rumors were true. It was enormous, several times bigger than Kmart and A&P combined. And all under one roof with better prices! Bikes and toys, jeans and sneakers, jewelry and camping supplies, and groceries galore. It was a shopping paradise.

Mom and I spent over two hours shopping that afternoon. We almost had to get a second cart, which I witnessed several other families doing. Mom purchased more nonperishables than I ever saw her acquire at one time. As usual, my job was to man the shopping cart. By the end of our shopping spree, I was sprung. My legs screamed and my back ached as I pushed the cart through the Meijer mecca. We loaded the trunk and placed the excess in the back seat.

When we arrived home, it took twenty minutes to unload. Once all was stowed away, Mom delightfully made us a snack. Ham, butter, and Velveeta cheese sandwiches with Pepsi on the rocks. It was delicious.

They say money doesn't buy happiness. I always wondered if "they" were poor and ever had to use food stamps. With age comes wisdom. Eventually, I realized true happiness does not come from money or how much you can buy. What money does buy is security. That welfare check and those food stamps bought my mom some time. A full fridge and pantry provided security. That security gave Mom a reason to smile.

Chapter Nineteen

DENISE

Mom wasn't always motherly. That's not to say she was a bad mother. She always fed and clothed us, helped with homework, and went above and beyond to provide our basic needs. She just wasn't much fun.

When we entered our teens and twenties, Mom was at her best. She shined when we became old enough to hold a meaningful conversation. That's when we learned that her greatest gift was the gift of gab. She listened to our concerns, then gave us options, advice, and guidance.

Before then—particularly from ages six to twelve—Mom was especially dull. My siblings back me on this. They, too, remember Mom coming up short in the fun department. She never got on the floor to help build a blanket-pillow fort or a house made of playing cards. She lacked enthusiasm for make-believe and never took us on adventures through the woods or engaged in the silliness of a child's daydream.

Thank God I had Denise. Where Mom dropped the playful ball of parenting, my sister scooped it up and scored. Nine years my senior, Denise wore several hats during my grade-school years.

As the only girl, Denise was automatically Mom's assistant, feeding and watching over me and helping Mom in the kitchen. She was also good at making us three younger boys disappear when the adults needed the main level of the house to themselves.

Life wasn't all work for Denise. She actually enjoyed taking me places and always made the best of her nanny position. When she developed an interest in photography, I became her leading subject, willingly subjecting myself to whatever funny and peculiar position she requested for picture time. Mom saw most of it as goofy tomfoolery. But I'm sure it made her smile.

Sometimes, Denise staged me in the driver's seat of our car with my little head barely poking over the steering wheel. Other times, she took shots of me and our pets in the backyard. The year Rick graduated high school, Denise dressed me in his cap and gown and a pair of adult glasses for a classic shot. I was swimming in the enormous gown, and the cap almost entirely covered the top of my head. There is a picture she took of me when I was in seventh grade. In it I'm sitting on an old two-wheeled hay rake. My head is tilted, and I am wearing this stupid grin on my face. I adore that picture.

Denise also played games with me. Memory, Monopoly, Chutes and Ladders, and Connect Four were in regular rotation. She taught me to shuffle cards, build card houses, and play card games like War, Crazy Eights, Go Fish, and Speed. When I got older all of my siblings pitched in and taught me how to play Euchre, a Michigan tradition.

With Denise by my side, I was allowed in the kitchen. I chopped nuts for brownies and forked the tops of peanut butter cookies to give them that signature criss cross design on top. She showed me how to make pudding and popcorn too. The best part of cookie time (and a kid's birthright) was licking batter from the beaters and bowl.*

Becoming a Working Man

As I got older, Mom went back to school. Denise and my other siblings and friends filled in the parenting gaps. At age nine, Denise gave me my first job. She made me waterboy for the flower gardens she planted around our home. I wasn't very good at it and I didn't care for flowers, but it taught me how to earn money.

In my early working days, Denise helped me get real jobs. She,

---

*For kids' sake, I hope this tradition continues forever. Don't give me any paranoid crap about a miniscule amount of raw egg killing kids either.

through a friend, got me one of my first big boy jobs working at a concrete paver plant. The ironic twist was it took me away from my first full-time job Rick had helped me get. The first official part-time job I had was with Denise. I think it was her idea too. I heard her tell Mom, "If he stays home all day by himself this summer he'll do nothing but get into trouble."

Denise ran it by her boss, and I became Denise's part-time assistant. She'd been promoted to weekend store manager and convinced her boss she needed me. It was 1986, one of the weirdest summers of my life.

Denise worked. I spent a third of the time working, a third of the time talking to her, and the final third goofing off. I collected two dollars an hour under the table without feeling too guilty.

The store was a combination gas station–convenience store–bus station–bait-and-tackle shop. Situated on the southeast side of Brighton on Grand River, the store was near one of Dad's favorite watering holes, the Cozy Inn.

The corner store was owned by a friend of Dad's, who, coincidentally, helped Dad start a business on the same corner. Unfortunately, the lure and proximity of the Cozy was too much for my father. That, coupled with Dad lacking perseverance, led to the demise of what could have been a really solid entrepreneurship. North Country Pasty made the best meat pies around using Mom's recipe. But alas, it wasn't meant to be. The business folded quicker than a government-subsidized solar company.

I wasn't lazy. But I couldn't be confused with a steady, hard worker either. I worked at the store. I just didn't look for work that needed to be done. I pumped gas, sorted empty bottles and cans, stocked the cooler, and took out the trash. When the store was in good shape, I did things for the owner like lawn maintenance and landscaping. When Denise and I caught up on all our duties, we ate dinner, listened to music, and prepared the store for the following day.

It was a weekend summertime job for me. Not a bad deal. Sometimes the owner, Miles, took me on his boat after work on nearby Island lake. The job and boat time kept me from getting into trouble. It also put a couple bucks in my pocket, and it was kind of fun.

Regular customers came in to chitchat. Patrons, not quite sober from the night before, waltzed in shirtless and shoeless. They plopped down two dollars in nickels, dimes, and quarters. That and six empty cans got them a fresh six pack of American lager, AKA, the mountain beer.

Run, Denise, Run

In high school, Denise dated a cross-country runner. Convinced of the merits of running by her new beau, Denise began running. She didn't do it for any team. She just ran to exercise and increase her endurance. For the first time, my sister enjoyed something that was physically challenging.

She started running a couple of laps around the camp. Since we lived on eighty acres, she ran a good distance without crossing the same path twice. Then, to the dismay of Mom and Dad, she began running up and down our gravel road. It was two miles to Grand River and back. Denise knew this because she drove Mom's car there—before she had her license.

Running was more than physically rewarding for Denise. It was therapeutic, her alone time.

Early on, I watched for her to return from her runs. Soon as she got within eyesight, I hopped on my bike and rode beside her for the last stretch. She would finish fast and then slow down after passing the mailbox to begin her cool down. At this time I began questioning her on all things running and other things too.

As Denise's running progressed, my approach changed. I left my bike by the garage. When she reached the far edge of our property, I joined her for her final dash to the mailbox. Then I walked with her during the cool down. My little legs struggled to keep up at first. Once I got older and taller, she invited me to come along for the entire run.

Our first joint run was her standard two-mile jog. Half a mile from home, my legs were lead, and my lungs burned. I hadn't paced myself and had no idea how to breathe properly. I slowed down. To help me keep pace and get me home, Denise slowed down. "Whatever you do, don't stop," she said. "Keep moving! If you stop, you'll never make it home. No walking either. Keep running!"

At Denise's command, I kept running. I was soon running at a snail's pace. The mailbox loomed in the distance. "Now go as fast as you can," she yelled, "and don't stop until you pass the driveway!"

With that, Denise took off. I chased after her, pulling strength from a reserve I didn't know I had. I didn't catch Denise, but I passed the mailbox faster than I thought possible. She ordered me to keep moving, to spend time cooling down. We would walk and talk, sometimes for as long as a half mile up and down our gravel road or driveway. At the time I didn't know what endorphins were, but I always felt great during cool down. The emotional and physical combination of reaching a goal and winding down our muscles and lungs afterward was a great reward.

Cool downs changed with the seasons. In nice weather, we took the back way home through the woods. On these days, Denise pointed as we walked, directing my attention to birds' nests high in the trees or a whooping crane hidden in the cattails.

In the spring, Denise showed me the stages of budding flowers and trees as they exited another long Michigan winter. We tiptoed by the pond. While I tried to catch tadpoles, Denise called attention to a sunfish building a nest nearby.

In the fall, we took in the wide range of colors on trees scattered along our fence line. We cleaned apples with our shirts and taste-tested them for ripeness.

My sister filled many voids from early elementary through high school and beyond, voids that were later refilled with garbage from my peers and cable television. Granted, Denise and I did watch some TV shows together. Most were produced before 1970: *The Three Stooges*, *Twilight Zone*, *Night Gallery*, *Leave It To Beaver*, and *My Three Sons* were a few of our favorites.

Denise taught me the value of work, the discipline of pushing myself, and how to laugh and have fun.

Thanks to her encouragement, I kept running. Eventually I kept pace with her. I even beat her in the final dash home now and then. She didn't teach me how to win or lose. She taught me to look around during the race, have fun, and always finish strong.

Chapter Twenty

GOING TO WORK WITH MOM

When I was a kid, I got nervous stomach pains over asking someone to help me do something. The thought of anyone going out of their way or changing their schedule to accommodate little ole me created feelings of guilt and embarrassment. I still get the same feelings as an adult. I get a downtrodden feeling about any circumstance in my life that causes a kink in someone else's day.

My mother went back to school in 1980. Thanks to grants and government assistance, she enrolled in a four-year business/accounting curriculum at the Livingston County satellite campus of Cleary College, tuition-free. This meant Mom had less time for her family.

However, the effects weren't felt by everyone. My older siblings were busy. Rick was living in East Lansing. Tom, Vic, and Denise were consumed with high school, part-time jobs, and hanging out with friends. If I had a need, Dad—who was still living with us—took care of it. Kind of.

At first, Dad supported Mom's return to school. He figured if one of his business ideas took off, he would have a live-in accountant and business administrator. That support was short-lived. Once he realized Mom was smart enough to do more than cook and clean, Dad's insecurities took over. My father had two evil friends, Jealousy and Contempt. These friends showed up when Mom went back to school and didn't leave until Dad left with them a few years later.

Mom loved her time at Cleary, making friends and exercising her brain—a brain that was on life support since the late '60s. Her grades were excellent, and her confidence got a much-needed shot in the arm. A much-deserved bonus for spending thirty-five hours every week at school—less time with Bill Simpson.

My father could see the writing on the wall. His wife was less vulnerable. It was becoming apparent that Dad needed Mom more than she needed him. So, Dad's self-defense mechanism kicked in and he did what he did best. He went into attack mode.

He griped when chores weren't finished around the house. He complained about Mom staying after school to study with friends. He bitched when Mom's night class meant dinner wasn't on the table. During some of the bigger alcohol-fueled fights, Dad even accused Mom of having a lesbian relationship with a new school friend.

It all led to the beginning of the end of their marriage. Although some argued the marriage began dissolving moments after Elaine said, "I do."

Mom's Triumphant Return to the World of Work

Two years into Mom's courageous return to college, Dad moved out. No more bread winner. Honestly though, the bread my dad was bringing home could hardly be called a victory.

Mom's already busy schedule was taxed some more. After a fifteen-year hiatus from the work world, she had to go back. Pressed for time and cash, Mom considered settling for a two-year associate's degree. Fortunately, Mom was committed. Come to think of it, maybe she should have been committed to a special place with soft music and padded walls. Because her decision looked crazy to anyone on the outside.

In her biggest middle-finger gesture to Dad, Mom stayed in school and got a part-time job. A few months later, she got a second one.*

Tommy recently corrected me. For a short time, Mom had a third job while attending Cleary. So, in summation of the human spirit and proving you can do almost anything you put your mind to, Mom kept her family together while going to school full-time and working several part-time jobs.

Surviving was a group effort. My older siblings pitched in where and when they could. They encouraged Mom to finish school and get on with life after Bill Simpson. You know, A.B.S, or life after B.S., whatever sounds better.

The first job Mom landed was at Cleary College. Impressed by Mom's effort to remain in school, they made her the part-time morning janitor. Her workday began at six thirty. My bus didn't swing by the house until forty-five minutes later. Suddenly, I felt like a burden.

The bus that took me to Birkenstock Elementary didn't get to 1315 Euler Road until about seven fifteen. Just before Mom started working— the morning before, I believe—she broke the news to me. "Bedtime needs to be a little earlier this evening." "How come, Mom?" "Oh, I have to drop you at Betty's on my way to work."

With that piece of information, my stomach hit the floor. I instantly began dreading the next morning and every morning Mom reported to Cleary for janitor duties. But I had no say in the matter. My mornings would rotate between Betty's house and Jane's house.

Mornings at my home were spent eating where I wanted to eat, watching the cartoons I wanted to watch, and generally being left alone until it was time to go. Then a gentle, yet tired voice would call from the kitchen, "Time to get on the bus." I would carelessly stroll down our driveway, take time to watch some nature, and patiently wait for my chauffeur, Mrs. Spooner, to arrive. I would daydream, play games, or throw rocks over the fence and before I knew it, the bus would lumber down our gravel road.

Mornings waiting for the bus away from home were met with anxiety and shame. These mornings were sullen, nerve-riddled experiences. At home, I often had elaborate conversations with myself. I couldn't risk being caught by a non-family member engaging in that activity, and there wasn't anything to say to Jane or Betty. They didn't play with Hot Wheels or appreciate the violence and predictability of *The Flintstones* and *Tom and Jerry*.

I was on edge at both houses. Jane was always late telling me when to leave for the bus. Luckily, their driveway was short. If I ran, I could make it before the tall door squeaked close. Betty's driveway, on the other hand, was twice as long as ours. Five minutes before go time, Betty politely let me know, "Almost time to go." We took their mammoth, two-toned Chevy Suburban and waited in the heated comfort of the bow-tied boat.

Despite my apprehension, both neighbor ladies treated me like one of their own. If I was thirsty, they got me something to drink. Sometimes they made me toast with jam, and they never made me feel awkward about being there. I did that on my own. I got embarrassed when I used the bathroom. I was uptight about moving from the couch and hoped the whole time I was there they would simply leave me alone.

It sounds awful, and it was. But honestly, I only endured these away-from-home mornings a couple times a week for a few months.

Goodbye, Birkenstock

Near the end of fourth grade, I got more bad news. Birkenstock Elementary, the best elementary school on the planet, was closing its doors at the conclusion of the 1981–82 school year. It would be the end of an era. No more visits from brother Tom at recess. No more sled hill. No more costume-filled Halloween parades through the trailer park next door.

The day it turned from vicious rumor to official fact, I got off the bus, slowly walked up my driveway, and cried. It was the first time I remember being truly sad.

My nervous stomach lasted all summer.

There was true comfort spending time with my friends, the teachers, and everyone else at Birkenstock Elementary. The janitor George was even a beloved guy that you could chat with as if he were your grandpa. My time at Birkenstock felt like time spent with family. Much like the end of a holiday weekend or the conclusion of a visit with kith and kin, I mourned that my time at Birkenstock was over.

For the fifth graders it was no big deal. They were headed to middle school anyway. But my friends and I still had one more year. For us, the end came one year too soon. The Tigers of Birkenstock transferred to other schools. Most of us ended up at Latson Road Elementary, the school we loved to hate. I'm not sure where our sour feelings toward that school originated. I didn't know a single kid who went there. The whole bag of negative feelings my friends and I had for that school up the road was probably simple: It wasn't Birkenstock.

There was, however, a silver lining to the untimely school transfer. No more waiting for the bus at the neighbor's house. No more guilt-riddled mornings with Jane or Betty. Cleary College was less than a mile from Latson Road Elementary. So, years before Take Your Kid to Work Day was a thing, Mom introduced me to the janitorial circuit at Cleary College.

Hello, Cleary

Working mornings at Cleary meant I still had to wake up earlier to leave with Mom. I was happy to do it because I was no longer imposing on the neighbor ladies. Not much better than sitting on the neighbors' sofas, I spent my early mornings in the student lounge at Cleary. Most importantly, I was alone. With no one judging me, I relaunched my habit of talking to myself.

Mom and I would walk down this long hallway, and she would deposit me in the lounge. Some mornings she got herself a small coffee for a quarter. Occasionally she would spring another quarter for me to get hot cocoa. On mornings when Mom felt extra guilty for dragging me to work, she kicked a dime to get my cocoa topped with whipped cream.

I had seen simple, refrigerated vending machines before. You know, the ones that slide your sealed beverage down a shoot after pressing a button. Not much mystery there. This machine though? This machine that made the coffee and cocoa sent my young imagination into overdrive.

I would ask Mom, "How does it do it? How does a machine, a vending machine, make something that usually takes a stove or a pot or a kettle or a Mr. Coffee?" Mom would give me a tired look that said, "You've got too much time on your hands kid." She wouldn't say it though. Mom's simple reply was, "I don't know. It just does."

Mom left me there and began her workday. I spent the next ten minutes sipping cocoa and analyzing the machine. I would ponder all the different ways this rectangle box could possibly make coffee and cocoa with no eyes and no hands. My first guess was the most cartoonish. I peeked behind the machine, convinced I might spot a small person hunched over the box, anticipating the next hot beverage request. The machine was too heavy though, and I couldn't get a good enough look behind it.

Well then, it must be a robot. "Yeah," I thought, "that's it. The eyes and hands are on the inside and it's just a nonverbal robot." Sometimes I left my imagination there. Other times I was so curious as to stick my hand up the shoot to see if I could feel a pair of metal hands or the smooth face of a tiny droid. Nothing. I could only get my hand up into the machine about ten inches.

That machine bewildered me. It also fueled my imagination and gave me joy. Mornings with cocoa and ten cents of whipped cream were a little more special.

After a few weeks, I blended in with the institution, sitting in the hard plastic chairs with my thoughts and cocoa.* As I became more comfortable there, I wandered the halls and scouted out my surroundings. I walked through every open door and played with staplers, messed with overhead projectors, and doodled on white boards. Because the campus was so small, I occasionally ran into Mom. She always asked what I was doing. I always gave the same lie: "I was just going to the bathroom." She never bought it, but she never questioned it either. She had other things to do.

Eventually, I grew bored with my snooping routine. I found Mom and asked if I could help. Mom hesitated, then said, "Well, I don't see why not." That morning, I became the unpaid janitorial assistant to Elaine Simpson. My only benefits were mother-son chitchat, developing a greater appreciation for Mom, and cocoa topped with whipped cream.

In this new role, I dumped small trash cans into a larger, wheeled can Mom pushed around campus and straightened chairs as Mom dusted window sills. Once a week, we cleaned the bathrooms. I wiped sinks and

---

Students and teachers got used to seeing a ten-year-old sitting alone. Their double takes turned to polite questions that turned into acceptance.

mirrors in the men's room and picked up trash. There was pride among the tiny college's staff and students. As a result, the campus stayed pretty clean. Most mornings cleaning with Mom were not much more than trash duty and Mom refilling paper towel dispensers and checking the toilet paper supply.

When we worked in a classroom where Mom had class, she always pointed out her seat. I would ask something stupid like, "Why did the teacher put you up front? Do you talk too much in class?" "No, in college you can sit wherever you want. I sit up front, so I don't miss anything," Mom explained. "Wow!" I said. "No assigned seating? I might like college."

If a lesson was still on the board from the day before, Mom gave a brief summary. When Mom talked about her education and the Cleary curriculum, she always perked up. She was very proud of the journey she was on. That pride, combined with her desire to have a slightly better life for herself and her family, provided steadfast motivation.

Just before classes began, Mom drove me to Latson Road Elementary. It was neat not having to ride the bus. I thought, "This is what it feels like to be rich. I'm a car rider!" My dream, my vision of pomp and circumstance took a hit when my driver and I pulled up in our rusty, burnt orange, 1974 Ford Galaxy.

No Time to Walk

One particular morning at Cleary did not go as planned. Mom and I got in ole orange, and Mom turned the key only to hear that oft-heard *click, click, clickety clickety, click* a Ford starter makes when when met with a dead battery or other electrical issue. Mom didn't even pop the hood. She got out of the car, looked at Latson Road Elementary through the distant trees, and challenged me to be Forrest Gump years before we knew the name. "You've got a little less than ten minutes," she said. "If you run, you can make it, Stephen." I knew she was serious because of how she said my name, so I ran.

I didn't have confidence in many things as a fifth grader, but I could run. Almost a mile by car but a little shorter as the crow flies. I zigged and zagged through a field of tall grass and picker bushes, careful to avoid all obstacles bigger than me. I snagged my jeans getting around the rusty fence guarding the school and kept going. When I scooted through the double doors and into the fifth-grade coat room, I had time to spare.

While going to work with Mom brought us closer together, it was an exhausting, stressful time. Years later, Mom reaped the rewards of her perseverance, graduating magna cum laude. Soon after, she traded her multiple part-time jobs for a new career.

For her commitment, I raise a toast to Elaine Elizabeth Simpson. Here's to accomplishing goals, facing life's challenges, and sipping hot cocoa with whipped cream.

Mom's diploma from Cleary College.

Chapter Twenty-One

BACKYARD SPORTS

When I was young, my family rotated between poverty and just scraping by. We got enough toys at Christmas to stay occupied for a few cold winter days. Birthdays added a plaything or two. But if it wasn't raining, our entertainment preferences led us outside. Sports were a big part of our childhood, even if we had to invent our own.

Michigan's challenging climates added to our backyard sports. Grueling, hot summers in the early '80s made our field of dreams steamy. When games went late, dusk brought a welcome layer of fresh evening dew. October's cool, crisp air provided an extra snap to our football games. Springtime generated muddy, rain-drenched, sneaker-destroying fields that were perfect for some games. However, rain-soaked hockey in early March is sloppy and not much fun. Pucks don't like puddles. Ice skates don't either.

During my childhood, weekends were for cleaning. Fun, games, and sports had to wait. If you weren't cleaning, you were in Mom's way. If you planned to sleep in while Mom cleaned, think again. If she concluded you weren't pulling your weight, her subtle suggestions turned into loud, semi-violent declarations. "Get up and stay out of my way!" If we didn't get the message, she would change it up. "Get up and get out of this house right now!"

As the baby, I never wanted to irk Mom, so I always climbed out of bed and shuffled away before she reached my room with the vacuum.

Tommy was the same way. Victor, on the other hand, was stubborn about his beauty sleep, especially in his teenage years. Too many cheap beers the night before often caused lingering hibernation.

Ready or not, Mom flung open our bedroom door and rammed her 1970's red-and-chrome Hoover into every piece of furniture in our room. We dubbed the loud machine the Iron Horse.

We always knew when Mom guided the Iron Horse into Victor's direction. "Victor Loring Simpson!" she screamed over the vacuum. "Get up right now before I pull every hair out of your precious little head!" Playing his part as expected, Victor would slither out of bed and join the rest of us outside.

Then came the chores. Mowing grass, trimming trees, raking leaves, cleaning dorms and bathrooms, and emptying trash all took priority over play time. But once we finished chores, it was game on.

Balls and Bats and Occasional Contact

We played any game involving bats, balls, mitts, and whatever other equipment we had at the time.* If girls were hanging out with my brothers or my sister was there, we played softball. Otherwise, we played baseball or some version of baseball. I preferred softball. The underhanded pitches were easier to hit, the co-ed game rules were more flexible, and the competition wasn't as fierce. This gave me a chance to have an impact at bat and in the field.

Once my siblings reached (or neared) drinking age, these laid-back games featured cold beer at every base. Less competitive, the games were essentially outdoor parties. For my brothers, playing hard and scoring runs came second to teenage drinking and showing off for girls.

---

*During the 1983 Camp Luther Vista baseball season, my brothers renewed a friendship with an old church acquaintance, Greg—a.k.a. Kegger. He had the summer job of a lifetime. He was a bat boy at Tiger Stadium and brought us real baseballs from batting practice with the blue stamp indicating *OFFICIAL BALL* AMERICAN LEAGUE. Greg also brought used bats that had cracks or were considered past their prime. The most precious item he brought was a black bat with red writing. The barrel read, "Glenn Wilson"—the Tigers' right fielder for two years. It was a thrill to use Wilson's bat, the best piece of equipment we had.*

It gave me a little angst that the girls were given more than their share of balls and strikes to contact the ball. There was no such liberal bending of the rules for my friend Matt and I. If we got our third strike or popped out to the pitcher, we had a seat on the grass or took a base for another player. For the most part I was okay with my siblings' beer league games. I got to hang out with the big kids, and I still got to participate in some version of a game I loved to play.

As the years went by, my play improved while alcohol declined the play of everyone else. The games were fun though. So fun that laughing and kidding around far outweighed athletic action. Those alcohol-inspired softball games never really ended. A winner was rarely declared. People just casually left the hot field for a refreshing dip in the spring-fed swimming pond and never came back.

Boys-only baseball games were more intense. Most often we used a newer, fresh softball. As my brothers and their friends got older and bigger, our field got smaller. It got to a point that the left field couldn't contain hard balls being belted by the maturing teenage man-children. As the youngest available players, my friend Matt and I got picked last for these games. They had to let us play though. Otherwise, we would never get better.

The problem was that I was stuck with a ten-year-old hand-me-down Franklin glove. The web was weak, and the pocket was paper thin. Those heavy, large softballs caused the web to fold out, resulting in dropped catches. If I did catch it, I winced in pain.

A kind stranger accidentally remedied my problem in the summer of 1984. After a group left camp, we scoped out the dormitory for forgotten treasure, and I hit the jackpot. Some overly eager city kid packed too quickly and left his brand-new Rawlings glove under his bunk. That wonderful glove fit like a dream and gave me some much-needed confidence.

When players were too scarce for an actual baseball game, we played 500. One batter pitched to himself, and everyone else chased down balls for points. Pop-ups or long fly balls were worth 100, line drives 75, one-bouncers 50, and ground balls 25. Balls bouncing out of or over your glove cut from your score. First one to 500 became the batter.

I participated but wasn't allowed to win. Positioned just past second base and fielding mostly ground balls, it was a tall order to get 500 before the big kids. That was the goal. They didn't want me at the plate. On the rare occasion a flyball was mishit just past second base, a taller brother or one of their friends would sneak behind and snatch the can of corn just above my glove, robbing me of the coveted 100-point catch.

Sometimes the older kids spiced things up a bit with full-contact 500. Flying elbows, violent collisions, and glove slapping were a few moves in this short-lived game. It was as exhilarating as it was scary. Being little and elusive, I was the recipient of a few soft rollers that would bounce away from the free for all. Two teenagers down, one bleeding, twenty-five points for me.*

Hoop Dreams

I've loved basketball since making my first basket on a "big boy" rim. Dad didn't even like the sport. Out of all the sports his boys played with friends and family, basketball was Dad's least favorite. That said, he always wanted to be the man of the house and do nice things for his kids. So one spring, he and Uncle Joe headed to Kmart to give us basketball at home.

The backboard was made of plastic fiber that didn't seem weather resistant. The rim was as vanilla as it could be. The whole thing only took a few hours to install. Uncle Joe added two pieces of wood on the back for added support. Dad bolted the steel brackets to the roof, leaving all that sports glory hanging off of our eight-and-a-half-foot tall garage. Not exactly like the gym, but better than nothing.

Despite our pavement-and-gravel driveway, we had some good times shooting hoops at home. Full-paced games were out of the question because you had to shuffle your feet over the potholes and through the

---

I used to love the NBA, but the sport has changed. In the '80s and '90s, the game felt real, like it mattered. Now it feels like a three-point contest with uncontested dunks. They sprinkle in an occasional block or steal to keep the old timers engaged.

gravel to stay upright. Our little court was great for HORSE or PIG, but one could really wreck an ankle trying to drive the lane.

I learned to play basketball off of that garage. It was the first place I shot hoops with all my brothers, giving our little court meaning. But it didn't last long.

One afternoon, we short Simpson boys were shooting hoops outside, and Denise's high school boyfriend, Drew, joined us. The tall, lanky long-distance runner drained a couple outside jumpers before demonstrating his driveway court skills. On a rim he could grab without jumping, Drew drove down the lane with authority and slammed the basketball home. He landed on his feet eloquently, the rim in his hands, a jagged piece of backboard still bolted to the back.

The chip-wood and fiberglass backboard from Kmart snapped like a twig. All that remained on the roof was four-fifths of the backboard and a football-shaped hole where four long bolts once held the rim in place. Because of Dad's lack of interest in basketball, there was no second chance for at-home hoops. The rimless backboard remained on the roof, never to be enjoyed again.

The bright spot is that this created another family tradition I look back on fondly. With no hoop at home, Rick and I drove around seeking a new basketball arena. We visited a few school playgrounds with no luck. The rims were either too short or constructed with unforgiving double-iron rims. As if the metal backboards and crappy rims weren't bad enough, the goals usually had dangerous, ball-destroying chain nets that offered no satisfying *swoosh* sound.

Eventually, with help from Tom and Vic, we found our new basketball court. For the remainder of our years at Luther Vista all basketball games would be "away." It was a five-minute trek from our driveway court. The church on the corner of Hyne and South Hacker Road in Brighton was our new basketball home. There was rarely anyone there Monday through Saturday. Even when church members were present, they didn't give us a second look. The paved blacktop was smooth and clean of debris. There were no gravel potholes like those that riddled our driveway. The court was surrounded by large oak and maple trees, a shady resting spot between games. This was important, as the court's black surface got pretty toasty on a hot summer day.

On spring Saturdays and several days a week during the summer (other than Sunday), Rick took me to church for the gospel of one-on-one roundball. Lessons covered moving your feet on defense, maintaining your dribble, and using the glass when necessary. Sermons included the importance of making baskets from the baseline, the knock-away steal, and the unblockable eight-foot hook shot.

When our chores were finished Rick would summon me to his car. He said few words, as it was understood that it was time for hoops. Basketball in hand and large ice water on the floor mat or wedged between the parking brake and the seat, we went for a little ride.

Rick's Little Red Vette

At this point in the early to mid-'80s, Rick again had the best and newest car in the Simpson family fleet. But everything is relative and my brother's fire-engine red Chevrette was no flagship. It was a base model, two door hatchback purchased from our neighbor Mark. He customized the little Chevy by adding rear louvers, tinted windows, and an $800 aftermarket sound system. Not exactly a professional installation, it blew a fuse every time you hit a large pothole. Mark's attempts at turning the car into a poor man's sports coupe were foolish gestures but made it marginally more glamorous than most Chevettes on the road at that time.

This car was so slow it was scary to drive. The power produced by the 1.6 liter was scarce, and it could barely get out of its own way. Even with a four-speed manual transmission, it struggled to reach sixty miles per hour in less than fifteen seconds. As for highway travel, pray for a long, flat on-ramp. Preferably one that went downhill. If GM and the Feds at the Highway safety bloated government agency had a conscience, this four-wheeled buggy would be banned from all interstates and dubbed "unsafe at most speeds."

No cup holder or storage, no A/C or power anything, no optional equipment whatsoever, and all the ride and handling characteristics of a bumper car at the county fair. Even the brakes sucked on that shitbox. But it was cheap to buy, cheap to run, cheap to fix, and easy to work on.

Some good times were had in that car though, and one bad one. It took us to shoot hoops, and Rick occasionally paid me to wash it for him. The car was part of the family. We would (after a quick fuse replacement) jam out to classic rock in his "Vette" all the way to Hyne Road. When I saw Rick put the ball in his red Chevy, I got excited. I knew we were going to shoot hoops.

A Final Memory

The one bad Chevette memory was also the final one. After work one Friday Rick picked up Victor near Southfield. He was bringing Vic home for the weekend when they smacked an old lady in the rear. She hit her brakes doing fifty on Grand River for no apparent reason. Victor ate some dash and Rick ate the steering wheel. Neither was using a seatbelt. It was a different time.

Amazingly no one was seriously hurt. No ambulance was needed. But the car ambulance took Rick's Chevette to the junkyard. After a three second investigation by the insurance adjuster, whatever was left of the car was declared a total loss.

Down, Set, Hike!

As the months slipped toward September, basketball treks to Hyne Road were replaced with school, homework, and my favorite ball of all— the brown-leather, laced, oblong one synonymous with autumn, crisp air, changing leaves, back to school, and the beginning of harvest season.

In a word, football delivers. It brings a bit of everything: unity, separation, hatred, joy, heartbreak, pain, and glory—all in a single game.

The greatest thing about football is all you need is a ball and a place to play. Six to sixteen people means a pretty good game. Three to five people can have a light scrimmage, with the odd or old guy designated as all-time quarterback. Two people can have a game of catch, and I often practiced kicking all by myself.

As a young boy with few nearby friends, I played entire football games alone. I relied heavily on the running game and always came up big in the kicking game. These solo games usually ended on a three-point try. With the clock ticking down, I positioned the ball on an impromptu tee made of dirt and grass clippings, imagined the ball getting snapped, and blasted it. As it sailed through the uprights in my head, my fellow Lions patted me on the back and peppered me with high fives.

Light snow added even more atmosphere and detail to my legendary games. I marked off every ten yards by dragging my feet in the snow and wrote LIONS in the end zones with my snow-covered feet.

Fun as these games were, backyard football with actual people was even better. The fence that ran parallel to our gravel road served as the back of the west end zone. The other end zone rested between two trees near the house. Sidelines were marked by fallen tree limbs.

Then there was the cement patch. It was on the goal line in the east end zone, twenty yards from our back door. It had a look of being there for decades and was at one time the foundation for a bird house or flagpole.

The two-hole piece of cement had an element of home field advantage to it. Most people who came over to play were leery of this unmovable landmark that promised mangled ankles and stubbed toes. We Simpson boys weren't afraid of it. Instead of avoiding the concrete, we used it as a screen on slant passes to the end zone.

Weekend gridiron games at Luther Vista were always a good time and were often grueling competitions. We played on Saturday afternoon following our caretaker duties or Sunday at the conclusion of the Lions game.*

We only needed six or eight players to get a contest going. Most weekends we had enough kids from down our road to accomplish that. It helped that the home team showed up with four players. Well, three and a half counting me.

---

*Sooner if our "professional" gridiron heroes became unwatchable or had little to no chance of winning the game. Dramatic double digit, come from behind victories were a rarity in the 1980s version of the NFL. Comebacks for the team wearing Honolulu Blue were in two words, very infrequent.

Some Friday afternoons after school, my brothers and I practiced. Rick always encouraged me after a nice catch. He would add a bit more hand clapping after a successful long over-the-shoulder catch or if I snagged one of his harder thrown balls. There would be a hint of disappointment on a dropped ball. Often when I failed, Rick had me run the play again.

During one practice session, Rick turned me into a punt returner. "On this next one," he said, "run it back and see if you can get by me." It was a version of a twisted game Rick played on the twins when they were young. Rick tormented Tom and Vic, daring them to run by him through a narrow passageway in our home. The twins had numbers, but Rick was bigger and smarter.

So, I stood on the opposite end of the field awaiting Rick's kick. I had some speed and could cut and juke. Besides, we were outside. This would be no problem, right? No sharp objects or concrete basement walls for Rick to crush me into. Just soft, thick grass in a wide-open field.

My confidence dropped the second the ball left my brother's foot. It was his highest, longest kick of the day. It soared over the power lines that cut through our yard. I took a few steps backward, then a few more. I heard Rick closing on me. By the time I caught the ball, I only had time for three steps—two forward and one to my right, away from Rick. He cut to his left, and my nose exploded into his chest and shoulder.

Blood splattered Rick's sweatshirt, as my mind went black. My eyes closed. When I came to, I pointed at Rick's shirt. "Is that mine?" I asked. "The blood—is it mine?"

Once I regained consciousness, Rick's fears transitioned elsewhere. *What would happen if Mom found out?* Rick ripped off his shirt and used it to clean my face. He picked me up and set me on my feet. "How do you feel? Looks like you just got the wind knocked out of you and a bloody nose. It happens," he said, the words moving at the same speed as Rick's sprint toward me a minute earlier. "Victor gets nosebleeds all the time. You'll be fine."

He was right. I was fine. No medical attention needed.

Of all us boys, Tommy was most likely to make a big play. Get him in space on a fly pattern or pitch it out to him wide. If he turned the corner, he was gone. No one could catch Tommy, despite the fact that he rarely wore shoes during games.

Two of my brother's friends, Jeff and Chris, were hockey players. These thick dudes brought a certain flare to backyard football. These boys were swell fellas but they had an affection for violence and hard physical contact. So much that they were never allowed on the same team. When they hit someone and brought them to the ground, the soil vibrated.

Some rules were implied, not stated, to protect me and my friend Matt or any other grade schooler on the big guy field. Oh, we could still get tackled hard, but no gang tackling the little men. For us smaller kids, the game was *elude* on offense and *force direction change* on defense. Kind of like the kicker or punter after some blown special teams play. Change the runner's direction and hope someone behind him makes the tackle.

I once tried to prove I was one of the older kids by attempting a solo tackle. I caught a full-speed thigh in the face that weighed as much as my entire body. I slowed him down enough for Victor to make the tackle. It was a moment of pride that left my ears ringing the rest of the day.

One of our more intense games involved Tom's friend Wally. During one play, Wally flared out to the flat, caught a short pass, and turned up field. Rick charged over to make the tackle. As Rick went for his textbook tackle, Wally's wrestling instincts kicked in. He pulled away, a little maneuver that resulted in Wally's heavier, larger body slamming Rick's skull into the hard Michigan turf.

Like so many of our backyard football games, the game that early Autumn Sunday was preceded by watching Detroit Lions Football. It was September 27, 1981. The Lions played and won that day, beating the Oakland Raiders 16–0. We all watched the entire game before heading out back to play our own version. The Lions pitched a rare shutout. The defense was stifling, and Billy Sims had over 100 yards and a touchdown. It was a memorable game. But a few moments after Rick tackled Wally and for several hours after that, Rick couldn't remember a moment of that glorious game.

For the hour following Rick's bell ringing, my brothers and their friends quizzed Rick on the day's events. He couldn't remember watching the game, who they played, or how they won. He didn't know what day it was or why everyone kept asking him questions. He was unsteady on his feet, struggled to recall anything besides his name, and looked odd. Of course, this was decades before *concussion protocol* was a household term. No one knew what to do or how serious the situation was. Rick wasn't bleeding, no bones were out of place, and besides a headache and some nausea, he seemed okay.

Going to the doctor or hospital on your own two feet, not bleeding? It wasn't even considered. Rick just walked it off. It scared Tom, Vic, and I. Before that day we always thought Rick was indestructible. I never saw him hurt before that afternoon. After the tackle on Wally, backyard football was done for the day.

Looking back, Rick recalls not being quite right for about two or three days. He now admits we should have told Mom, and he should have gone to the hospital. But over the years we had a saying in the Simpson household, a saying I still use in my house and in my family to this day. "Just as nothing kills a buzz like a ride in a police car, nothing ruins a weekend like a trip to the emergency room."

Chapter Twenty-Two

MY FIRST DIRT BIKE

I n 1984, I spent the West Virginia portion of my summer with Dad on Uncle Joe's mountain property in Braxton County. Thankfully, my West Virginia stay was shorter than usual.

The Tigers were having a record season. I wanted to get back to *Detroit News* box scores and game summaries. The two TV channels we had only showed Pirates or Reds highlights. I was missing the four guys who brought the Tigers to life: George Kel and Al Kaline on TV and Ernie Harwell and Paul Carey on the radio.

The boys from Detroit were leading the pennant race. Yet I had no newspaper, no "This Week In Baseball" with Mel Allen. No games or Detroit sports shows on TV and no older brothers for post-game commentary. My hometown Tigers were having the season of a lifetime, and I was out of the loop, suffering FOMO before that was even a thing.

But the summer wasn't going to be a bust. I was committed to that. While on the trek from Michigan to West Virginia, I made myself a promise. I decided that sweating my ass off with Bill Simpson in a single-wide trailer would not be my only Mountain State highlight. I just had to figure out how to make good on my promise.

This particular year things were awkward in W.V. I always guessed that my dad either owed Uncle Joe money or they were not getting along. Dad and I arrived in Frametown the day before Uncle Joe and his family left for California. For crashing at Uncle Joe's house, Dad agreed to work on a list of projects. Dad and I were also responsible for day-to-day maintenance of Uncle Joe's vast property.

I helped care for the dogs and cats and did yard work. When it came to large-scale home improvement projects, I played the role of a lazy sidekick who did his best to stay out of the way.

After breakfast Dad would start on a project. He was putting aluminum skirting around the base of the trailer. I handed him tools and if he were in a dark corner, I held the flashlight. After an hour or two of me sitting in the grass trying not to look too bored, Dad would just say, "I got it from here, Stefen (Stefen was Dad's nickname for me). You can head down to the creek and get cooled off. But watch out for copperheads!"

In all my years of traveling to West Virginia I never—not one time—saw a single copperhead. They were always on my mind though. Every time I visited West Virginia. The way my dad and his family talked up the copperhead snake, you would think they lurked around every corner. Hid under every rock. It got to where I was looking for them just to see what they looked like.

The First Taste of Glory

After a few days of chores and boredom, I built up enough nerve to ask Dad about the Aquarius blue motorbike half-tucked under the steps outside. It appeared unridden and neglected for some time. Did it run? Was it a Kawasaki, Yamaha, Honda? How much power did it have? Did it have a clutch?

I held back most of my questions and opted for a short Q&A session instead. "Hey, Dad," I said during dinner on my third West Virginia night. "Is that bike near the front steps—um, is that Uncle Joe's?" "I don't know son, it might be." "Would it be okay if I looked at it, took the plastic off?"

"You aren't wanting to ride that old thing are you, son?" Dad picked at his teeth. "Hell, it's been sitting there so long I bet it doesn't even run."

Half a minute into my sly inquiry, my father killed my dream. Simpson pessimism is both predictable and depressing.

Dad must have been bored like me and a little curious too. After we cleaned up from dinner we stepped outside and approached the little blue mystery. He removed the plastic, sending some dirty old rainwater cascading onto our shoes. Not a good start. But then I spotted the key in the ignition. This was a good sign. Cobwebs and a layer of dust tempered my excitement.

Dad unscrewed the gas cap. Fresh fumes wafted up, confirming the bike had fuel. Another good sign. Without a word, Dad hopped on the bike and went through a series of actions. He moved quickly and knowingly, like it was his daily routine: kickstand up, key on, gas on, choke lever down, kick-starter arm folded out.*

"It might take a few kicks," Dad grunted. "No telling how long this thing has been sitting."

He gave it one kick, then a second. On the third, he twisted the throttle, and the dusty bike came to life. It sounded great. After about thirty seconds, Dad opened the choke, pulled in the clutch, and put it in first gear. He turned the throttle slightly and proceeded down the driveway, smiling in the saddle of my dream.**

Dad rode up Uncle Joe's driveway and down the gravel road. He returned in a few minutes and motioned for me. I wanted to run, but casually walked towards him. I was so excited. I was already visualizing all the dirt I was gonna tear through on that thing.

The bike was a 1972, Honda SL70, Not to be confused with the tiny wheeled, ugly CT "trail" 70 minibike. The SL 70 was designed in Torrance, California, during the mini-cycle craze to compete with Yamaha JT Enduro bikes. The Yamaha was faster and lighter, but the Honda had better suspension, a four-stroke motor, and a reputation for lasting longer and being more dependable.

**Coincidently the first motorcycle my dad ever owned was made by Honda and dubbed the Honda Dream. Dad bought it brand new in 1964. It was a Honda Dream 305. He didn't have it long though. Two things killed "Dad's Dream." My oldest brother, Rick, burned himself on a motorcycle that belonged to my dad's friend. The shine of the chrome exhaust was too tempting to his little hand. This did not sit well with Mom. A few months later, Mother dealt another blow to Dad's motorcycle dream. Late in the fall of 1964, Mom told Dad she was pregnant. That news meant Dad had to have a toy sale. For most of their childhood Mom believed—no, was certain—that Dad hated buying toys for the twins. That's likely because upon and before their birth, Dad was forced to sell most of his.*

"I had to make sure it ran," Dad said, "and that the brakes worked."

As long as he got up and let me have a turn, I'd buy whatever lie he was selling. He scooted toward the fuel tank and motioned for me to climb on behind him. "Well, this sucks," I thought to myself. But it beat listening to the bug zapper on Uncle Joe's back porch, so I got on.

Pushing through the gears on the old dirt road, Dad yelled back at me: "Don't let your feet drag, but don't get them close to the back wheel or the exhaust pipe either." I looked down and noticed the passenger foot pegs. I flipped them down and comfortably rested my feet. Dad said nothing, but I think he felt a little stupid for not noticing them before.

After a nice, dusk-lit ride up the mountain, Dad parked the bike near the steps and cut the motor. "I'll cover it back up before I go to bed. Right now, the exhaust is too hot."

"That's it?" I said. "You're not even gonna show me how to ride it? You're not even gonna let me start the damn thing?" Edit: I only thought these things. I wasn't stupid enough to tell my old man how I felt. The early evening temperature was ninety-two with sweat-drenching humidity. I was pretty hot too.

"You want some milk and cookies before bed?" Dad asked, feeding my anger.

"I'm not eight years old, you son of a bitch," I screamed. "I could give two shits about cookies right now. I want to ride that motorcycle!" Again—these words never escaped my mouth. I valued my life too much.

As we sat sweating on the back porch consuming our milk and two dry, shitty, tasteless oatmeal cookies (Dad's favorite), I only had one thing on my mind. Dad nodded to the bottom of the trailer. "Help me finish the skirting tomorrow," he said, "and then maybe I'll show you how to ride that little Honda. Night Stefan, don't forget to brush 'em."

I slept no more than three hours that night. As I tossed and turned, all I saw was that little blue Honda. Speeding through the yard, climbing hills, tearing up dirt as I shot through a trail. I was consumed.

The next day, it was hard to contain my excitement. The anticipation of riding the motorcycle gave me more energy than a night of restlessness stole from me. Eyes on the prize, I was motivated to finish the trailer skirting project as fast as possible. After four hours of morning labor, it was time. Dad went inside to wash up and told me to fetch the gas can in the shed.

I pushed the bike to the driveway and topped off the tank as instructed. Fifteen agonizing minutes later, Dad finally strolled out of the house. He wore blue jean shorts, a clean black T-shirt, and a big smile.

Dad gestured for me to get on the bike then went over the startup procedure and riding instructions. My patience was wearing thin, but I stayed quiet. If I talked back it would just irk my old man.

"Make sure it's in neutral and kick it over," Dad finally directed. After being ridden just yesterday the Honda came to life after only two kicks. "First gear is down. Pull the clutch in and put it in gear. Slowly release the clutch and give it a little gas."

I put it in gear, and it lurched under me, then stalled after traveling a couple feet.

Dad smirked. "That's okay," he said. "Do it again. This time, give it a little more gas and let the clutch out slower."

I started the bike. This time, not wanting to disappoint the old man, I gave it more throttle. The back wheel spun in the gravel, the front wheel pulled off the ground, and I sped down the driveway into a trail of high grass. It was better than I imagined. There was just one hangup. Dad didn't want me going beyond first gear until I got the hang of it.

After a day of tooling around at nine miles per hour, I asked if I could put in second. Dad said it was okay, but he said it with some trepidation. "Keep it in second!" He would bark out. Almost like he knew there was no stopping my trail-bike fever once I got it out of first gear.

Birth of a Rebel

I was cruising now. Second gear propelled the little Honda to almost double the speed. My confidence grew. Third gear came without Dad's instruction or permission. I hit twenty-eight miles per hour before running out of trail and having to slow down.

Defying my father by skipping to third gear without his knowledge was gratifying and nerve-racking. It was one of my first solo rebellions.

Powerful as I felt in my revolt, it had immediate repercussions.

As usually happens in life, the karma train made a stop that day. It turned my dirt bike trail riding upside down.

I was scooting through a dark valley in third gear. Tall grass lined both sides of the path I'd beaten down over several days of riding.

The thing was so big and dark that I thought it was a dead limb. I slowed down, but not enough to avoid hitting it with my front tire. When I did, that limb curled his head and hissed at me. I screamed and gave the little Honda all it had. I was so scared I shifted into fourth gear and kept my feet off the foot pegs to avoid the rest of the killer snakes!

Dad ran from the trailer to catch the runaway Honda and its rider. I slowed down, and Dad caught the bike by the handlebars. He pulled in the clutch, as I jumped off the Honda like it was on fire. I flailed my arms and nervously spouted off details about my slithery encounter.

"Slow down and say it again," Dad said.

I repeated the story, making sure Dad understood the gravity of the situation. Dad straightened up and headed to the trailer. When he returned, his Sears & Roebuck J.C. Higgins bolt-action 20-gauge shotgun was slung over his shoulder.

"Show me where," he demanded.

I ran down the trail, Dad a half a step behind. "Dad," I said with a shaky voice, "he was big and fast. I ran over him pretty hard. Do you think he'll still be there?"

"He'll be there." Dad said it with a confidence that suggested he knew the snake personally. If the seven-foot reptile was still there, I almost expected Dad to have a conversation with him, maybe invite him up for a beer.

Near the scene of the crime, Dad stopped and barked for me to do the same.

"Where is he, Dad?" I asked. "I don't see—"

Before I got all the words out, Dad chambered a cartridge and blew the snake's head clean off. He immediately regretted it.

"Shouldn't have done that," he said, surveying the still-wiggling body. "That was a black rat snake—best snake you can have on your property."

Mom peers at Dad on his Honda Dream in front of our Southfield home.

He explained that rat snakes eat varmints like rats and mice and some say they help keep the copperheads away.*

That day ended in typical fashion. Dad and I sat on the back porch enjoying milk and oatmeal cookies.

"Stefen?" "Yeah Dad?" "When you shot up the hill after you ran over that snake, you were going pretty fast. Were you in third gear or forth?"

Over the years, Dad told this story more than 100 times. Every time, the tale ended the same way. Dad would shake his head slowly from side to side and mumble, "I should have never shot that old rat snake."

I didn't answer. I was caught.

"Good night, Stefen," Dad said. "Don't forget to brush 'em."

The day before my West Virginia stay ended, Dad called to me. I put down one of Uncle Joe's many cats I was playing with.

Dad pointed to the blue Honda. "Just how do you think we are going to get that in the back of this car?"

I tilted my head. "Where are we taking it?"

Dad smiled. "To Michigan," he said. "It's yours now. I bought it from Uncle Joe!"

Like that, I became the happiest kid in the world.

Once back in Michigan, I trekked over every square foot of Camp Luther Vista on my blue trail bike. And, unbeknownst to my mother I rode it up and down our gravel road too. The action packed memories I still have are very real. When my twelve-year-old self was on that bike I was in heaven.

All of the joy that little bike brought me was short lived. Without Dad to keep it on a maintenance schedule, it gave out in early November of 1984. I still get a little sad when I think about it. That little Honda wasn't just my first dirt bike. It was also my last.

Forty years later, I'm still waiting to replace my beloved SL70. My friends and family give me shit about my dirt-bike aspirations, but I don't care. "You're over fifty years old," they say. "What are you gonna do with a dirt bike?" Ride. I still long to ride in the dirt someday. Hopefully soon, when circumstances are right, I'll get another dirt bike. It may seem childish at my age but I'm not ready to give up on my dirt bike dream. I will ride again.

Chapter Twenty-Three

JOY RIDING, LITTLE BOY FLYING

During our seven years and three months at Camp Luther Vista, there was never a shortage of things to do. Expensive toys and ATVs would have been great, but it may have caused us to not appreciate what we did have.

During the latter half of 1984 I had my own dirt bike. That was awesome. Then for a few months that fall my sister's boyfriend, Marty, brought his dirt bike to the camp, doubling our two-wheeled good times. His Yamaha IT175 was perfect for the camp. Even though it was too tall for me (I could barely touch the ground when sitting in the crease between the gas tank and seat), I had my share of fun on it.

In sixth and seventh grade, I often had weekday afternoons to myself. No adult supervision. On those days, I drove or rode anything that had gas, keys, and a motor. A few afternoons I was even brazen enough to sneak Marty's Yamaha out of the garage and rip through the gears like I was running from the law.

Riding the much bigger bike took courage and strategy. First, I had to stand on my brother's weight bench in the garage to climb on and start the bike. Once it was running, I had to get off the bike, raise the kickstand, and climb back on via the weight bench. In a single motion and without tipping over, I pushed away from the bench, released the clutch, and took off through the garage door.

If I wanted to bring the bike to a complete stop, I had to be on the side of a hill or near a tree or stump. My little left foot could just tippy toe the earth below. The whole ordeal was complicated by the 175cc's weight. That Yamaha was much heavier than my SL70. I should have, could have died riding the Yamaha. I would take it out on our road and make it scream. One gravel rut or pothole would have sent me flying 100 feet or more.

When I finished a joy ride, I idled back into the garage and brought the bike to a stop next to the weight bench. It was the perfect crime. Unfortunately, like all criminals, I pushed too far. I got cocky. My last ride featured perfect dirt bike weather: sprinkling rain. I came into the garage hot and tapped the brakes. But the sprinkled rain coated the tires, sending me sliding past the weight bench. The bike fell on me, and the handlebars slammed into the cement garage floor, breaking the clutch lever. My first official lay down and the end of my days riding the Yamaha.

Building the Beater Fleet

The Simpsons always had a car or two with enough mechanical problems to not be street legal. We loved tearing around camp in those old beaters. Dad may have loved it more than any of us. He once went through a phase that more than tripled our Beater Fleet.

It was the early '80s, a year or so before Mom kicked Dad out of the house. Ole Willy had a crazy idea. One by one, VW Bugs appeared in our driveway until we had a small, rolling museum of Punch Bugs. There were even two or three of the German insects decorating our front lawn. Dad had a plan. He was going to build a dune buggy.

We were going to be a really cool dune buggy family. I bet Dad had fantasies of trailering his new toy to the dunes near Lake Michigan. He had been bitten by the dune buggy bug. Dad was getting old, but he still wanted something to play with. Mom would never allow street bikes, and a boat big enough to fit all seven of us was out of Dad's price range.

I can imagine the conversation between my parents once the first couple of Volkswagens showed up. "Bill, what are you doing with those ugly little foreign cars?" "What, 'Lain?" ("Lain" is how Dad mostly referred to Mom. It was shorter than "Elaine" and he could bark it out quicker in one syllable.) "Oh, those little Bugs. I only paid fifty bucks apiece for 'em. I was thinking of either fixing 'em up and selling them or maybe making the best one a cheap first car for the twins. You know, and keep the other ones around for parts, that's all."

Mom bit her tongue to preserve family harmony. She didn't concern herself with what Dad was doing until she thought it necessary to intervene. Mom was not stupid. She had a planned procrastination she used while dealing with Dad and most other things too.

One of the best things that came from the dune buggy project was driver's education. All the Bugs had manual transmissions. Two of the Bugs ran and were used as camp cars, but they weren't safe for highway travel. It gave Tom and Vic an opportunity to hone their driving skills and it gave me a chance to watch and learn. The car they drove around the camp most often was a heaterless rust bucket with an AM radio and no brakes. Like all Bugs of that time, it had no power steering. Unlike other Bugs of the time, this one had no floor.

When the dune buggy frame showed up, we all cued in on Dad's master plan. The tubular two-tone blue frame had no wheels or tires. It consisted of two bucket seats, a rear bench seat, and no more than one working seat belt. It had a steering wheel, a Hurst shifter, and three tiny pedals dangling above the steel grate floorboard. To my eyes, it looked awesome. Mother disagreed.

A few days later, Mom finally acknowledged the arrival of the dune buggy frame. Eventually, like always, the main bone of contention popped up during conversation. Money. We didn't have it.

"That blue thing looks like it's missing a few parts," Mom said. "How much did it cost?"

Whatever else was said didn't matter. The dune buggy stayed.

Soon as the weather broke in spring, Victor helped Dad build his custom dune buggy. It was a cold, exciting night when Dad cranked it up for the first time and drove it solo around the camp. It was almost dusk, and that handmade machine backfired orange flames from the teepee-style exhaust.

After an inaugural circle around the camp buildings, Dad gave his sons their first rides. Tom, Vic, and I hopped in like kids in a 60's beach movie. Tom squeezed beside me on the rear seat and stretched the only working seatbelt across both of our laps. Victor took shotgun as a reward for helping with the creation.

We zipped around the camp for a bit, then Dad wanted to see what it could do on the open road. No lights, no windshield, no problem. We zoomed down the back roads of Genoa Township for nearly an hour. Guided by the light of a full moon, Dad idled the buggy back to our house.

Over the next month, we were a full-fledged dune-buggy family. Dad let Rick and the twins drive it too. Crazy as it was, the buggy brought Dad and his boys together. Denise, on the other hand, only rode in it once or twice, and Mom wouldn't get near the thing.

When summer arrived, the dune buggy's days were numbered. So was my parent's marriage. Dad went south for several months to look for work, leaving the dune buggy's care in the hands of Tom, Vic, and their friends.

That poor thing never had a chance. It was air-cooled, had a small oil leak, and had taken a beating. Tom and Vic were playing a chase game around the camp with their friends. It involved fireworks and water balloons—something I believe they called King of the Dune Buggy.

On one of July's hottest days, the buggy ran nonstop without anyone checking the oil. As Vic drove through our yard with several of his friends standing on the frame and clinging to the buggy's rails, the engine started smoking. Vic let off the gas just as the buggy backfired for the last time. In an instant, we were a dune buggy family no more.

Flying Like Superman

Most of the time, we made do without dune buggies or dirt bikes. Good times came courtesy of beater cars, a riding mower, a hay wagon, and the fleet of tractors in the barn.

If I was bored, I tooled around the camp on the riding mower looking for grass to cut. After cutting a few patches I would take the mower hill climbing or mud puddle splashing. Any obstacle I thought would be fun to traverse was in play. I put that ten horsepower Craftsman through a gamut of lawn tractor challenges.

We also had the three large Ford tractors, which I was not to operate unless Dad was around. My older brothers used them all the time, for chores and goofing off. When they did, I tried to tag along. Burn barrel dump trips happened after any large group left the camp. We collected all the barrels of trash and ash and headed to the dump. It wasn't great fun, but it meant a tractor ride. I couldn't begin to lift the barrels onto or off of the trailer's steel floor. Sometimes though, I put my back against the front wall of the trailer and used my feet to slide the barrels into the removal position.

Dad and cousin Billy on the red Ford tractor in front of our fishing and skating lake.

One day when my brothers were hauling trash to the dump with the tractors, we learned the basics of gravity. We also discovered that tractors and other farm equipment aren't built for racing.

Victor drove the red tractor. He was towing a single-axle utility trailer, which I jumped into as he headed to the dump. Tommy was cutting grass on the older, yellow tractor.

The timing was perfect. Tommy finished his grass grooming just as Victor and I dumped the last burn barrel. Nothing was said. The race began of its own accord.

Once the grinding of gears began, I didn't have a choice. It didn't matter that I was scared. I had to stand in the trailer and cheer Victor on. After all, I didn't want to lose.

Rough and bumpy, the racecourse weaved through the front orchard. The finish line was always the same. If you were on bikes, in beater cars, or driving tractors, the end came as the path narrowed between the pond and canal. There was barely room for two bikes but only room for one of anything on four wheels. The slower of the two would either slam on the brakes or be forced into the woods at the edge of the canal or into the pond. It was our Lutheran Church Camp version of Chicken.

Victor was handicapped out of the gate. He was towing a trailer and his baby brother. Tommy had the slower tractor but got a slight head start. Grass clippings and rotten apples flew as the red and yellow tractors pounded over ruts, through tall grass, and around apple trees.

As the narrowed path came into sight, the old sickle attachment on Tommy's tractor flopped around like a swordfish out of water. Tommy slowed his yellow beast. He couldn't risk having to tell Dad why the sickle bar broke off in the orchard.

Victor seized the opportunity and threw the throttle of the red Ford wide open. He looked back at me to share in his smirking glory. When he did, he slammed into one of the biggest rocks on camp property. The front of the tractor jumped over the boulder, and the rear followed. Thanks to its high clearance, the sturdy Ford cleared the obstacle unscathed. The single-axle trailer and its passenger had a different experience.

I stood in the trailer, squeezing the front wall as the tractor launched and the trailer bolt—Why didn't an adult put a nut on that bolt?—shot out. I followed suit. Suspended in mid-air, the next thing I saw was the right rear tractor tire inches from my forehead.

When I regained consciousness, Tommy's dumb grin stretched across his whole face. "You flew just like Superman!" he exclaimed.

Victor was too scared to talk. Thankfully, I only got a scrape on my arm and a scratch on my face.*

Whatever you believe, something or someone was with my brothers and me that day. How did I miss the tractor tire with my face? How did the barrels stay in the trailer, and I flew out? How did I get launched twenty feet or more up and out of that trailer, onto the hard ground, with only minor injuries—a short-term loss of breath and a few scratches? My brothers Tom, Vic and I never really talked about it again.

It probably also caused my first concussion. I don't remember what happened immediately after the accident.

Chapter Twenty-Four

GRADUATION DAY, CELEBRATION YEAR

Some years come and go without much fanfare. Others leave a stamp on the world. Nineteen eighty-four was legendary! It was so big that it was written about and anticipated years earlier by George Orwell.

While Orwell's novel left readers with little hope for the future, the actual 1984 brought hope to the Simpson family. For possibly the first time, our future bordered on bright. It wasn't just a great year for the Simpsons though—1984 was a great year for a city and our nation.

That year, Los Angeles hosted the Summer Olympics. Team USA destroyed the competition, winning eighty-three gold medals and 174 medals overall. Carl Lewis, Greg Louganis, and Mary Lou Retton all had historic performances.

While we were busy winning, fourteen Eastern Bloc countries boycotted the games. It was a calculated, predictable response to America's boycott of the 1980 Summer Olympics in Moscow. Sadly for them, no one here cared that the Eastern Bloc countries weren't represented.

Our gutsy competitiveness reached beyond the athletic arena. We were making a comeback in industry as well, fighting our way out of the doldrums and uncertainty of the 1970s and once again separating ourselves as the biggest boy on the block.

Want a unified America? Go back to 1984. That year's presidential election was the last real landslide. Incumbent Ronald Reagan was not loved by all, but he won forty-nine of fifty states. An overwhelming majority felt he deserved another four years.

Reagan wasn't perfect, no president is. But his bold leadership was sincere and unwavering. Reagan was a proud American. His faith and strength spurred a renewed appreciation and respect for our military. In the mid-'80s this country walked with a swagger that was absent for quite a while.*

Can you imagine waiting hours in line for a couple gallons of gas? The oil embargo in 1973 led to the Congress-initiated Energy Policy and Conservation Act of 1975, which caught US automakers off guard.

The Corporate Average Fuel Economy standards, or C.A.F.E., established higher fuel economy requirements for passenger cars. The intention was to double the average fuel economy of every new car fleet to 27.5 miles per gallon by the 1985 model year. Detroit was not ready.

Japanese automakers were already producing cars on par with or better than the big three. Now, almost overnight there was a new challenge for Detroit. Build them better, safer, and more economical. It was a tall order on short notice. It was too much for the stubborn Motor City corporations to handle. American-made cars from the mid-'70s through the early '80s, with few exceptions, looked bad, ran worse, and were not any safer or better on gas than they were a decade before.

By the middle of the 1980s, Detroit actually had a few winners. This fueled a new confidence in the Big Three. Fired from Ford in 1978, Lee Iacocca was courted and hired by the competition almost immediately. His energy and foresight brought Chrysler back from the dead. Iacocca approached Congress and requested a guaranteed loan. He was successful but cost-cutting concessions had to be made to seal the deal.

At Chrysler Iacocca was reunited with another former Ford employee, Hal Sperlich. Together they launched two major projects. The very affordable, front-wheel drive K-car platform was launched in 1981. The

---

Compare this to the previous decade. The '70s gave us disco, Watergate, the Nixon resignation, horrific fashion, record inflation, skyrocketing unemployment, Jimmy Carter, the Iran hostage crisis, an energy crisis, and disco. (Yes, disco was bad enough to mention twice.) We needed a reset.

K-car line took Chrysler off of life support. Ugly, boxy, cheap looking, basic transportation. The only two significant qualities of the new models were front-wheel drive and slightly better fuel economy. But sales were good, and Chrysler was on the comeback trail.

On a personal side note I owned one of these vehicles. My three boxes sitting on four wheels was a 1986 Plymouth Caravelle. It was diarrhea brown with tan cloth interior. I can personally attest to this car's toughness and front-wheel-drive prowess.

My brother Victor and I once spent the better part of a December morning trying to get the car stuck. It was during a rare family vacation near Traverse City. A few Simpsons scraped together enough money to rent a neat little loft cabin for our Christmas celebration. Eight inches of fresh white powder adorned the northwest Michigan landscape. My brother and I were sent out to get supplies. We ran that little Plymouth into every snowbank we could find. The low torque four-cylinder motor could not be contained. The front wheel drive beast barely spun a tire as I threw it into R and slowly, steadily backed away from multiple snow-filled embankments.

The next major project Chrysler embarked on was so big it sparked a family transportation transformation. More than a new vehicle line, it quickly became an American icon. In late 1983 the American minivan was introduced to the world as an '84 model.

While at Ford, Hal Sperlich was unsuccessful in convincing his stubborn FoMoCo bosses to take the then-dubbed "Mini-Max" project seriously. Apparently Henry Ford II was disinterested in a restyled version of a small van. Despite all of the success that Toyota was enjoying with the concept in Asia and Latin America, the Mini-Max project at Ford never made it to the factory.

Chrysler, wanting to keep the K-car momentum going, took a chance on Sperlich. Hal Sperlich was given the green light to give birth to his baby. Lee Iacocca was the pitchman, and Sperlich the father. Together they made automotive history.

The early 1980's resurgence of Chrysler provided hope and inspiration to a city that had, in recent decades, not had many reasons to be optimistic. Through the summer of 1983 and into the spring of 1984 the Motor City had another inspiring story brewing.

Baseball Dreams

Sparky Anderson, the Architect of the Big Red Machine in Cincinnati, brought his brand of baseball to Detroit in June of 1979. Shortly after his arrival, he unapologetically proclaimed the Tigers would be a pennant winner within five years. It only took a few short seasons to turn the slumping Tigers into contenders again. In 1983 the Tigers had the third-best record in baseball but finished second in the division. The Orioles of Baltimore won the east and were the eventual World Series Champs.

The following year the Detroit Boys of Summer started the season with a bang that lasted all year long. After forty games, they had a mind-blowing thirty-five victories.

It was the first year, the first summer, I fell in love. Her name was Baseball, and she wore a large D in an olde English font. From pretending to hit like Darrell Evans or field like Trammell or run like Kirk Gibson in our back yard to pitching tennis balls against our garage emulating Morris or Hernandez, I was deeply infatuated. I listened to games on car radios and Mom's clock radio and watched every time the Tigers were on TV. I learned to detest west coast road trips. Their late start times made it impossible to watch or listen to the entire game.

Every post-game morning, I hunted down the *Detroit News* and scooped up the sports section like Lou Whitaker fielding a routine ground ball. Then I took the sports section to the lawn and relived every inning as I chowed down on Rice Krispies.

Lightning in a bottle is an understated way to describe Willie Hernandez's success that year. The Puerto Rican leftie won the American League MVP and Cy Young Award and led the Tigers to a pennant and a Championship. In thirty-three save opportunities, he only dropped the ball once. He closed the door on two World Series games, giving up only one run.

When you are young your mind is free of worry and the day-to-day troubles that adults concern themselves over. The '84 Tigers are still my all-time favorite team. Being a kid that summer made an already magical season even more special.

My brother Rick enjoyed a very memorable season when he was young. He was only nine years old at the time but retains vivid memories of the scrappy '68 Tigers to this day. That team was both historic and dramatic. The 1968 World Series went seven games, and the Cardinals were in complete control until game five. Game seven was scoreless until the seventh inning, and both starting pitchers pitched the entire game.

The '84 Tigers were so good the World Series was almost boring. The only disappointment came during the final inning of the final game when I turned to my mom. "If the Tigers win it tonight," I said, "can I stay home from school?" In one word she diminished the joy of an entire baseball season: "No." This short answer was followed with a directive to get to bed "as soon as the game is over." At least Dad wasn't there to holler "Brush 'em" as I sulked to my front porch bedroom.

Throughout childhood, the phrase "Brush 'em" was linked to all things good and bad about my father. The bad: The overall way he spoke at us, not to us. My dad was no Ward Cleaver. His idea of a sit-down conversation was, "Pass the gravy." The good: Somewhere, deep down, Dad really cared about us. He wanted us healthy and able to keep our own teeth. Dad lost all his teeth in his early twenties and had to get dentures in the Army. He considered that one of the worst experiences of his life. So, when Dad yelled, "Brush 'em!" to us at bedtime, it was stated with passion and purpose.

Crawling to the Finish Line

Another real-life contrast to the depressing Orwell novel was my favorite band, Van Halen, releasing their sixth studio album. Appropriately titled "1984" it began with an odd yet optimistic sounding instrumental and ended with Eddie's ear-slamming guitar in "House of Pain." This album was anything but sad and hopeless.

Hits like "Jump," "Panama," and my favorite, "Hot For Teacher," propelled the album to its peak at number two, behind only one of the most popular albums of all time. Michael Jackson's sixth studio album, which spent a record thirty-seven weeks at number one is still, I believe, the best-selling album of all time.

My brothers, the twins Tom and Vic, were Van Halen fans before I knew what rock music was. How appropriate that 1984, the name of Van Halen's new album, was the year they escaped that taxpayer-funded prison called high school.

I was in sixth grade when I watched my older brothers completely check out from high school. Years later, I had my own bout with senioritis. It kicked in for me on my sixteenth birthday—March 18, 1988. I had my license, a car, and a little freedom, and I didn't give two shits about school.*

Tom and Vic both found their niches during high school. Tommy found a home in the culinary arts program. The students of HHS ran and prepared food for the Highlander Restaurant, and Tommy loved it. Tommy seemed happy when he was there, and he felt part of something.

Victor had skills no other Simpsons possessed. Mechanically minded, he was an expert at taking things apart and figuring out how they worked. He was good at drafting too. The trades corridor of high school almost kept Victor's full attention.

But being good at a few things couldn't stave off an epic case of senioritis. During the 1983–84 school year, Tom and Vic averaged one missed day of school every other week. If they weren't absent, they were tardy. If they were in class, they were sleeping due to their hectic work and party schedule. Their shotty attendance combined with their D+ GPA left my mother wondering whether they would graduate. But somehow, they did.

I think maybe the officials at Howell High School were simply sick of seeing them in the halls and knew that keeping them around another year wouldn't help anyone. This was as good as they were going to do. In June of 1984 they received their high school diplomas.

As I write this, my daughter is in the middle of her senior year in high school. Thankfully, she's a better person than her uncles or father ever were. Her bout of senioritis is mild and inconsistent. It's growing stronger as we approach May, but Stephanie has maintained a respectable GPA and done more than just show up.

Afterward, there was more relief than excitement. Even Dad's appearance—which wasn't guaranteed, as he failed to make Rick's graduation seven years earlier—couldn't kill the dull vibe.

A Real Cause for Celebration

The twins' participation trophy couldn't compare to another major milestone that June. Dad wasn't invited to that commemoration. And Mom couldn't clap, because she was holding the trophy.

On June 9, 1984, Elaine Elizabeth Simpson graduated magna cum laude with her four-year degree in business administration. The journey was long and filled with obstacles, but she persevered and reached her destination.

For some students, kids in their early twenties, graduating college with a four year degree might just be another stepping stone. Go to class, study, repeat, leave with a diploma four years later with a degree in Horology, Art History, or Parapsychology. Now go take on the world. My mother took on the world while earning her degree.

What makes her accomplishment so extraordinary?

1. She started college at age forty-five, when some students are mailing in their final student loan payments.

2. She had little support from her spouse. Instead, Dad demeaned her efforts, calling her out for not being a good wife and mother.

3. We lived in poverty from Mom's first day of class to her last. The entire time, we had little extra money for clothes or anything else needed to attend higher education.

4. Between classes and studying, Mom raised four of her five kids almost exclusively alone.

5. She worked multiple part-time jobs to support her family.

6. Our family had no dependable transportation, so she frequently hitched rides to school or burned through our money to maintain the junk we had in the driveway. She eventually accepted her father's gift of a ten-year-old Ford.

7. While in school, Mom found the courage to end her broken marriage, separate from her husband, and—the year before graduation—

finalize her divorce.

8.   Mother swallowed her pride to become part of the janitorial staff at Cleary, cleaning up after students and staff at the college she attended. While admirable, this was not an exercise in confidence building.

9.   She was under constant pressure to keep good grades to maintain government assistance that made school a possibility.

In one Finnish word, *Sisu!* As Wikipedia puts it, *sisu* means "stoic determination . . . going beyond one's mental and physical capacity." Over her four years at Cleary College, Mom embodied sisu, demonstrating the motivating power of desperation. Ultimately, she proved to herself and her family that you can do

Mom at graduation.

most anything you put your mind to.

A single picture sums up Mom's accomplishment. Wearing her cap and gown and holding her diploma, Mom's prideful smile outshined the entire day's events. She projected a glow of confidence we'd never seen in her before. She was no longer a tired, downtrodden, single mom with no future. For the first time in ages, she had hope, self-assurance, academic accomplishment, and a degree. This was worthy of celebration.*

It's also noteworthy that I kissed a girl for the first time in the summer of 1984. But its effect on me wore off faster than the resulting relationship. Besides, it happened in West Virginia, and my heart remained in Michigan. My love belonged to Mom, my siblings, and the Detroit Tigers. Bless You Boys! Bless you, Mom.

Chapter Twenty-Five

THE SLOWEST EVICTION

L egendary as 1984 was, it eventually had to end. The life-altering events of that year brought changes and challenges that all of us knew were coming, but none of us were ready for. After the parties and celebrations were over it was time for the next chapter. The evolution of a family trying to get out of its own way.

What the Simpsons lacked in planning and preparedness, we made up for with a complete disregard for direction and forethought. Tom and Vic graduated high school with no idea what was next. Like blindfolded partygoers, they stuck pins in their future and hoped for the best.

There was no deliberation or kitchen-table conversations that drove the twins out into the cruel world. But they had to do something, so they did.

The military path should never be taken lightly. Uncle Sam doesn't have a slogan that declares, "The many, the confused, the career-path challenged." Joining the armed forces is honorable. For many it is a decision reached after intense consideration and self-evaluation. In my opinion it is a choice that needs to come from the heart and soul. You need to be worthy of the uniform.

The unfortunate reality is our military needs more than just a few good men. We need thousands and thousands of good men and women. These young people don't get paid well, must endure rigorous training, are away from home months or years at a time, and are essentially owned by the United States of America. They must take orders, never question authority, listen to all instructions, and comply.

In a knee-jerk move, Tommy signed his life and freedom over to the U.S. Marine Corps. He wanted to be a Marine, and he was physically capable of getting through the training. But Tommy's free spirit suffocated, unable to tolerate the mental gymnastics young recruits are subjected to. While he knew mental toughness was necessary, he couldn't grasp the demeaning path the Marines built to obtain that toughness.

The problem was compounded by his childhood. While Dad talked down to both twins throughout their childhood, Victor and Dad bonded over Victor's mechanical skills. Tommy had mechanical aptitude, but it took a few minutes to teach Tommy. Dad was not a patient man. So, Tommy spent the better part of his adolescence as an afterthought to Dad. When Dad wasn't bitching about Tommy, he was yelling at him.

All this came to a head a few weeks into boot camp. After he was made to feel like crap day after day, my brother put his hand through a plate glass window. He was finished being ridiculed by Dad, his drill instructor, and everyone else.

There was no plane ride back home like the one he enjoyed on the way to San Diego. When the government sends you home early, you take the bus. Tommy said that the time it took to get home were the longest three days in his life.

Victor left home for trade school before Tommy joined the Marines. Despite Vic's poor grades and school records, a place of higher learning accepted Victor's application—another miracle. Thanks to our family's financial status, Victor qualified for enough financial aid to get through the first semester, and Mom sent him packing. Eager to take on the world, Victor left the nest and flew to the armpit of the Midwest: Columbus, Ohio.

As the Bible story regarding Belshazzar goes, the writing was on the wall. I would not be as lucky as my older siblings. Massive parties and sports with friends around Camp Luther Vista were not part of my high school years.

The land, the baseball field, the swimming pond would not be enjoyed by me as a teenager. All things that Tom, Vic, and Denise took for granted. Our departure, our removal from the camp as caretakers began the day Mom kicked Dad out of the house.

Here Comes the End

Early on, Dad returned to camp occasionally to help out. He stayed in a small cottage by the barn for weeks at a time, possibly hoping for reconciliation. My parents' rent-free living arrangement with the church was contingent on both parties being part-time, live-in caretakers. With Dad fading from the picture, that contingency grew weaker each day.

Mom was busy finishing school and working multiple part-time jobs. When the church learned of our crumbling family dynamic, Mom told a few white lies to delay the inevitable. She was desperate to keep the happy family charade going as long as possible. At least until she graduated from Cleary.

As Dad's diminished status became evident to the church, Mom received a letter that outlined the caretaker contract and Mom's inability to live up to it. She delayed some more but eventually admitted that Dad was no longer living on the property.

Graciously, the church had compassion on the single mom struggling to get by. They didn't throw her and her kids out on the street—not right away, at least. After all, we were still doing some maintenance on the property, and we weren't destroying the place. A new agreement allowed us to stay. We just had to pay a small amount of rent and perform certain caretaker duties.

Then came the spring of 1985. A few church members grumbled that the Simpsons pulled a fast one on them and had taken advantage of the church's generosity for far too long. With a new camp season looming and my family going in about six different directions, the church pulled the plug on our month-to-month rental agreement.

A mother never wants to see her child sad or disappointed. And my mother never wanted to be the reason or cause of her child's sadness. Mom knew it was time for her and I to have a conversation.

My mom was a world class procrastinator. She had put this talk off as long as possible. I was in denial, but Mom knew I wasn't stupid. She knew I was catching on to our impending eviction. She not only needed to tell me, but she felt like she had to persuade me into thinking I had a say in where we lived next.

Now remember, this was a time before moms were made to feel bad for working and not spending every waking moment with their minor children. When I was a kid we didn't have much say in anything. I would not be making any final decisions on where we ended up, but I would tag along. Mostly because it was something Mom didn't want to do by herself. She also wanted to give me the illusion that my opinion mattered.

I threw as much guilt at her as possible. My core argument: I didn't want to change schools. I didn't want to be separated from my friends and end up attending Brighton Area Schools, our hated crosstown rival.*

Mom sympathized, but my friends at school were not high on her list of concerns. So, in the spring of 1985, Mother and I began looking for a place to live. Mom got her first full-time job after graduation, but it was an entry-level job with entry-level pay. Our options were limited.

While Mom was learning to juggle a new job and caring for me on her own, Livingston County was growing fast. Home prices were high, and interest rates were even higher. Buying a home with no credit and no down payment was a dream reaching as high as the Fisher Building.

Shopping for a rental was equally frustrating. The rent price of every nice house was beyond our budget. If it was affordable and a decent place, it was in the wrong area. Affordable rentals in the right area required gigantic deposits or didn't allow pets. Either was a deal-killer. Mom didn't have a stack of cash for a deposit, and she felt so guilty about tearing me

---

When it came time to relocate my own family, my wife and I were determined to make it as painless as possible for our daughter. Together as husband and wife we talked it through and agreed on the parameters of our plan. First we wanted there to be only one move. If we were going to make our daughter change schools, it needed to be one time only. The next objective was to make sure our daughter wasn't at the bottom of the school's totem pole. No change of schools entering the first year of middle school or high school. Being a freshman sucks. Being a freshman in a new school sucks more. Finally, the new school system had to be smaller than the one we were leaving. With communication, hard work, and dedication, we executed this plan flawlessly. It remains one of my proudest accomplishments as a husband and a father.

away from Camp Luther Vista that she committed to finding a place where we could keep our little dog Barney.

Defeated and exhausted, we entertained the possibility of living in Mom's 1982 Ford Escort. Before resigning to that fate, we went to check out one more possibility on a rainy, gloomy, Michigan afternoon.

The Start of Trailer Life

It wasn't a house, and it wasn't a rental. As real estate decisions go, it was about the worst available option—a thirteen-year-old double-wide trailer with monthly lot rent. But Mom was desperate, and we needed a place to call home. Besides, it was near Camp Luther Vista, which meant staying in Howell Public Schools.

When we got out to look at the trailer, it felt like we were being watched. At camp, our nearest neighbor was a quarter mile away. In the trailer park, I could almost stand on one porch and touch the next trailer.

It was brown and white with ugly metal awnings over the two front windows. A rusty shed sat out back. Despite my visible objections, we went inside.

The kitchen had carpet and a hole under the counter where a dishwasher once lived. The worn-out abode had exactly two things going for it: a wood-burning stove and multiple bathrooms. We'd been a one-bathroom family since the beginning of time. A second bathroom was a significant upgrade The trailer sat on about one-twentieth of an acre of land that we would never own. A faux Styrofoam beam ran down the middle of the living room hiding whatever actually held the double-wide together.

We were there for ten minutes when Mom asked about pets. "There are a few rules about pets, but they are allowed," we were told. "There is a monthly pet fee and dogs can only be twelve inches tall." My heart sank. I was sure Barney was at least fifteen inches tall.

As I reeled from the possibility of losing Barney, the lady showing us the home told us about the amenities. "There is a playground with a basketball hoop and a private lake for swimming and fishing," she said. "You and your son should go down and have a look. Then swing by the office on your way out to pick up some paperwork."

Mom gave me the cup-half-full treatment. I gave her the silent treatment as we surveyed the subpar amenities. "Look," Mom said, "they have a basketball thingy and a swing set." I said nothing.

Two weeks went by without another word about moving or the trailer. I convinced myself that another miracle occurred, and we were staying at Camp Luther Vista. The miracle was undone on a Saturday morning. I was pouring cereal into a bowl and Mom sat beside me. "I'm buying the trailer in Sylvan Glen," she said with a crackle in her voice. "We move in a month."

"No!" I yelled. Crying, I ran outside, got on my bike, put a leash on Barney, and took off. Memories ran through my mind, each more bittersweet than the last. I couldn't believe it was over. This home, this eighty-acre playground would no longer be part of my life.

Barney and I traveled nonstop for nearly two hours. I was hot, and we were both thirsty, but I didn't care. I was a little surprised that mom had not come looking for us, but I was thankful. I didn't want to talk to her or anyone else. I needed to pout, sulk, and cry in solitude. When we reached a paved road, one that I didn't recognize, I decided it was time to turn around and go home.

The next few weeks were trying times. My relationship with my mother became strained. I was only in my first year of teenagerhood, but I was rookie of the year. My attitude and demeanor matched a seasoned sixteen- or seventeen-year-old. When it came to the whole moving and packing thing, this thirteen-year-old wasn't doing shit.

A few days before the move, I packed exactly three boxes. It was an asshole move. While Mom cleaned and packed, I took off. Sometimes, I was gone for hours at a time. The little I did pack was crap I didn't want Mom to see: fireworks, ammunition, a lighter and a small knife, some girlie mag pics, and a stack of small bills.

A week before our move date, Mom gave me more unwelcome news. Dad was coming up to Michigan. Not to help move but to recover some of his possessions. You know, before Mom burned them.

For some reason, Aunt Terri came along for the ride. You couldn't find two more unlikely carpool members. Dad and Aunt Terri despised each other. To make their ride back to West Virginia a little more civil, Mom had an idea.

"Oh, you don't want to help with the move? Okay," she said, chewing on the bitterness I'd nursed for weeks. "Go spend a month with your father. Maybe that will improve your attitude."

I had overextended myself and my teenage ways. Now instead of spending weeks exploring my new trailerhood, I would be spending an undetermined amount of time with my grumpy father. I didn't move one box into our new trailer home. I got shipped out of town like a crate destined for Hell.

To West Virginia and Back

I was in West Virginia for a painfully long six weeks. While there, Dad took me on the road with him. He also took me to a bar with no windows. And he bought me a new ten speed. If my math is correct, I outlined the entire summer's highlights in three sentences.

That summer spent with Dad in West Virginia was different than most. It extended deep into August. So deep that I remember the school by Grandma's house in Barboursville conducting summer football practice and doing test runs with the fleet of buses. "Am I going to miss the start of school in Michigan?" I wondered.

My father's financial status was bleaker than usual that year. He couldn't even afford to take me back to Michigan.

I was out riding my ten speed when Mom arrived. I remember rounding the corner and spotting that ugly Escort in Mamaw's driveway. I jumped off my bike and ran to greet Mom with a big hug.

We spent a few minutes catching up and then got to work on the new bike carrier she purchased. It was a sixty-dollar Sears Special. Mom insisted it was a steal, even with the 21.9 percent interest rate.*

Dad could have cut several middlemen out of the entire purchase if

---

*Over the next few months, Mom spent hundreds of dollars paying for that bike rack. All to get my ninety-nine-dollar Huffy home.

he'd simply given Mom money toward a new ten speed from Sears. We could have bought it in Michigan. I would have gotten a better bike and Mom wouldn't have had to carry debt for six months on a bike carrier we would never use again.

This is a classic example of how the lower-middle class sometimes stays so low for so long. Buying the ten speed when Dad chose to was never about finances or economics. It was about him seeing my face when he surprised me with it. That was something my father truly enjoyed doing.

While putting the rack on the Escort, Mom let me in on some family dirty laundry. "We have to get on the road early in the morning." "That's fine," I said, my attitude about living in the trailer now completely transformed after spending half a summer with Dad. "I can't wait to get home!" Mom continued in her beat-around-the-bush voice: "Well actually, we're leaving early because we have a stop to make on the way home. A detour. Victor needs a ride home from Columbus," Mom said. "He quit school."

Good as Victor was with tools, electronics, and anything mechanical, he had weaknesses. He avoided and ignored his two roommates. He didn't like working and was not a self-starter. The curriculum at DeVry fit Victor. Everything else was a problem. After one semester of school and a summer working at Mother's Pizza, drinking beer, and playing foosball, Victor was coming home.

During the three-hour car ride to Columbus, Mom and I talked about anything and everything except Victor. I gave her the three-sentence highlight reel of my summer.**

She was so eager to tell me the details about the crazy hit movie she went to see. It was the blockbuster of the year, something Dad could have easily taken me to see for about $7.50. But that might have been fun and a good memory, so no, it didn't happen.

Back To The Future was the big hit that summer, and Mom spent

---

** *I actually only gave her two sentences. I left out the trip to the windowless bar. She told me about the trailer and living in Sylvan Glen. She also went on for a while about going to the movies with friends. Something mom had probably not done since the '50s or '60s.*

almost an hour talking about the film. She really had a good time seeing that movie because it took her back in time just like it did for the film's hero, Marty McFly. The clothes, the cars, the music, the way people carried themselves. It was one big nostalgia trip for anyone who grew up in the '50s.

Long Ride Home

Mom and I talked non stop until we got close to Columbus,. Then the car grew silent. We weren't sure what Victor we would see—angry-and-hot-tempered Victor, take-pity-on-me Victor, or reclusive-and-silent Victor.

We pulled up to the dirty, hot, trash-filled apartment parking lot. As expected, Vic's belongings and luggage were nowhere to be found. We approached what we thought was Victor's apartment and knocked.

Hot-tempered, unorganized Victor answered. He hadn't packed a thing. When Mom asked what he'd been doing, Victor went into a rage. Mom turned around and walked back down to the car.

Typical Victor. First he was going to make us wait for him. Then he was hoping Mom would take pity on him and help him get his shit together. She declined. When Victor came down with some rope and told mom he wanted to strap his foosball table to the roof of the car, mom threatened to leave without him.

I think he spent the next twenty minutes destroying the table and shoving it in a dumpster. His selfish thought being, "If I can't take it with me no one else is going to enjoy it either." Also, Victor had this way of taking the pain of his day and life out on inanimate objects. Doors, tables, chairs, walls—if he was in a bad enough mood, nothing was safe.

As afternoon turned to evening, we exited the apartment parking lot. Mom's Escort was loaded with Victor's shit—twice as much as he brought to Columbus. On the ride home, all of Victor's personalities made an appearance, putting the entire Victor catalog of emotions and mental instability on display.

The first hour on the road was tension filled and a little combative, but the thick evening air wore Victor down and a tired silence filled the car. Bus rides after a sports loss. Car rides after life deals you a setback. Coming up short after setting out on your own only to have to tuck your tail between your legs and return home to Mom and Dad. These trips always seem so much longer than they actually are. Although not as long as Tommy's bus ride from San Diego, Victor's ride home from Columbus was just as painful.

Mom bit her tongue and held off on the "What now?" conversation with Victor. He'd been through a rough patch. No need to worsen the wounds.

Part Four

TALES OF A TEENAGE TRAILER PARK BOY

Chapter Twenty-Six

NO AIR CONDITIONING, BUT WE HAVE CABLE

It was dark when Mom pulled the Escort into the very narrow driveway of our trailer park home.*

When Mom bought the 1982 Escort, air conditioning was an option. An option ours did not have. It was 1985, and Mom was a year or more away from getting her first car with A/C. Mom, Victor, and I peeled ourselves from the Escort's vinyl seats and poured out.

I hadn't been in the trailer since April. Victor and I figured it had to be better than the Escort. We were wrong. Soon as we opened the front door, it slammed us in the face. Dank, stagnant, and humid. Fortunately, living without A/C was nothing new to the Simpson family. Our previous homes didn't have A/C, so why break that trend?

There was a unit behind the trailer for making cool air. Someone painted the unit brown to match our glorious trailer. It was so big and old you might think that the A/C was installed first, and the trailer was then parked in front of it. The big rusty box was weathered from sitting in the sun. Wires dangling from one side made it clear it hadn't worked in quite a while. I suspect the last time that thing cooled the trailer, Gerald

---

Driveways frequently get overlooked. Prospective home buyers rarely spend much time on the thing that leads to their castle. As a result, driveways are often too short or narrow, or they're on a thirty-five-degree angle that makes getting in and out of the car a dicey experience. Do better, driveway makers!

Ford was congratulating Jimmy Carter.

Mom routinely avoided bad news whenever possible. I'm pretty sure she never even got a quote to see if it could be repaired, assuming it was way more than she could afford. Why get down about something that was financially unattainable? "We'll just sweat it out for a few years," Mom said.*

Victor claimed the living room couch and announced he was moving out in a few weeks. Tommy called dibs on one of the three frameless twin beds crammed in the master suite. I started down the hall to see my new room, complete with its own floor bed. Before I could get there, my brother Rick met me near the kitchen. Upon seeing me he announced the best thing I had heard that entire summer.

"We have cable!" he said.

Those three beautiful words lifted my spirits and gave me new hope. Double digits of channels and no snow-filled pictures that faded in and out with the weather. Crisp, clear television viewing was my new reality.

No more messing with rabbit ears or the UHF tuner to see a favorite cartoon or *The Three Stooges* clearly. Plus, channels that no antenna on any TV could access. I had the entire basic and extended cable lineup at my fingertips: MTV, TBS WGN, USA, The Weather Channel, Nickelodeon—so many choices, so few viewing hours. Also included with our promotional new subscriber deal, we got two digital cable boxes with remotes. No more pushing out of a comfy chair to change the channel.**

Mom kicked that can of BS all the way to 1996. For more than a decade, Mom lived in that aluminum box without working A/C—not even a window unit. Up to that point, the only thing the Simpsons owned with working A/C was a blue Oldsmobile sedan. Sadly, we never experienced the A/C. Dad brought the car home in mid-November. By the time it was hot enough to use the air conditioning, the car was gone. Seems the bank expected Dad to pay for the car every month.

**My first cable experience was at Rick's first apartment in Lansing. My second was at Denise's apartment. The best part was something called ESPN and the ability to watch sports on more than one channel. When one game went to a commercial, I simply switched to the other game. Magic!*

An Electronic Babysitter and Life Lessons

I even had a TV in my bedroom. This changed my life. I was a typical latchkey kid. No, check that, I was the textbook description of a latchkey adolescent. I came home after school to an empty home. This started in sixth grade at the camp. Mom worked and went to school. My brothers worked after school. In sixth and seventh grade I was being raised in part by after school cartoons and really bad movies.

Then, as I entered my teenage years in the trailer park, I got full access to a verifiable TV buffet. Uncut R-rated movies without commercials. Scantily clad girls in every other music video. Violent, profanity-laced action flicks on HBO. And don't forget Cinemax—or as the kids called it, Skinemax.

In the trailer, I quickly fell into an after-school routine: turn on the TV and flip through every channel several times before settling on the best choice that day. Once the show reached a commercial break or boring part, I headed to the kitchen for a carb-filled calorie fest to accompany my viewing pleasure. Ham-and-cheese bagel sandwiches were a staple. If my sweet tooth was active, I'd kill an entire stack of graham crackers dipped in extra-thick hot cocoa.

My after-school routine only got interrupted or shortened when a better option reared its head. A pickup basketball or football game at the lake were better options. So was riding bikes with other neighborhood kids. Sometimes, I'd leave TV behind to experiment with drugs or sneak beers with my buddy Dean.

While I missed the camp, the trailer park wasn't the worst place to finish growing up. I made friendships there that have lasted a lifetime. I bent some rules and got away with a ton along the way. I learned a lot about life in a very short amount of time.

I crawled out of my shell there, and I had fun. I should have and could have died several times from alcohol poisoning and pushing the limits of youthful immortality and gravity. Cable TV taught me a few things I shouldn't do. My pals taught me the rest.

Subscription television doesn't deserve all the blame for my crooked adolescent path. And I don't at all blame my mother. If she would have restricted my viewing I simply would have craved it more and found a way to circumvent her efforts. She consistently provided a good moral compass for me. I just threw it on the ground and smashed it with a hammer.

Chapter Twenty-Seven

MAKING FRIENDS IN THE TRAILERHOOD

My biggest fear about moving into the trailer park was not having friends. My second biggest fear was being the new kid. My gender, coupled with small-town geography, chased those fears away on the first day of school.

Sorry girls, but you know it's true. Especially during adolescence, boys make better friends. And because we don't thrive on drama there isn't a long friendship break-in period. My wife will vouch for me on this one. There's a reason *The Real House Husband* shows are outnumbered fifty to one by their female counterparts. Dudes are not as good at drama.

When we moved in 1985, Sylvan Glen Estates wasn't a vibrant, youthful community. There were kids living there but not many. The weird thing to me was that most kids in Sylvan Glen were all on one side of the neighborhood. Most of us lived on the same block of three or four streets. I think at one time our trailer park was exclusive to seasoned citizens and kids were not welcome at all.

Even into the '90s, years after we moved there, the front of the park was regulated to retirees only. The front east side was made up of about six streets. Those streets were quieter during the day and into the evening than the kid-friendly areas to the west.

I remember riding my ten speed through and around the "old section." A few geezers (usually cranky men) gave me dirty looks as I rode by. As if to say, "Get back to your section, you whipper snapper!" It was so quiet over there it was almost eerie. Summer afternoons, the loudest noise was the dull hum of A/C units laboring to keep the trailer homes cool.

When we moved into Sylvan Glen, I didn't know a single kid who lived there. But the trailer park was less than three miles from our house at Luther Vista and two miles from the retired Birkenstock Elementary.

On the first day of school, I learned I actually knew several kids in the area. I met new faces on that first day as well. Dean was new to Michigan and Livingston County. We had similar interests, so we quickly became friends. I'd known Jason and Brian for years. Chuck lived a street over and was one grade above the rest of us, but that didn't matter. Just like that, I had old and new friends who all lived a short bike ride away from 161 Shore Breeze.*

The bike ride to nearby friends was shortened with the cut throughs and back trails. Those same shortcuts and hidden paths were pivotal for getting into and out of trouble. On our bikes we navigated over and around stuff that cars and the park manager couldn't traverse. Old Dale, the asshole trailer park manager, repeatedly patched a fence section the trailer park kids beat down with their feet, bikes, and skateboards. Then he dangled a locked chain from two posts to keep us off a dirt cut-through trail that led to a retaining pond and Dean's house. It was an attempt to keep teenagers from driving down there to smoke pot or make out.

The chain wasn't much of an obstacle. Dale left room between the posts and the thick brush on both sides. We could sneak past without even dismounting our bikes. When he realized his folly, he moved the posts until they touched the brush. So, Dean and I stood on the chain. Our combined weight pulled in the posts and lowered the chain until it was only a foot off the ground.

A well-executed bunny hop was our ticket in and out of the trailer

---

*No, that's not a typo. We lived on Shore Breeze. Our landlocked community in lower middle Michigan had a catalog of Florida-inspired street names. Lake Breeze, Breezeway, Gulf Stream, and—my favorite—Tamiami Trail. The street names catered to the retirees and snowbirds, some who spent their winters in Florida. Other old timers didn't have the means to own two homes. They just wished they lived part-time in the Sunshine State. The street names made all of them feel like they were in Florida, I guess.

park prison. I was fast on my bike, but my chubby, husky frame made it difficult to clear the rusty metal. Nighttime jumps were the worst. The little trail was creepy in the dark, and all I wanted was to get through it quickly without getting off my bike. If I went too fast, I might not clear the front tire. Jump too early, and the chain snagged the back tire like a fish, sending me over the handlebars.

I would like to say something in my defense. While I wasn't great at jumping and doing tricks on my bike, I had a severe handicap during my first year in the trailer park. My bike was that piece-of-shit Huffy ten speed Dad gave me in West Virginia. Everywhere Dean, Chuck, and Jason went and everything they did on their BMX bikes, I did on a ten speed. I kept up, but it wasn't easy.

My First Major Purchase

The human spirit is at its best when driven by clearly defined goals and aspirations. I had a goal. I wanted a BMX bike. I yearned for it.

Like most dreams that come true, timing and a little luck were on my side. My legally blind neighbor, Mr. Glynn, had too many trailer park lawns to cut and was looking to downsize his operation. He offloaded some clients to me. In the spring of 1986, at the age of fourteen, I officially had a side hustle. Cutting two lawns every eight days raked in about eleven dollars.

Within a few short months, I saved fifty bucks. About that time, Jason got every teenage boy's dream job. He began working at a bicycle and skateboard shop. After a few months, Jason's own aspiration took shape. He set his eyes on a pink and white MT racing bike.

Once he brought home the shiny new two-wheeler, he didn't have much use for his old Mongoose anymore. Negotiations were brief. "Can you give me fifty for it?" Soaked in sweat from walking to Jason's house, I gave him my entire life savings.**

**Why walk to Jason's House? I didn't have an option. If I rode the Huffy to his house, how would I get both bikes home? Impressed that I walked the entire trip Jason softened. "Just give me forty."*

The ride home was my first real self-worth moment. I'd made the biggest purchase of my life, and I did it by myself. I was the very proud owner of a used Mongoose with mag wheels, a rear handbrake, and a Redline competition handlebar neck. A great deal from a good friend. And a ten spot left over to buy a front hand brake.

Now that I had a BMX bike, I could join in all the BMX games I'd missed out on before. I kept the Huffy though. It was better for long distances and riding to girls' houses.

Our most beloved BMX game was Foot Down. The game took place on the rectangular patch of blacktop by the lake. Black, tar-soaked railroad ties outlined the blacktop to prevent cars from driving onto the grass. Every game of Foot Down started by pulling two ties across the entrance to establish boundaries and prevent cars from pulling in. Then, the game began.

The general premise: Ride around and beat the crap out of each other and our bikes while staying on the black top. Players could bunny hop onto the black ties to escape or initiate an attack. Fall onto the grass or go outside the perimeter, and you're out. Players who put a foot down on offense or defense were out and insulted. Last rider standing on the pedals wins.

Kicking, punching, slapping, tail-whipping—it was all on the table. Nothing was off limits. Surviving without needing medical attention or having to push your broken bike home was a small victory.

Foot Down was something that just four of us did together: Dean, Jason, Chuck, and me. It was an intimate game and you had better be good friends with all participants. Tensions ran high but at the game's conclusion, we were always boys again.

Smoking Hoops

I hung out with other kids in and around the trailer park also. We played pick-up football in the fall and hockey in the winter on Grand Beach Lake. In the summer, we rode bikes and raided each other's pantries and refrigerators. We swam in the lake, played some hellacious half-court basketball, and a few of us experimented with THC-inspired frisbee.

But basketball with the fellas was my favorite trailerhood activity. Despite my below-average stature, I was an above-average playground basketballer. I was fast and could find the open guy, shoot, and play defense. While there are many reasons I wish I was taller, basketball is one of the main ones.

However, I know who I am and what I come from. I never expected to be over six feet tall. Mom was an inch taller than Dad at five-foot-five. I didn't want a miracle. I wanted to be average. Five-nine or -ten would have been fine. But it wasn't meant to be.

Fortunately, our version of streetball featured short white boys with average ability and way-above-average competitiveness. Ironically the two tallest participants, Dean and Jason, were the most average players on the court. I don't think Dean even liked basketball. He played because everyone else did. Both Jason and Dean were good at rebounding, putting back layups, and blocking shots. Because their height stood out amongst the rest of us, we usually made them play on opposing teams.

Aggressive and hack happy was the style of play. No ticky-tack complaints about a hand being touched during a shot or someone bumping an elbow. Fouls were rarely called unless one guy was around. Ernie was his name, and crying "Foul" was his game. We made life so rough on that guy he literally took his ball and walked home a few times.

But I remember having success when Ernie and I were on the same team. His game was fundamentally solid, and he was good at finding the open man. He was not well liked though. As a result, street ball was a little harder on him then it should have been. Kids can be cruel. Ernie was a smart kid though, and I bet he is somewhere having the last laugh. No doubt having a great life, pulling down a six-figure income while I'm stuck behind the wheel of a tractor-trailer.

Chuck was an outlier. He had real basketball experience from playing on a team for a couple years. He had a good outside jumper, a great fade-away, and a few classic moves he used to shake off defenders. Chuck and I played at the lake more than anyone else. Our games were on par, but Chuck's longer limbs and experience gave him the edge.

Similar to Dean and Jason, Chuck and I rarely found ourselves on the same team. It made for better basketball but it kind of pissed us off. When we were on the same team the game seemed easy. I would get hot from the outside; he would draw the defense in and toss it back to me for the open shot. With my speed I could catch up to long rebounds. Chuck would anticipate me getting the ball, disappear in the crowd, and reappear all alone on the baseline. I would hit him with a pass, and—*Swoosh!*—nothing but nylon. Much like playing with my brother Victor, we knew what we were doing before we did it.

But most of the time Chuck and I were on opposing teams. Our friendship took a backseat during those games. We weren't mean or nasty when we played against each other. It was just more of a business atmosphere. Both of us being ultra-competitive, we turned off the humor and friendly banter and went to work. We didn't talk much during the game and even afterward, out of respect, the winning player kept gloating to a minimum. Less than two minutes later, Chuck or I would say (before most of the other players were ready), "Let's do it again! Who's taking it out?"

On a typical hot summer day, we shot hoops for hours. The action picked up about four in the afternoon. By that time, kids were finished with chores and part-time jobs, and a few adults would join in after work. When any three of my older brothers were around they would come down and play too. Then when dusk turned to dark, the adults bought beer and introduced us to marijuana.

I love those trailer-park summers. I want to shoot hoops every time I think about them. Then I get a little depressed. I know from just observing and by what my nephew tells me that it doesn't happen as much anymore. Boys and young men don't get together for a few sweat drenched hours of blacktop balling. The rigorous physical competition made us all stronger and boosted our endurance. Unorganized, rough, self-governed activity that was completely void of any parental supervision. It was a blast.

Going through eighth grade and my high school years at the camp might have been one big party. I spent a decade being bitter at the world and pissed off at my mom because of something I felt I missed out on. However, the friendships I enjoyed and the life experiences I lived through in the trailerhood are irreplaceable. Sometimes life is just as simple as acknowledging that "Everything happens for a reason."

Jason showing off on the Mongoose he later sold to me.

Chapter Twenty-Eight

MOM GETS SICK

As a kid, I thought my parents were indestructible, borderline immortal. They got colds and fevers, but nothing kept them out of the game for more than a morning or an afternoon.*

In many ways, Mom was tougher than Dad. The only clues that she was under the weather were excess Kleenex usage and a rougher, more drawn-out smoker's cough. If we made her laugh, she would have an uncontrollable choking fit. Her hacking lasted several minutes. It was painful to watch and hear.

Dad usually powered through illness and hangovers alike. Close to Christmas, when he was trying to earn extra money, Dad diligently made it into work. He only called out once or twice a year. Those few occasions when Dad stayed home sick were blessings to us all. He would stay in bed until dinner, giving the world and our living room a Bill Simpson-free day.

When Mom was sick, she kept it a secret. She didn't seek pity or consolation; she pressed on. That's what she did during our first winter in the trailer. She pressed and pressed until she got pulled into the emergency room.

It all changed when Dad hit the big five-oh. Overnight, his body started breaking down. Shoulder pain, gastrointestinal issues, and high blood pressure were all consequences of his lifestyle. By that time, he'd smoked for thirty-five years and drank heavily most of his adult life. Pile on a not-so-stellar diet and nonexistent fitness plan, and his shoddy health shouldn't have surprised anyone.

Rick, the oldest child and geographically nearest to Mom's work, got the call. One of Mom's coworkers reached Rick and described her condition. "Your Mother is having some kind of health issue," Mom's coworker explained. "She is talking gibberish, has slurred speech, and no energy. She also has an unquenchable thirst."

Rick made the twenty-minute drive to Walled Lake in fifteen. Mom was a mess. Her speech was slow and nonsensical. Rick had to coax her out of the office. She could hardly stand up as she shuffled her feet to the car.

For some reason, Mom insisted on being taken all the way to Mcpherson Hospital. Other, bigger hospitals were near her work, but she opted for the forty-five minute drive to the other side of Howell. Mom was a creature of habit, so she wanted to go to the hospital she was familiar with, we guessed.**

Rick pulled into the ER entrance and got Mom in a wheelchair. The staff there diagnosed Mom immediately. It was the sugar—diabetes. Shortly after receiving the news, Mom barked at Rick to go home. "I'll be fine," she insisted. "Watch Stephen and make sure he gets up for school." Mom, in typical martyr fashion, shooed Rick away.

Guilt ate at Rick as he left the hospital. He followed the command to "Honor thy mother," but he still thinks about it to this day. A mild twinge inside him asks, "Should I have at least stayed in the lobby?"

On the Simpson Guilt Train, my big brother sells tickets, carries luggage, and drives the engine. If I thought Mom was nearly immortal, Rick thought she hung the moon. Rick's history with my parents started thirteen years before mine. He had seen the not-so dynamic duo during the 60s. They got kicked in the face by life dozens of times before I was

---

**During the 1980s, Mcpherson Hospital had a legendary reputation for providing bad service. Longtime Livingston County residents nicknamed it "The Chop Shop." Staff there once spent an hour trying to pull a sewing needle out of my foot. Finally, they looked at the x-ray one last time and realized the needle was broken in several pieces under my skin and bone. They removed the pieces that were easy to access and sewed me up. "Sorry, that's all we can do. Those tiny metal fragments in your foot shouldn't cause any significant problems. If they do, come on back and we'll fix you up!"*

even born. But Bill and Elaine always kicked back. They always stayed afloat no matter how much water they took on.

For years I harbored thoughts about what Mom went through that first night in the hospital. More than afraid, she was terrified. Her health was never an issue.

I'd heard stories about Mom's mental health, especially after the twins were born. "Mom's state of mind was shaky for a few years," I heard. But physically, Mom was always as tough as nails. The hospital visit showed cracks in her strength. She knew when she left the hospital, her life would never be the same. She thought, "I'm not gonna like any of it but I'll go along with it. Just don't tell me to quit smoking."*

For most of her adult life my mom's diet was consistent but not very diverse. She primarily lived on sweets, coffee, cigarettes, bread, butter, cheese, and fasting. Mom didn't have an appetite for lunch or breakfast.

Before the time of digital communication, waiting on updates about anything made time stand still. You would hear about a friend in a car crash and that was it. For hours you waited and waited for scraps of additional information.

When I got home from school that day, the phone was ringing. "Rick is taking Mom to the hospital." That was the only thing I knew until Rick walked through the door.

That January day was dark, gloomy, and cold—a depressing, typical Michigan winter day. It seemed quieter than usual though. Like the world was in mourning after hearing Elaine Simpson was on the disabled list for the first time.

Rick came in and gave me the news. I remember immediately asking, "What's diabetes?" At age thirteen the word *disease* rarely crossed my mind. I knew about the biggies thanks to television. Lung cancer, heart disease, Alzheimer's (Grandpa—September 1985), and—fresh on the

---

*This wasn't Mom's first warning sign to improve her health. A dozen years before, she received a signal from her mother's failing health. Grandma died before my second birthday at age sixty-eight. She loved sweets and ate them throughout the day. She passed that love to my mother, who passed that addiction on to me.

disease scene in the 80s—A.I.D.S.

So, I had a basic knowledge of the sexy illnesses, the ones TV and Big Pharma scared people with. I'd never heard of diabetes. I didn't know how to spell it or what caused it. I wasn't even sure how to say it.**

Sorry, B.P.

Now that Big Pharma and the media have collectively turned every disease from shingles to monkeypox to restless legs syndrome into Fright Fest Theater, pockets are getting stuffed. And overall health and disease prevention in this country is, wait for it, worse than ever. The oldest cliché in the world is also the truest. *Follow the money*. In 2021 the pharmaceutical industry earned a paltry $1.42 trillion.

In the 80s, diabetes was but a blip on Big Pharma's radar, so they'd not commercialized the disease just yet. No fear, no money. Now in 2022 every forth commercial is something about diabetes. Especially Type 2, adult onset diabetes. You know, the disease that for most people is almost completely preventable with diet and exercise! It's similar to many other illnesses Big Pharma, the CDC, and the media are currently highlighting to scare the living shit of people.

The best way to not need another prescription is to never get the illness. You know, prevention. But that's too much work and it doesn't make money. You can't give prevention away. But a pill with two dozen side effects including rectal bleeding, suicidal thoughts, and dizziness? That shit sells! The doctors earn kickbacks and get invited to high dollar junkets for prescribing Big Pharma's "cures."

Most doctors are essentially highly trained, highly paid salespeople. And the American consumer will buy anything. Especially if it means not changing their lifestyle.

Doubt me? Do you have full faith and confidence in the medical industry? You don't have to look back very far to see the evidence and the

---

***At the time, diabetes didn't get many headlines. The general population wasn't worried about becoming diabetic. It didn't bleed so it didn't lead. If it's not scary, Big Pharma can't profit from it. If Big Pharma isn't in the game then the mainstream media isn't playing along either. No news, no money, very little research, and no prevention.*

consequences of trusting doctors and Big Pharma. Bored on a Saturday? Spend a few hours researching the opioid crisis in this country. It was another thing that was completely preventable. Pay attention, people.

It's actually really simple. Many diseases are genetic, so if your family has a bad health history, you better put out that cigarette and take extra special care of your ticker. If a specific disease runs in your family you need to take actions to prevent that illness. And if both of your parents had diabetes maybe you should put down that doughnut, fat boy. Oh, crap—that's me!

Recovering and Renewed

Mom spent three days in the hospital getting her sugar under control. While there, she got a crash course in everything diabetes: diet, exercise, DIET, and medication. On her second day of hospitalization, I caved. I hated hospitals and preferred talking to Mom on the phone. She sounded good and promised to come home soon. Then Rick and Denise boarded me on the Simpson Guilt Train. They let me off once I swore to visit Mom at the hospital.

At the conclusion of just another day at McPherson Middle School, I walked to the hospital. I took my time. Hospitals made me nervous, and I didn't want to see Mom in a hospital gown. I didn't know how to act. I didn't know what to say. Very few good things happen at a hospital. TV taught me that.

But I made it there, eventually. Mom smiled ear to ear when I walked in. That made me feel worse, but only for a moment. She was anticipating my visit and excitedly educated me on her new diabetic lifestyle. Then she gave a short, rehearsed sermon on how to maintain a healthy blood sugar level. It was all so weird and out of character.

She looked at the clock and her face brightened. "Stephen," she said. "You need to watch this. You might have to do this for me someday!" With that, she pulled out a gigantic needle and stabbed it in her stomach. I wanted to run away and scream. Instead, I kept my thoughts to myself, which went something like, "Not on your life woman. I'm not sticking a needle in anyone."

Mom spent the next hour telling me all about diabetes. Everything from insulin to endocrine disorder to low sugar to hyperglycemia. She explained how she was going to drastically change her diet and start eating several times a day instead of just eating dinner. She demonstrated the key to living with diabetes before I left. The thing she would have to do every day, for the rest of her life. She checked her sugar.*

Lifelong habits that defined Mom had to change. She had to stomach lunch and breakfast every day, exchange Pepsi for Diet Pepsi and Schnapps and wine for scotch and water with a lime twist. Sweets needed to be swapped with low-sugar alternatives and artificial sweeteners.

I didn't understand why Mom seemed so happy about it all. A new diet, lifestyle changes, daily injections, and a new disease. Why did she seem happy? The joy followed her home. She was almost proud of her new condition for a couple of years. Like a badge of honor, she looked for opportunities to inject it into conversation: "By the way, I have Type 2 diabetes."

Like most things in our life, and this book, I didn't realize the truth until later. Mom wasn't happy about being a diabetic. She was relieved. She spent weeks, months, concealing how bad off she was. God only knows how long she spent suffering from exhaustion and dehydration and generally feeling like crap. In 1985 she spent the season of Christmas, her favorite holiday, worried, scared, and quiet. She kept it all to herself.

Back to the Old Ways

The mystery was over. Having diabetes is not the greatest thing in the world but at least now she knew what it was and how to manage it. Mom got a good dose of reality from her self-induced sugar coma and diabetes diagnosis. Over time, her fear and concern waned, and Mom began manipulating the disease.

The result was dangerously low sugar episodes and multiple 911

In time, this led to one of our most used backhanded slams. "Mom, check your sugar!" became our go-to phrase whenever we thought Mom was losing it or we didn't care to hear her opinion.

calls over a three-decades span. Mom pledged to change her ways, but her efforts never lasted long. She ate what she wanted most of the time, manipulating her sugar with extra insulin or medication. It was an almost constant battle, as she attempted to outsmart the disease.

Failing to monitor her sugar and eat as prescribed led to many close calls and one death-defying experience. During one low-sugar afternoon, she passed out behind the wheel. Her Taurus crossed the center line and rolled several times in the ditch—end over end. The crash ejected our family dog, Kobe, who ultimately died from sustained injuries. Mom survived with minor injuries. Thankfully, no one else was injured or involved.

After I looked at Mom's face in the hospital to confirm she was alive, I went to the salvage yard to clean out her car. The wreckage reminded me of something on *Super Dave* or an old driver's ed video called *Death on the Highway*. When I looked at the twisted hunk of metal that used to be Mom's silver Ford, only one word came to mind: *miracle*.

That was December of 2001. Afterward, Mom mismanaged her diabetes for another thirteen years. In that time, she witnessed a grand wedding, became Grandma to a couple grandchildren she adored, and

brought smiles to all around her. Six months before her own death, she was the star of the show at my mother-in-law's funeral. She was legendary that day.

Mom, you had no business surviving that car accident, but I'm glad you did. And while I didn't always like you, I always loved you. Your friends and family miss you dearly. I miss you too.

Chapter Twenty-Nine

OUTDOORS WITH WILLIE (PART TWO)

The never-ending onslaught of not-so-great events demoralized our family through the years. The original Simpson men—my dad and his brothers, Joe and John—kept a running score on bad luck occurrences. When they got together or talked on the phone, they often rehashed the miserable moments, naming the collective stories the Simpson Black Cloud.

Like a late spring storm rolling across the plains of lower Michigan, the Simpson Black Cloud is quiet upon approach but causes an enormous amount of damage in a brief period. The Cloud has impeccable timing too. It generally catches you off guard and pummels your spirit into submission with blow after blow.

Dad and His Toys

Dad loved outdoor toys. He purchased or built a recreational vehicle nearly every year. Boats, motorcycles, dune buggies, dirt bikes, campers, motorhomes—he wanted them all. And at different points in his life, he had most of them. The problem with big boy toys is, as anyone who owns one can attest, they aren't cheap. Toys that need a little fixing up may be cheap upfront, but they cost a lot to maintain or repair.*

Sometimes the money spent on adult toys bleeds over to other areas of life. A motor home, camper, or boat left out in the elements will never hold up as long as a covered one.

Too lazy to constantly take the cover on and off your toy just to enjoy it? Me too. Most people are. Now you have to get a car port. You have to do it right though. No half-ass job securing a do-it-yourself carport in the ground with tent stakes. Do it wrong and your aluminum "shield" will take off like a kite during the next storm or cave in around your Mustang convertible like a tin can. That'll set you back a few thousand dollars.

Got an HOA? Most of them frown at you putting your small yacht or forty foot motorhome in the driveway or in the backyard. Now you have to pay for storage. Or let it bake in the hot sun and dry rot in the free storage that the neighborhood provides.

I've heard dozens of stories of people who buy a new larger-than-life toy without even considering how to get the damn thing home. It doesn't matter how good the deal is on a thirty-six-foot travel trailer. If your 2008 Ford Explorer doesn't have the power, brakes, or suspension to get the job done, now you gotta buy a new truck too!

Dad never had money to buy toys at the New Toy Store. Ole Willie's toys were used, needed work, and often labeled "Mechanic's Specials." Dad only ever bought one toy brand new: his 1965 Honda Dream.

With a purchase price of about $600, it wasn't a crazy endeavor. But with Dad's income and our unimpressive economic standing, any nonessential cost too much. Once he bought the bike, he did what most men do after an irrational financial decision. He hid the bike from Mom by storing it at a friend's house for a few weeks. He needed time to warm Mom up to the idea of becoming a motorcycle couple.

Despite loving the bike, Dad was forced to sell his beloved Honda a short time after buying it. He kept the license plate though. Now, it hangs in my garage as a reminder to never stop dreaming.

Twenty years later, Dad was fully immersed in another dream: the boat dream. So, he bought a fixer-upper pontoon and got the forty-horsepower Johnson running in no time. He then started taking his new toy out on the weekends on Lake Chemung.

In the weeks after buying the boat, he tinkered with it until it was almost as good as new. There was only one tiny malfunction. Every time Dad took the boat out, the shifter cable stuck. After a few trips around

The license plate of Dad's Honda Dream.

the lake, the cable locked in position, forcing Dad to return to the dock at paddle-boat speed.

This was unexplainable and troubling to Ole Willie. The motor was an easy fix and made the purchase a steal. But that damn shifter-throttle cable! Convinced he could figure it out, Dad made another shortsighted decision. He started to tinker with it. On the water. By himself. Like the line from the classic movie *Captain Ron*, delivered by the legendary Kurt Russell: "If anything is going to happen it's gonna happen out there."

The boat was floating fifty feet from shore when Dad began his investigation. With the motor on and the throttle in neutral, Dad took off the cover and began snooping. He quickly diagnosed the problem but wanted to confirm his findings. He turned the wheel hard to the left, positioned himself over the motor, and jerked on the shifter cable with a pair of channel-lock pliers.

Eventually, Dad jerked hard enough to set the cable shroud free. This action immediately launched the boat forward at about one-third throttle. The equal reaction sent Dad over the stern of the boat and into the seaweed- and lily-pad-infested waters of Lake Chemung. Luckily, the wheel was still cranked hard to the left, so the boat crept past his head.

A below-average swimmer, Dad was no match for the sixteen-foot watercraft circling him like a hungry shark. But a couple things went Dad's way. The steering wheel slowly bounced back to center, causing the boat's circles to widen and get closer to the shore with each pass. As the boat got closer to shore, the motor clogged with seaweed and lily-pad debris. The motor slowed until the boat hit a low spot near shore and the prop buried itself in the mucky bottom of Lake Chemung. The trusty Johnson outboard sputtered and spat and stalled out. The Simpson Black Cloud popped in on Dad that day, but in uncharacteristic form, it didn't stay long.

Boat Fever

Another lake outing a few years earlier should have ended Dad's boat dream permanently. It's really kind of a sickness that some men get. Sometimes it stays with us for decades at a time. It destroys family budgets, causes tons of pain, and produces very little actual pleasure. It's called boat fever.

This time my dad had a new wife to go with his new boat. Yep, Ole Willie tied the knot. This marriage was not expected or understood, but it happened. In all the romance Dad could muster, he held the ceremony at the local courthouse. Dad told us after the deed was done.

As far as all of us could tell it wasn't a bad decision. Although the only thing Dad seemed to have in common with his second bride is they both liked being outside. Within a few months of meeting her, Dad had a new truck, pop-up camper, and of course, another boat.

There were several camping outings on nearby lakes that required two trips to bring both toys. He would tow the camper out on a Thursday night to set up and get a good campsite. He would then take Friday off and bring his wife and boat to the "Best spot out here!" It was one of my dad's many talents. He could always find the best campsite with the perfect mix of sun, shade, and privacy.

Dad and his second wife had a little place in Hamburg Township. Splitting the rent meant more money for toys and recreation.

One Friday night, he called me up. "You never get to see me much anymore," he said. "Too busy for your old dad, hey?" This was my loving father's way of saying A) he wanted to see me or B) he didn't want to spend another Saturday alone with his wife.

The next morning when Mom dropped me off, Ole Willie was

hooking the boat to the truck. Dad waved me over and began teaching me Boat Hook-Up 101 before a genuine father-son day!

Like most teenage boys I couldn't care less about learning how to do something that I couldn't care less about. But this was different. I was actually excited. I was going to learn something I wanted to learn. Because at age fifteen, I already had car fever and boat fever as well. Must run in the family.

Dad told me to crank up the trailer. "Raise it as high as it will go and I'll pull out the plug to drain out any water." He waved me away. "Get in the truck and back it up, slow. I'll holler and tell ya when to stop." My heart sank, and my throat dried up.

Because of how I was raised at the camp, I could and would drive anything with wheels. But this was Dad's new(er) truck, and I didn't trust myself not to mess things up. "You sure, Dad?" He pointed to the driver's door of his copper F-150. "Get up there."

Like all his previous pickups, this was a manual. This F-150 had the 300ci inline six with a four-speed manual. Because of the low-end torque, Dad only used first gear for parking and pulling something. If there was nothing behind him he would start out in second. Dad was flawless at driving a stick. He and Uncle Joe could both tell exactly when to shift just by listening to the motor or feeling the vibration of the gas pedal.

The super-low first gear came in handy for parking. Like many vehicles in Michigan, this truck's parking brake cable had fallen victim to Michigan's Salt Monster.*

Dad claimed he didn't need the parking brake. He insisted when the truck was in first gear—a.k.a. the granny gear—you couldn't budge it with a tank. The parking brake was not my concern when Dad told me to climb in and back under the trailer hitch. The long motion of the clutch

---

*Michigan is the belt buckle of the rust belt. Detroit and much of lower Michigan sit on a big salt mine, the primary weapon used to clear winter roads. Recently researchers at Michigan State and the University of Wisconsin found that Michigan uses roughly 450,000 tons of salt per year to keep the roads safe. This salt eats the metal on cars like hungry termites on a fresh piece of lumber. All exposed, untreated, unpainted metal is at risk.

pedal and backing over ole Willie was, however, on my mind.

Oblivious, Dad waved at me happily. With sweaty hands and a lump in my throat, I climbed in and got the truck in position after a couple tries. Dad lowered the trailer onto the hitch. "Cut the motor," he hollered, "and stick it in first."

Dad went over the last few steps like he was teaching a class. "Even though the trailer lights don't work, we'll plug them in," he explained, "just in case we get pulled over." This bit of intel was followed with more instructions—take some slack out of the safety chain, put the pin through the coupler to make sure it locks the hitch into place, and tug up on the trailer to make sure it stays on the hitch.

As Dad and I waited for his second wife, Carmen (name changed to protect the innocent), he anxiously described his nautical plan. "I found out years ago that there are connected lakes called the chain of lakes. We'll put the boat in at the marina and see how many lakes we can get to before lunch. Did you bring your swim trunks? We can pull up to a sandbar and get lunch ready while you go swimming."

And then Dad said the best thing yet. "Once we get out from shore and I get a bit more familiar with the layout of the chain, you can drive the boat. How does that sound?" I said "Yeah" so quickly it came out in a cracked voice. This was gonna go down as the best day ever spent with Ole Willie.

Dad pulled into the marina and positioned the truck in front of the boat launch. Carmen and I hopped off the bench seat as Dad looked at his side mirror and scratched his chin. "The lake looks a little down today," he mumbled.

I looked at the boat ramp and the lake. He was right. The lake was so low that only a third of the boat ramp was under water. But the low lake level or fast-approaching rain clouds couldn't dampen this day. It just meant Dad had to back the boat down a little farther than usual.

Dad backed down until the boat trailer was completely in the water. Waves created by nearby water traffic splashed gently against the Ford's rear bumper, but the rear tires were barely in the water. Dad cut the engine, threw it in granny gear, and went to release his pride and joy. He motioned me to help.

"Take the rope and walk over to the shore," he said. "I'm gonna unhook the boat and pull the trailer out. Wait until I'm up the ramp to tug it over to the dock." I gave a thumbs-up and took a step back. When I did, my right leg disappeared between two pieces of separated concrete in the ramp.

I sat in the shallow water on my ass, wet and embarrassed, my face twelve inches from the rear bumper. My left leg jetted out in front of me, and my right leg was halfway to China. "Stephen, Stephen!" Dad yelled. "You alright?"

"I'm alright, but I'm stuck, and I let go of the rope."

"Don't worry about the rope," Dad said. "Don't move, boy. I'll come over—"

Dad froze. We heard a sound that instantly brought terror to us both. It was the sound of wet rubber. It was the sound wet tires make when they lose traction on wet pavement. Dad and I were between the truck and the boat, and I was up to my crotch between two concrete slabs.

The granny gear was doing its part. Those rear wheels didn't spin an inch. It was the tires that let us down. The tires, combined with the lower ramp's moss-covered pavement, threatened my crotch and both of our lives.

After a couple of warning screeches, the tires lost their grip. "Look out!" Dad screeched. Fifteen years of life flashed before my eyes. Dad fell backward into the water, and my survival instinct took over. Possessed by an unknown reserve of strength, I kicked with my left leg, freed my right leg, and did a back roll off the ramp and out of harm's way. The rear bumper grazed my right foot as the truck slid into the water.

Truck, boat, and trailer were all in the water. There was nothing my dad could do. The water was only six or seven feet deep but the F-150's lack of buoyancy was no match. First, bubbles formed around the truck. Then a small gasoline cloud developed in the water where the truck began to sink. After a few minutes, only the truck's roof, camper top, and antenna remained visible. But the boat was okay. Still attached to the trailer, it fought to stay afloat as the truck attempted to pull it under. We stood on the shore watching the carnage in shock and disbelief. Dad was so pissed his face was a shade of purple.

Then the unthinkable happened. The boat began to sink. I suspect at this time Dad replayed the morning's events and realized he forgot something. In all the excitement, he never put the drain plug back in. I realized it too. But I wasn't going to utter a word about it—ever. At least not while Willie was still alive. Soon as the boat sank out of sight, it started to rain.

Surprisingly, the insurance company covered some of the truck's damages. Dad got it back after about a month in the shop, but it was never the same. It had electrical issues and the brakes locked up every time it rained.

The trailer and boat suffered a worse fate. When the truck slid into the water, the trailer jackknifed, lodged under the rear bumper, and got

Mom and Dad on his Honda Dream in the yard in Southfield.

bent to hell. Dad got it straightened with a tractor and some chains, but the trailer had a crooked lean to the left for the rest of its life.

Dad eventually got the boat running again, but like the truck and trailer, it was never the same. So, he sold the boat and trailer at a significant loss that was never discussed.

Unfortunately, there is no cup-half-full ending to this story. I never got to drive Dad's boat. I never even got to ride in that one. And to this day, I've not been out on the chain of lakes.

I can say that, once again, I lived. Oh, one other thing. If you come from a long line of cynics and pessimists like me, beware of your family's version of the Simpson Black Cloud. It can strike at any time.

Chapter Thirty

DAD TAKES ME TO A BALL GAME

When you hear someone say, "My dad and I went to a ball game," it usually means a baseball game. To gen Xers and all previous generations, it was assumed. Going to see a ball game meant you were going to see a duel on the diamond, which is a great tradition. Unfortunately, like most bond-strengthening traditions that involve a father and his kids, catching a game with Dad seems to be slowly fading into yesteryear. Increasing ticket prices combined with the overall expense of an outing downtown has made a day at the stadium a tall order.

A July 2022 *USA Today* article listed the average cost of a MLB trip between $125 to $300! There are over eighty home games every season. A family of four should really be able to enjoy a summer day at the ole ballpark for $100 or less.

Personally, I'm always trying to get one over on the man. This is why whenever my family and I go to a sporting event or a show I make a sizable request. "Hey honey, you bringing the purse?" The purse is a little tacky and the size of a small overnight bag.

My wife, who can at times be more frugal than I, doesn't mind at all. Except for that trip to the Knoxville Zoo in 2022. That day we asked too much of the purse and my wife's right shoulder. "Sorry Cookie, I can't carry that thing. I'm Dad. Dad has to take the pics with his superior smartphone."

You name it—beverage wise, we try to bring it all. Beer, airplane liquor bottles, soda, water, coffee, sweet tea. Nothing is off the table. And that goes for food and snacks too. Chips, sandwiches, chili, soup, whatever the event calls for. We once brought an entire box of chicken into a movie theater.

High school games are cheaper, but a trip to the snack bar takes forever and produces barely edible food. My daughter played all four years in her high school marching band. After the first few weeks of Frito pies and cold tasteless hot dogs we had enough. For the third home game in early September, we preheated and packed the ingredients to construct four fajitas. Complete with tortilla soup and a couple of Cokes.

When I was a little boy, I didn't go to the ballpark very often. There were several roadblocks that kept me from seeing games in person. The main one was my father. Dad wasn't a big sports fan. He was athletic as a kid, but as an adult, he enjoyed only two sports: boxing and auto racing.

Besides not liking baseball, Dad's main reason for not taking us to games was the same tired tale. It's why we never went out to eat, never went to the movies, and never went to the county fair. Money. As previously stated, Dad was tight with his wallet. He occasionally spent money, but only when he really liked something or really wanted us to have something. After all, why blow money on a sporting event when you can listen to it on the radio or watch it on TV?

Another obstacle from catching a game at Michigan and Trumbull was the logistics. Once we moved from Southfield to Brighton, it was fifty miles to Tiger Stadium. A 100-mile round trip was a lot of driving for a game.

The few Tiger games I attended before my sixteenth birthday came courtesy of my big brother. Rick was a huge Tigers fan. He and a friend once drove ninety miles to catch a Tuesday night baseball game. They even picked me up on the way. We had a blast!

Another trip was more of a bust. Rick and the twins decided the four of us should see a game. It was a late July doubleheader against George Brett and the Kansas City Royals. After hurrying through our chores, we took off for downtown Detroit. Rick's car was unavailable, so we rolled the dice with Tom and Vic's first car.

That car was a steal. Or perhaps it was stolen and never reported. It was a dark green 1972 Pontiac Lemans with two white stripes down the middle and several exhaust leaks that announced "Here comes trouble" miles in advance. At low speeds, exhaust came up through the rear seat, making any trip longer than a few miles a nauseating one.

The twins paid $400 for it, equating to about four dollars for each day it ran. It was previously abused by several other kid drivers and begged to be pulled over. Victor was pulled over countless times. It was also a car that Mom, Dad, and every other voice of authority resolutely warned the twins against buying.

They bought it. Mostly because they were told not to.

But we were going to see the Tigers play two, so none of the details about the Pontiac mattered. At least until we passed the Novi exit. Then the temperature needle launched to hot and the car overheated. After letting it cool down for an hour, we limped back to Brighton via Old Grand River, stopping every few miles to add water and let the car cool.

There was no baseball game that night. Not for me.*

Baseball was the first sport I truly loved. It was what most boys did when I was young—we loved baseball. Then as I got a little older my sports appetite expanded. Once I could shoot hoops with my brothers and was allowed on the field during backyard football, I added limbs to my sports tree. I especially started learning about the game of basketball and became a big fan of the Detroit Pistons.

George Blaha brought the simulcast to life on our nineteen-inch black-and-white Magnavox. During the winter months I watched a ton of NBA basketball. Sometimes I would shut all the lights off during the game so it was the only thing I could see, tuning out my messy room and any homework I may have had.

Through the early to mid-80s, Detroit fans watched the home team progressively trend upward. Year after year under Chuck Daly, the Pistons

---

While baseball was my first love, I started an affair with the Pistons in the winter of 1983. It was Chuck Daly's first year coaching the team, and most of the Piston's future stars—Bill Laimbeer, Isiah Thomas, and Vinnie Johnson—were in the infancy of their NBA careers.

got a little tougher, a little grittier, and a little better. By the '87–88 season every other team in the NBA knew that the Detroit Pistons were a team to be reckoned with.

The 1986–87 season was epic, ending in heartbreaking fashion via the worst pass ever. It still hurts. Let's not talk about it anymore, okay?

A Celtic Christmas

I was a typical teenager. A resentful, cocky, misunderstood product of divorced lower-middle-class parents. Custody was granted to my mother without a fight from Dad. So, despite living with Mom, I spent as little time with her as possible.

I spent even less time with my father. He was far from the "See ya on the weekend" divorcee dad often depicted in movies. After his second marriage dissolved a year after promising "'til death do us part," Dad moved into a small rental a few miles from our trailer. Even though he lived five minutes away, I only saw Dad once a month.

I was a know-it-all fifteen-year-old punk who had little time for his parents. Birthdays, holidays, and a once-a-month visit to a hamburger joint was the extent of visits with my father. I looked forward to our occasional Saturday morning breakfasts at Cheryl's Place in Brighton. But that was more about the food and less about bonding with Bill.

In my defense, I was a busy kid. I had part-time jobs and side hustles. In the summer I mowed lawns and hung out with friends at the lake. In the fall I had football practice and games. In the winter I shoveled snow and spent afternoons in the back of the trailer, as far from authority figures as possible. Oh, and starting at age fourteen, I started experimenting with alcohol and marijuana. It all kept me pretty busy.

Dad loved us kids. He just wasn't skilled or motivated to be a good dad. He barely knew our interests, unless it was also something he liked.

Late November 1987, with Christmas fast approaching, Dad didn't have a clue. All my siblings were adults, so he was only worried about getting a gift for me. Based on the end result, he got some help.

To Dad, a piston was an internal part of a motor that moved up and down. To Mom, the Pistons were my favorite basketball team. Somehow, this information reached my father, and he completed the transaction that made Christmas memorable.*

Christmas day 1987 was a Simpson-only Christmas. But Mom made the rules. She decided when and if Dad came over.

The front door of our trailer park home crept open and Dad stuck his head into the living room. In a crackled, slightly hung over smoker's voice, he uttered, "Merry Christmas." It was late afternoon and it was already getting dark outside. My siblings were off doing other things, so it was just me, Dad, and Mom.

Dad, not sure if he would be invited to stay, didn't waste any time. (Or maybe he just wanted to get back to whatever watering hole was calling his name). After a minute or two of small talk, he handed me an envelope.

"I just wanted to stop by and give you a little something, Stefan," he chuckled. The business envelope read "Simpson" on the front. I didn't know how to react. This was a Christmas first. An envelope? I looked down, trying to guess its contents, wondering if this was just part of growing up—smaller gifts without wrapping paper.

I tentatively opened the envelope and my jaw dropped. There in my hands were two glossy, freshly printed tickets to see the Detroit Pistons. And not just any Pistons game. My dad, maybe without knowing the full significance, secured tickets to a showdown with the hated Boston Celtics!

It was a surprise that I never imagined, especially from my dad. My excitement and joy lasted a full five minutes. Then a dreadful dose of reality seeped into my brain. There were only two tickets, so I was going with one other person. My mind considered all possibilities of who would take me to the game, but I kept coming back to the same conclusion.

Even after their divorce, Mom invited Dad over for the big holidays. He would make it over on or close to Christmas day, or the day we had relatives over. It helped create a larger buffer zone. Uncles, aunts, and cousins provided a Swiss-like neutral territory that helped limit flare-ups between Bill and Elaine. Dad was sometimes invited to the outdoor cookout holidays like Memorial Day and the Fourth of July. The extra space outside had a similar peacetime effect.

Dad was proud of his purchase. He saw the excitement in my face as I clinched the tickets. As much as he hated crowds, car rides, and basketball, he wanted to see—in person—how much I appreciated the gesture. I was going to see my favorite team with my not-so-favorite person. Dad.

A few weeks went by. I prayed Dad would have a change of heart. That he would call me with some B.S. excuse why he couldn't take me to the game. I was ready to accept any excuse, no matter how unbelievable or drowning in horse shit it was. If all went as I hoped, Dad would ask Mom to take over his responsibility. Then Mom would guilt Rick into it, and Rick and I would have a great time.

It did not go as planned. Ole Willie let me down, in reverse. He wasn't paying that much for something without checking it out for himself.

The night of the game, I sat by the living room window when Dad pulled up to our trailer. "Dad's here," I yelled to Mom and shot out the door. I ripped open the car door so fast it startled Dad into a nervous laugh. I giggled with excitement.

On the way to the game, Dad talked about his week delivering pallets around Detroit. I acted like I cared. He asked me about school, and I replied with standard answers guaranteed to put an end to the conversation. I had one thing on my mind, and it wasn't the C minus I had in World History.

After enduring a day of traffic, Dad took 23 to M59 and skipped the freeway. His plan failed like mine. Soon after we passed the Oakland County Airport, traffic came to a complete stop.* Dad released a frustrated sigh under his breath. It took half an hour to travel the last five miles. Dad made a sarcastic joke about the World's Fair having less traffic. "How many people are going to this damn game?" he asked.

---

*This was just one reason I thought Dad would bow out and have Rick take me to the game. This outing had five of the fifty-two things my father truly detested. Heavy traffic was near the top of his list. By the end of the night, we were also going to wait in lines, deal with crowds, be in a noisy arena, and pay way too much for anything my father was willing to buy. As I wrote that last line I realized something. I'm just like my dad in far too many ways. But I still love going to loud, packed venues.

My only experience with events at the Silverdome was attending a few Detroit Lions games. So, traffic didn't seem that different or heavy to me. I knew NBA games didn't have as many people at them, but I didn't give the numbers much thought. I was too anxious and excited about seeing the Pistons.

We waited in line to park, and Dad backed into a tight spot where he was directed. We squeezed out and started toward the big white dome. I could feel the charged-up vibe in the air as we made the long, cold walk to the stadium.

We entered the Silverdome twenty minutes before opening tip—just enough time to hit the bathroom and get a couple of drinks if Dad would open his wallet. Ten minutes later, I was through the restroom line. Dad flagged me down. He was holding a beer, soda, a package of peanuts, and popcorn. "The prices for food are pretty damn high here," he said, passing a Sprite to me. "We'll stop and get a burger on the way home."

We walked the tunnel toward our seats, the noise getting louder with each step. I arrived at the rail that overlooked the court and gazed down. Then I did a complete circle with my eyes and didn't believe what I saw.

Even though some of the crowd had still not made it to their seats, there were fans everywhere. People near the top of the third level sat, stood, talked, and danced. A couple beach balls bounced around the dome before the fun police confiscated them.

A curtain like wall was used by the Silverdome during NBA games. It was pulled around the stadium, shutting the court off to help fans and the TV audience forget the game was inside a football stadium.

Dad settled into his second-level seat. I remained standing, taking it all in. I smiled ear to ear as the first few bars of "The Final Countdown" played over the loudspeakers. To this day, that song gives me chills every time I hear it.

The crowd erupted as the starters were announced, the loudest cheers reserved for when Laimbeer and Thomas trotted onto the floor. Everyone was standing, yelling, clapping, and pumping their fists. I joined in, but not to my full frenzied potential. I didn't want Dad to get weirded out by my fandom before the game even started.

233

The crowd quieted for the opening tip. After a good defensive play, a steal, and an easy fast break bucket for the home team, the place erupted. So did I.

Dad would have to understand. I couldn't stay reserved any longer. The fans were loud, obnoxious, and out of control. Dad sat in his seat with a look of uncomfortable awe and a sincere grin. He could see I was having the time of my life. He got a good dose of pride knowing he got me a great gift that I truly enjoyed. The mid-fifties curmudgeon that was my father didn't make an appearance the rest of the evening.

At some point, the PA speaker made an announcement: "The Pontiac Silverdome and the Detroit Pistons are proud to announce that tonight, we have set a new record! The paid attendance for tonight's game is 61,000!"

The crowd absolutely lost their collective mind. Dad, realizing he was part of history, stood up and slow clapped. His moderate excitement added to my fervor.

The Pistons and their fans applied more pressure through the fourth quarter. Even the Celtics could feel this one getting out of hand. During another extended timeout, the atmosphere reached an almost violent level as fans took out their playoff frustrations from the previous year.

The pinnacle came when a fan, apparently with money to burn, launched a green, brand new Celtics jacket into the crowd. The iconic clovers on the sleeves were instantly ripped off and flung down like floating debris after an explosion. The rest was torn into 100 pieces in a matter of minutes. Dad watched it all, mouth half open. I cheered the destruction until the tattered jacket hit the bottom level of the dome.

The Pistons won convincingly, cruising to a 125–108 victory. Before the final buzzer, Dad had the jitters. He wanted to leave—to beat the traffic. I was staying until the buzzer. My look must have made that clear, because Dad never voiced his request to leave early.

As we walked toward the car, Dad listened as I recalled every moment of our special evening. We got in the car and he turned to me. "Have you ever had a slider?" he asked. I didn't even know what a slider was.

On the way home, we stopped at one of Dad's favorite burger joints:

White Castle. Or as Dad called it, White Castilly. As we were pulling into the Pontiac location, Dad told me that he once watched his friend Big John eat twenty of the legendary burgers in one sitting.

Before getting out he asked, "Is this okay or do you want to go somewhere else?" Little burgers with onions, my stomach was thinking "nasty." However, this guy just took me to the best basketball game I might ever see in my life, so my heart said, "No, Dad, this is fine, I wanna try it!"

My dad loved onions in and on everything. A few years before our memorable Pistons game, Dad ordered us a pizza with onions and pepperoni. When it got to our table I said I don't like onions. He told me to try a slice. "If you don't like it," he said, "you can pick them off." I tried it and really liked it, but I couldn't let Dad have an "I told ya so." I picked the onions off just to not be wrong.

I was a few years older now, riding a big high from the dismantling of the Celtics by my beloved Pistons. So, I was in a great mood and prepared to try anything with an open mind. I was also really hungry. I'd had a Sprite and a few handfuls of popcorn over the last eight hours. If I get fries with the sliders, I thought, then at least I know I'll like something.

Dad brought the tray to our table, and the aroma hit me like a freight train. I took a bite, and it melted in my mouth like beef and onion candy.

After my second bite, I grinned. "These are great, Dad! And thanks for taking me to the game." Dad chewed on his burger. "Happy to do it, son."

That night was special. But it wasn't the start of something new. A few weeks later, I went back to being a teenager, and he went back to being Bill Simpson. That said, Dad truly enjoyed treating me to an NBA game and post-game sliders that night. The smile he displayed until he dropped me off was real. It is one of my all-time favorite memories of Dad.

I'm not a big fan of the Detroit Pistons anymore. The 2005 season was the last season I really paid attention. That said, I still love a warm White Castle fresh off the grill. Make mine a double, extra onions, extra pickles. Thanks, Dad.

Chapter Thirty-One

CUTTING MY WAY THROUGH HIGH SCHOOL

When you move into a trailer park it doesn't take long to meet your neighbors. In some parks you can touch the trailer next to yours with one foot in your driveway—if you're lucky enough to have a driveway. While moving a couch in your living room, your buddy has to brace himself against the rail of your neighbor's porch. We were lucky at Sylvan Glen to have good neighbors and a few feet of breathing room on both sides.

The trailer to our starboard side changed hands frequently. On average about every two or three years someone new lived there. But they were always nice. Occasional neighborly exchanges were had, and peace was maintained.

Before our second summer in the trailer, a hairdresser moved in. Lisa was a single mom that every single trailer-hood guy under forty wanted to get to know. She was sweet, attractive, and very nice. Despite her mature age, my friends and I had a crush on her too.

The Glynns lived next door the entire ten years Mom was at the trailer park. The Glynns were an older couple that fit the original concept behind Sylvan Glen. They were both in their mid- to late-sixties, and Mr. Glynn was legally blind.

Our first year there, we didn't say much to Mr. and Mrs. Glynn. Then one late May evening, Mr. Glynn knocked on our door. My summer and subsequent summers were altered that day. I like to think for the better.

When Mr. Glynn spoke, he looked at your face but not your eyes. He wasn't being rude; he just couldn't see your eyes that well. Mr. Glynn, or Eddie, as he was known by the old timers in the park, was a nice man of few soft-spoken words. He was of average height and despite being very round, his gut didn't jiggle when he walked. Instead of a typical belly that hung over a man's pants, Mr. Glynn's stomach somehow held his pants up. I honestly don't know how he walked without tipping over.

Considering his shape, age, and disability, what Mr. Glynn did in his spare time seems incredible, if not inspiring. It's a story you hear from retired guys all the time: "I just do it to stay busy."*

My first full summer living in the trailer park was fast approaching. Mr. Glynn knocked on our door, then climbed down our porch. In our trailer park, that's what you often had to do. Most of the time the "porch" was really just four fiberglass steps, a less-than-sturdy handrail, and a small landing just big enough for either one person or one half-open screen door, but not both simultaneously.

I opened the door to see Mr. Glynn standing with one foot on the ground and his right foot on the first step. He was bent over and leaning forward, gripping the handrail for balance.

"Is it Steve or Stephen?" he asked in a gruff voice. I told him Steve was fine, fearing I was in trouble for something. "I got a business proposition for you," he said. "Are you interested in making a little money this summer?"

Any fear of trouble washed away. "Sure, Mr. Glynn!" I replied, only to suffer a feeling of dread immediately afterward. "Oh shit," I thought, "what did I just agree to?"

The wisdom behind the statement is severely underrated. The resulting action(s) behind the statement is most likely responsible for prolonging the lives of retired, elderly people everywhere. It gives them purpose. I imagine it helps well-seasoned marriages last longer too. You know, "til death do us part." You can either live and stay active or choose to wait and die. And as long as you can still get around, speak, and interact with others, you had better keep moving and stay in the game.

I knew what Mr. Glynn did in his spare time around the trailer park. I often spotted him walking behind his Craftsman push mower, heading to or from a customer's home. His cutting hours were mid-morning and early evening. He spent the middle of the day in the shade of his shed, listening to the radio and maintaining his silver Sears and Roebuck mowing machine.

"I'm getting up there in age, and I'm afraid I have more lawns than I can handle this year," he said. "There are a few—one large lot in particular—that I just can't do." He invited me to meet Mr. and Mrs. Hayes the following evening. "If you do a good job for Mr. Hayes," he offered, "maybe you can pick up a few more customers this summer."

Mr. Glynn turned to leave. I gathered myself and asked him for more details, skipping the most important question: How much does it pay? He answered a couple questions, cut off the conversation, and walked away, leaving me to wonder, what I was getting myself into.

Mom's face lit up when I told her about my new gig. Before I told the full story, I knew Mom was in on it. I'd been played.

Here Comes the Entrepreneur

The seven-minute walk from Shorebreeze to the Hayes's trailer home felt like an eternity. I had questions, but I had no idea how to bring them up to my stoic neighbor.

As we approached the roundabout median near the front of the park, Mr. Glynn threw a few more surprises my way. On top of mowing, I'd be weed eating and bagging up the clippings.

A few Simpson-esque bumps in the road were starting to rear their ugly head. I was no stranger to cutting grass. I did plenty of that at Luther Vista. But if you waited too long between cuttings, the clippings clumped up behind the mower. Bill Simpson would frown, and we boys would have to do a few hours of raking. As much as I hated raking, I shuddered at the thought of bagging clippings. Stopping a lawn mower every five minutes to bag clippings is not what I wanted to do this summer.

Plus, he wanted trimming done too? I don't want to say trimmers are fancy or a luxury, but we never owned one. Since I didn't have a trimmer or a bagging mower, why was this guy, Mr. Hayes, going to pay me to cut his lawn? "Mr. Glynn," I said, "I don't own a trimmer."

"You worry too much kid," Mr. Glynn responded, without so much as a nod in my direction.

Mr. and Mrs. Hayes came out through the side door as we walked up. They were clearly expecting us. Lyman reached out his hand to shake mine, and I didn't see it right away. Eddie bumped my arm as a "wake-up call." Realizing my error, I quickly, nervously, shook Mr. Hayes's hand.

"I'm not sure what Eddie told you about our situation but let me show you the mower you'll be using," Mr. Hayes explained. It was one of the greatest things about the greatest generation. The men of that time did not B.S. you when it came to work or a job. They communicated with clarity and conviction.

Don't get me wrong. I know the WWII folks could shoot the shit with the best of 'em. They were great bullshitters. Mostly because they had the best stories to tell. But when it came to work or business, it was straight to the point.

I spotted something red and shiny as Mr. Hayes waved me toward his backyard, where a brand new, self-propelled, bagging lawn mower awaited me. Mr. Hayes added gas to the mower and walked me through the startup procedure. Then he gave the starter cord a single, easy pull, and the mower started. "This lever inside the handle that looks like a brake," he yelled over the purring motor, "makes it go. Use it to go forward and release it when you need to stop or pull the mower back." He tugged at the lever, sending the mower lurching forward so quickly it almost got away from him.

I listened the best I could, but it was difficult. I was in awe. A mower that starts on the first pull, has a safety cut off, and pushes itself? This was a Cadillac compared to the mowers I used. Mr. Hayes cut the motor and showed me how to deal with the grass catcher.

"Weather permitting," he said, "we like the grass cut once a week."

He promised six dollars for each cut and an additional dollar every other week for cutting the little extra lot in the back and trimming. Before I could admit to not having a trimmer he pointed to an electric

Toro trimmer hanging on a hook in his shed. Then he pointed to two fifty-foot extension cords on a shelf. "There's an outlet toward the back of our trailer to plug it in," he said. "The key to the shed is hanging on a hook under our porch. If we aren't here when you come over to cut, I'll leave the money under the gas can in the shed."

And that's how it was back then. He never asked if I wanted the job. I'd known him for ten minutes, and he already trusted me with his brand-new lawn mower and the entire contents of his shed. I went through a very brief interview process and was hired on the spot. Back in the day no one turned down a chance to make money. I took my very small part in the multibillion-dollar lawn industry.

A week later I returned for my first week of mowing. I had to stop mowing three times to bag the clippings. I also cut the extra lot and trimmed around the trailer, shed, flowers, and trees. It took an hour, and the seven dollars I earned were all mine. Suck it, Uncle Sam!

To anyone under thirty reading this, seven dollars may not seem like much money. Keep in mind two things. I was only fourteen years old. And minimum wage in 1986 was $3.35 per hour.

I had just finished trimming and was wrapping up one of the fifty-foot extension cords when I heard a screen door open and shut. Mr. Hayes gingerly walked down his porch steps but then walked toward me with purpose and a slight limp. I smiled and asked with trepidation, "How does it look?"

He looked around at his lawn and replied, "It looks great. Nice job. Do you have a minute, Steve?"

"Yeah, sure, Mr. Hayes."

He pointed across the street to a single-wide, older, yet meticulously maintained trailer with a full screened-in porch. "Our friend across the way, Mrs.Brown, is looking to have someone cut her lawn this summer."

Like the previous week, no one asked if I was interested in the gig. It was assumed that if I was willing to cut one lawn, I was willing to cut two.

Mrs. Brown was on her porch tending to some flowers. She looked up and darted out the screen door with the speed and agility of a woman

240

half her age. At the time I guessed that she was in her late sixties or early seventies.

Mrs. Brown was a short, petite woman who spoke very clearly. I believe she was a widow, but I can't remember many details about her life. Unlike Mr. and Mrs. Hayes, Mrs. Brown rarely spoke about her personal life.

She greeted me and Mr. Hayes with an energetic smile. Mr. Hayes excused himself. "See ya next week, Steve," he said as he left me with another aging stranger.

Mrs. Brown motioned me to the side of her trailer that faced the street. "Let me show you the backyard," she said, "and then you can get started." Her ten-cent tour concluded at her well-organized shed.

Inside was a bagging push mower. The green machine was maybe six or seven years old but was in like-new condition. Mrs. Brown proudly pulled it out of the shed. It was the odd style Lawn-Boy with the offset front wheel.

Mrs. Brown went over fueling, startup, and the operating procedure like she was reading it out of the owner's manual. It was an older mower with a two-stroke motor. "You have to mix the oil and gas just right," she explained. "Push the bulb exactly three times and then give it a pull. It should never take more than two pulls."

She was correct. It started right up. Mrs. Brown raised her voice to get over the mower. "When you get done cutting the grass I'll show you the trimmer and where I keep the extension cords. Just knock on the screen door when you're done."

That was the entire discussion. I was suddenly responsible for cutting her lawn too. There was no mention of money or an offer to come back another day if needed. I just got to work.

Her lot was about half the size of the Hayes's, and it only required two stops to bag clippings. But Mrs. Brown insisted I do the trimming every time. When I finished, Mrs. Brown was inside at a little round table with what looked like a glass of tea. She invited me in and told me to have a seat.

Always the observer, I noticed a little coin purse next to her iced tea.

My mind went to scenes from the legendary movie *Caddyshack*. First came the scene where Judge Smails asks Danny if he wants to mow his lawn. Then I thought of an earlier scene during which the judge tips Danny fifty cents for lugging his clubs around all day.

"You did a nice job, Steve. Can you make it over here about every seven to ten days?" Mrs. Brown asked. "How does five dollars sound?"

She took a crisp, folded five-dollar bill from the little purse and handed it to me. I thanked her and turned to leave.

"Steve," she said, holding out another dollar. "Here is a little something extra. See you next week."

Thirteen dollars for an hour and forty-five minutes of cutting, bagging, and trimming grass, without spending a penny on gas. I didn't even own a lawn mower, gas can, or trimmer. Yet I earned more than twice the minimum wage without leaving my neighborhood. My love affair with capitalism began that day. America, what a country!

A few weeks later I added another neighbor to my client list: Mrs. Couch. I even convinced Mom to buy a newer mower and saved up to buy my own little electric trimmer. News of the lawn-cutting kid spread like wildfire through the trailerhood.

By the end of July, I was cutting ten lawns on a weekly basis. I had no idea how it happened, but the clients kept coming. Looking back, I can easily define my three keys to success: price, accountability, and relationships. Big companies charged at least fifteen dollars per lawn. My base price was five dollars, and the most I charged was ten.

Accountability was appreciated by the old folks and hard for me to avoid. If I made a mistake or was late getting to someone's yard, they all knew where I lived. Also, there was no caller ID, and we didn't own an answering machine. Therefore, any call for service was not ignored.

But the major key to my success was the relationships I built with customers. I talked to these people. More importantly, I listened. I hearkened to their stories of yesteryear. I listened to their lists of health ailments and concerns about the state of the country and the world. I heard countless stories about children and grandchildren I never met. When the work was done, I didn't take the money and run. I gave them what they wanted most—a few minutes and an open ear. Some welcomed me into their homes and offered me a cold Pepsi and a story or two.

Like any business that takes off too quickly, it became difficult to provide the same level of service and attention. But I always made time for my original customers. Talking with and listening to stories always gave me a sense that I was doing something good. During my teenage years I didn't get that feeling very often.

Eyes on the Prize

Granted, my primary objective was money. I needed it to buy the one thing I wanted. I had dreamed about exactly two things more than anything else since my eleventh birthday: dirt bikes and cars. I had my dirt bike at the camp, and it was great, but that Honda didn't last long. Now that we lived in a concrete trailer jungle where motorcycles were outlawed, my chief aspiration involved four wheels instead of two. And I didn't just want a car sometime. I wanted it the day I turned sixteen. But I wanted something nicer than Tom and Vic's old Pontiac that kept me from seeing my first and only double header.

As easy as it was to self-motivate during my first summer of cutting lawns, it was even easier the second summer. I turned fifteen in 1987. I was a year away from getting the most coveted piece of plastic any teenage boy possesses. Thanks to my very detail-oriented friend Dean, I was on my way to the joy and freedom of public road automobile operation. But to be honest, growing up in rural Livingston county, I had been driving cars on everything but the interstate since I turned thirteen. I'm not sorry, just honest.

I didn't pay much attention to things in school and extracurricular activities such as Driver's Education. I kept track of the school calendar in anticipation of any days that indicated "no school." I knew about football practice and football games and that was about it. I knew driver's ed existed; I just didn't know how to pursue it.

My friend Dean did. He bugged me about it weekly. He wanted to ensure we were in the class together. We signed up on the first day it was offered. Without Dean I would have just let that key summertime opportunity slip right through my daydreaming mind.

Between driver's ed, cutting grass, and household chores, my schedule was packed. That made it harder to get into trouble, but not impossible.

After a few hours of mindless lessons, driving practice, and death-on-the-highway videos at Howell High School, Dean's sister would pick us up. We usually had homework, which we knocked out in record time. It was easier than standard-issue homework. And unlike algebra, there was a tangible, practical result of completing driver's ed homework. It put us one step closer to attaining our learner's permits.

After homework, Dean tended to chores, and I cut some grass. While mowing lawns I pondered the limited catalog of cars that cost less than $1,000. Thinking about my potential first car made lawn cutting fly by.

In year two of my lawn-cutting service, I picked up a few more lawns and got up to roughly fifteen customers. However, being a teenager was getting expensive. Mom provided the basics, but I had to cover extra-curricular stuff like junk food and other recreational essentials. As a result, I became more proficient at using the automated teller machine than saving cash.

When the grass-cutting season ended, I picked up extra cash raking leaves through October. That left five months of spending money without making any via lawn care. I added as much part-time work and as many odd jobs as my social agenda and lack of transportation allowed. After football season, I worked twelve to fifteen hours with Rick at Universal Electric. Once Uncle Sam took out his FICA slice, I brought home about fifty bucks a week. I made the same at The Doughnut Shop, another job attained courtesy of Mr. Glynn.

Together, these jobs gave me enough to purchase my first automobile.

As bad luck would have it, when I turned sixteen, Denise was dating a used car salesman. We shared the same first name and a passion for four-wheeled American steel. While I buried my head in every AutoTrader I could get my hands on, Steve was secretly keeping an eye out for my first car.

Or should I say *boat*—because that's what I ended up with. Steve came across a trade-in at the dealership that could be had for a song. They were asking $900, but to win favor with the family and do something nice for Denise's little brother, Steve sold it for $750.

My first car. A crushed-velour, slightly less-equipped version of the automobile Ricardo Montalban so elegantly represented in the late 70s. The Chrysler Cordoba. Mine was a golden brown '76 model. It was a luxury car dubbed "The New Small Chrysler." It weighed almost two tons and was eighteen feet long. Thanks to the decade-old car's tired suspension, the car drove at an odd angle, making it difficult to see over the hood.*

I have a few fond memories of that car.

One of the most memorable journeys with the Chrysler was with my pal Josh. It was our first official, unsupervised trip to the Motor City, and we took the 100-mile round trip on a school night to catch a Tigers game.

Thinking about it now makes me question my memory and our parents' states of mind. But I know it happened for two reasons.

1. It remains the coldest baseball game I've ever been to.

2. Toward the end of the game with the stadium almost empty, Josh and I snuck down to the lower deck rail and grabbed a handful of dirt and gravel from the field. Back inside the appropriately nicknamed "Cordoobie," we placed our score in the ashtray. The gravel stayed in the ashtray until the big Chrysler's last day of operation, two months later.

On my second unsupervised trip to Detroit, I took a bunch of friends to the Freedom Festival firework show on the river. The Chrysler got us there, but it didn't quite get us back. Cars need oil changes, and I had too much fun that summer to be concerned with such things.

Fortunately, having transportation for the rest of the summer wasn't necessary. My main source of income was within a half a mile radius of

---

Other notable facts about my Chrysler: It got subpar gas mileage (about 10 miles per gallon), had an extremely inaccurate fuel gauge that floated on the dashboard like a bobber on a windy day, and included the factory eight-track player. Speaking of—Dean's sister donated four tapes to my pitiful cause. My entire secondhand play list consisted of Led Zeppelin IV, Black Sabbath Paranoid, AC/DC Back In Black, and a nonworking Judas Priest tape. The sound was bad, and I wedged a match book under the tape to keep it from jumping tracks.

161 Shorebreeze, so I really didn't need a car. Besides, my girlfriend that summer had a car that I borrowed while she was at work. All my friends had cars too. So, I got by.

The Hunt Resumes

Fortunately, I wasn't without transportation for long. Dad, for whatever reason, had two pickup trucks: a newer Dodge Dakota and the F-150 we put in the lake a few years earlier. With football season around the corner, life was about to get busy. Everyone in my family was too busy to take me to practice twice a day.

Mom leaned into Dad, who loaned me his old truck for a good portion of my junior year. Somehow, even this gift was a trap. I learned after accepting the truck that the terms were simple. I use the truck for free, and Dad finds my next vehicle. Once again, Bill Simpson wanted to be a hero and save the day. Dad yearned to demonstrate his automobile expertise by finding the perfect set of wheels for his teenage boy.

When the junk man picked up the Cordoobie, I traded the title for thirty-five bucks. Not a good start to purchasing my second car. Eager to get out of Dad's formerly waterlogged truck as soon as possible, I went back to spending less, mooching off my friends, and cutting grass as if my life depended on it. I did not want to spend my last two years of High School driving Dad's brown camper-top-clad F-150.

Dad was equally motivated to find my next vehicle. He preferred having his F-150 outside his apartment where it was safe. Dad loved us, but he had trust issues. With our track record of vehicle care and maintenance, I can't blame him. Then I gave him another reason not to trust me.

For years it was the most dangerous intersection in Livingston County. In between Howell and Brighton, eastbound travelers on Grand River had two choices: veer to the right to get on eastbound I-96 or veer left to continue on Grand River, AFTER and only AFTER coming to an immediate and complete life saving STOP! The stop was necessary because oncoming cars were zooming off of I-96 inches from your front bumper at highway speeds. There was a red blinking light and two large stop signs. The traffic accidents at that intersection were legendary.

At this point, I need to remind readers that Dad's brown Ford truck once spent several hours completely submerged in water and was never the same afterward. Keep that in mind.

It was raining after school in early November. My friend Josh and I were headed to my place. Probably for some Bible study or to work on homework together. (Laugh out loud.) I approached the ridiculous intersection and began to veer left while depressing the brake pedal. Nothing happened. I quickly and more forcefully pressed the brake pedal again—and again, nothing happened. With the wheel still slightly turned left, I slammed both feet on the brakes. Thank God for the stop sign on the right.

The brakes locked up and never released, sending the truck into a sideways spin toward the intersection. The passenger door and side mirror of my father's truck slammed into the stop sign, bringing us to a halt and keeping us from entering oncoming traffic.

After making sure Josh and I were okay, I started the truck back up and pumped the brakes like they were on fire. They released, and I slammed the truck into gear. I finished running over the stop sign, and Josh and I proceeded down Grand River.

Terrified to tell Dad about the damage, I avoided him for weeks. When I visited him, I parked the truck in a way that hid the evidence of my driving crime. A month later, I finally got the courage to tell Dad, knowing he would find out eventually. He wasn't even that mad. It was almost like he expected me to mess his truck up one way or another. Once again, he was right.

It only took a few months of driving Dad's truck for Dad to find me a "winner" for my next vehicle. Only it wasn't a running winner. It was a cool, faded apple-red, 1967 Ford Custom F-100. It had white wagon wheels and a three-on-the-tree standard transmission. I had to wait several months for Dad to correct its mechanical issues.

When I did start driving it—wow! It got looks and compliments everywhere I went. Every week another stranger asked if it was for sale. It also came in handy for the lawn-cutting business. Despite the perks, it was slow, handled slightly better than a Ford tractor, and wasn't a practical daily driver.

Through cutting more lawns and convincing Mom to help me out, I bought a car, too. The white '78 Buick Regal had a shade-tree mechanic-built 350 in it. That car was fast—too fast for the brakes and suspension and a kid who only had his license for a year. The rear tires on that car only lasted a few months at a time. Additionally, the back glass leaked, the power steering locked up in the rain, and the engine randomly overheated without warning. But man, I had fun in that car.

I was a seventeen-year-old high school student with two vehicles, a growing business, a part-time job, a new girlfriend, and football in the fall—way too much shit on my plate! Something had to give. I chose the thing I was least interested in: my academic career at Howell High.

I picked up so many lawns in the summer of 1989 that I took on an employee, sort of. I'm not sure what circumstances led to my brother Victor being unemployed and completely lost in life, but I had more lawns than I could handle, and he needed beer money.

Victor put himself in charge of equipment repair and maintenance. He also cut the ten lawns near the back of Sylvan Glen that didn't require as much personal attention. Victor's best quality was his purchasing power. At twenty-four years old he brought the one thing to my lawn business I could not provide: a legal ID. At the end of each lawn-cutting day, he took my truck and bought beer for us and my friends too. Again, I'm not proud of the things we did, I'm just being honest. It was all about the party and having a good time.

With everything going on, it was a miracle I "earned" my diploma. Some days I woke up and pretended I was going to school. Once Mom left for work, I went back to bed. When I woke up hours later, I cut grass.

Occasionally, an elderly customer asked why I wasn't at school. I got good at lying. They usually bought what I was selling or they enjoyed my company too much to dig any deeper.

My lackluster attendance sent me over the threshold of what I called the Tom and Vic Rule. I know I'm wrong here, but I have to blame someone. I swear the school system implemented a ten-absences rule in

1985, immediately after my brothers graduated—despite being absent a third of their senior years. The rule was simple. No matter how well you did in a class, once you accumulated ten or more absences in a semester, you received two letter grades instead of one. Those letters were NC, a.k.a. no credit. I had the mindset that once I lost credit there was no reason to continue going.

This didn't sit well with the family. Most of my siblings and Mom rode me about graduating, so I earned just enough credits to pass. It took summer school, night school, and gracious teachers, but I made it. In the process, I let everyone down in my life, but I squeaked by in the standard four years. There was no way I was coming back for a fifth year.

At the time, I had no regrets. I was working, providing a valuable service to senior citizens, and having the time of my life—or so I thought. It took me exactly three semesters of high school to realize I didn't want to be there. I started partying. I stopped growing as a person, and I just didn't care.

Much like a delayed hangover, those regrets eventually reared their ugly heads. Nightmares plagued me for nearly two decades. I was haunted by my high-school missteps. In dreams, I tried to do things differently. I went to class, studied, and worked hard at football practice. But every time, I would be left running between school, jobs, lawns, football, friends, and parties. I would try to stay on top of it all. But the dream always ended the same—me failing at everything, disappointing everyone, and waking up in a cold sweat of regret.

Decades removed from my foolishness, I repeat the old saying with strong conviction: "Stay in school." Actually, do more than that. Go outside your comfort zone. Talk to and befriend people outside of your circle. Get involved and be the best version of yourself you can be.* File petitions. Involve your parents and others. Ensure your time

---

*This may involve pushing back against the elites that run the public school system. If you feel the government employees who administer ridiculous policies and procedures are not acting in the best interest of the student body, speak out. If some grouchy, old, no-fun, over-educated fool decries "No pre-ceremony beach balls," stand up and say, "Hey, Mr. Hand, this is OUR time TOO"!

isn't dominated by one-sided agendas that stunt your personal growth and infringe upon your values, beliefs, and freedoms. The citizens of the community fund that school system. The kids and parents should have a say as to what goes on behind those doors.

Your high-school years happen only one time. Hopefully you can revisit them often with a smile. Because once you grab that diploma and exit stage right, it's over. There is no going back.

Chapter Thirty-Two

IF WILLIE AND ELAINE WERE ALIVE TODAY

At the risk of chasing away dozens of readers, I'm going to get a little biblical. I admit I'm only a tiny bit familiar with the Good Book, but I know it's full of great wisdom and everlasting truths.

There's a statement that appears numerous times throughout the Bible. It is seriously simple and should never be minimized. Of all the regrets I have, I wish I made it a more significant part of my life.

"Honor your father and your mother."

No matter how religious or agnostic, everyone has one absolute, irrefutable thing in common. We all come from two people. If you love them or even if you hate them, the fact remains, your mom and dad made you.*

Most of us do know how we got here and who made our being a reality. For us the instructions are clear: "Honor your father and your mother." Without that man and that woman, where would you be and how would you have gotten here? No matter how awful any two parents might be—without them, you wouldn't exist.

Now that we have all the qualifiers out of the way, here it is, one more time: Honor them. Note that it doesn't say *love* them. It doesn't say

---

I feel for the exceptions out there—those who grew up not knowing their parents. I'm not sure how I would deal with that. To those unfortunate souls, take comfort that you got a seat at someone's table. And honor the ones who made you or the ones who took you in.

respect, *cherish*, or *like* them. It doesn't say *agree* with them at all turns, but rather to give them honor.

At this point, I'm sure some readers will argue I didn't treat my parents with the respect they deserve. That I was crude toward my father and—at times—far too sarcastic with my parents. And maybe I was. Maybe I should have kept a few things to myself.

If you feel I should have kept quiet at certain points, I have a question. Is there anything in this book that dishonors Mom and Dad? Did I make anything up? Did I lie about who my mother and father were?

If Mom and Dad were alive today, they certainly would take exceptions with things I've written. They would do this out of embarrassment or wanting to remember the past in a better light. They both would be defensive about certain details pertinent to our upbringing. They would believe and argue that they did a better job than some of these pages depict. But to me, this book is the ultimate badge of honor. Like many couples of their generation, my parents had the deck stacked against them. Between them they had one high school diploma, no idea what they wanted out of life, and few examples of good, loving marriages to mold their relationship after.

There were no support groups or parenting classes. Marriage counseling was in its infancy. In the '50s and '60s, seeking outside help with domestic problems was seen as weakness and failure. Any problems were dealt with "in house." During their first fifteen years together, my parents were winging it.

They used that same off-the-cuff approach when it came to raising their children. Making a kid is the easy part. Now we have to care for this living, breathing seed? We have to provide for these souls—provide things we barely provide for ourselves? To this day, I would give $1,000 to see Dad's face the moment he found out his wife was pregnant with twins! Any parenting knowledge they possessed came via on-the-job training.

In the early twentieth century, low-income parents weren't concerned with their kids' psyche, self-confidence, or social adaptiveness. The only priorities were in this order: food, clothing, and shelter. All other child rearing was performed on accident or of desperation. Yes desperation. I imagine many parents thought, "If we put all our eggs in one basket and raise little Johnny a tad better than the rest of 'em, maybe he can dig us out of this hole we've dug ourselves into."

Dad's mom, Mamaw Dixie, was full of knowledge and faith with a dash of piss and vinegar sprinkled in. Once while walking with Tommy and Denise at Luther Vista, they came across a Michigan rattler (Eastern massasauga rattlesnake) slithering across their path. Before my brother and sister could react, Mamaw Dixie was beating that satanic creature into the ground with her cane. As any good brother would do, Tommy later showed me the remains.

Mamaw had the survival skills of a Navy Seal, could clean any stain, and make a meal for ten with leftovers and scraps. But was she a good mother? Did she raise her kids right and teach them all she knew about parenting? I have no idea. But she kept her kids alive and surely passed some life skills to her offspring.

Mom's dad was probably the best parent of my four grandparents. He had a calm, calculated, endearing demeanor and spoke only when he meant it. But I don't know what kind of parent he was to Mom and Uncle Bill.

Money was tight when Mom was young. Grandpa was a frugal man who made every dollar stretch as far as he could. He kept things way past their intended lifespan and even used and reused paper towels until they fell apart in his hands.

If he got upset, he rarely showed it, and he was a good listener. But did any of those characteristics get passed down to Mom?

Thankfully, they did. Mom was usually slow to anger, and she generally listened when we had something to say. She presented us with options as young adults and taught us to consider multiple solutions to problems. You know, the old "There's more than one way to skin a cat" speech. It's a very cliché lesson that bailed me out of several jams.

She must have gleaned this wisdom from her father, but I suspect she didn't heed all his words.

Mom was rebellious and stubborn as a young adult. Through her early twenties, she disregarded what any adult had to say, including her mother and father. I'm sure William Simpson was not Grandpa's first choice for a suitor. The wedding pictures illustrate his feelings quite well.

Black Sheep and Light at the End of the Tunnel

Ignoring all of the obvious, bold, large print signs, Bill and Elaine married and started multiplying. They did have one original plan after my oldest brother arrived on the scene. They wanted three and only three kids. My parents . . . Even when they did take time to plan, things still got messed up.

So now the moment of truth has arrived. The grades are out. Would Mom and Dad be happy or proud of any of us? Would they consider any of our lives good and successful? Did we achieve better lives than they enjoyed? Just how far did we fly?

The short answer: We all grew feathers. While this isn't a Hollywood feel-good story with a nice little bow at the end, it's not a horror show either. None of us ended up in prison.

When it comes to most things human, nothing has to be forever. People can change. Even the darkest souls can find meaning and see the light. Any life can be saved, and any person can find purpose. But for those with little faith and no clear path, the journey back can be long and complicated.

Throughout the history of my family, three of us have been the family's black sheep. Although out of embarrassment, prayer, and hope that things would change, none of us ever officially carried the black sheep label. To my siblings and other family members, calling myself out might seem like a stretch but, if the wool fits, right?

I was a petty thief in my middle school years. I didn't steal for fun. I stole due to a lack of funds, and I stole things that were illegal for me to purchase and possess. I started practicing the art of truancy my freshman year of high school. One attempt landed me in the back of a police car. That should have raised some red flags.

Like most rebellious young men, I spent a couple of nights in jail. I drank too much, used numerous illegal substances, and in my twenties considered "having a good time" my only hobby. I always had a job though. Couldn't let the party bus run out of fuel. Sometimes I would cut just enough lawns to buy half a tank of gas, a bag of breadsticks at Gus's, and a twelve pack or a bottle. *Party on, Wayne!*

Speaking of buses . . . I totaled three cars before turning twenty-two. I've been in two motorcycle accidents. At the absolute worst possible time I had my driver's license taken away. Convincing my employer that I could still drive a commercial vehicle with a court summons hanging over my head was one of the worst Mondays of my life.

I have, on occasion, distanced myself from family—even my daughter and wife. I've battled depression and for years at a time walked away from the church and my faith. I can't stand authority, and I question rules and the bureaucratic assholes who create them.

Does my past qualify me as a certified black sheep? I bet most families out there would be talking about me behind my back. As plans are made for family gatherings, would my name be last on the invite list or left off all together? During the holiday season, maybe my address and phone number would be curiously misplaced. The disgrace and embarrassment my family endured from my poor choices never lasted long. I was the youngest of five, and to the youngest go the spoils. The spoils came in the form of cover-ups and excuses. I rarely got the book—at least not the entire book—thrown at me.

I'm not proud of my list of mistakes. I often wonder how—or why—I'm still alive. I still don't have an answer. But I credit God and some luck.

For years, Tommy was considered the real black sheep. He battled demons, struggled to stay on the right track, and still fights with self-destructive ways to this day. But like me, Tommy was graced by some gifts from God.

From his earliest days to well into his forties and fifties, Tommy has had a dynamic personality. He's full of energy, optimism, and hope. Everyone he meets likes him, and he never runs out of things to share and talk about. Tommy's personality has saved him time and time again, acting as a life preserver in the rough seas of life.

Tommy and I agree—neither of us deserve the breaks we've received through life. By the grace of God, forgiveness of our sins, faith, and good fortune, we are still on the path. It's a path littered with forks, narrow shoulders, hairpin switch backs, and the occasional U-turn.

The Call of Heartbreak

I love Tom and Vic. I have faith in Tommy and myself that we can redeem ourselves and accomplish something worthwhile. For these reasons, I can't label any of us as black sheep.

That said, chapter fourteen discusses the third black sheep in this story. But I wrote that chapter over six years ago. A more accurate description of Victor is dark gray. In his twenties, he let himself down and those around him a handful of times. But his downward spiral grew serious in his mid-thirties.

Victor was not evil. No one considered him worthless. He was just different. He didn't always fit in, and he kept too many things inside. Victor was hard to get to know or talk to, and he didn't listen well. But he's my brother, and I love him.

While working on this book one Saturday in late January, I received the phone call I dreaded for years. It was the Oakland County Medical Examiner's Office. They informed me that Victor, my long-lost brother, passed away.

If you knew Victor and lost touch with him, I'm sorry if you're just learning of his death. He died tragically young, completely alone, and—to my knowledge—with very little faith in God.

He passed away in his early fifties. At the time of his death, he hadn't contacted family for several months. Some family members hadn't spoken to him in years. We don't know how he died. I believe he simply gave up.

As much as it hurt, his death wasn't surprising. I'd expected that phone call for some time. He had several health issues, some which were irreversible. He suffered from alcohol and prescription medication abuse. He suffered from lack of direction. He suffered from mental illness. But most of all, he suffered from too much pride. He was always going to do things his way, even if it killed him.

If we knew how bad things were with Vic, we would have tried to help. We would have done anything to make his last days comfortable.

But for reasons only known to him, he left us in the dark. Our contact information hadn't changed in years. On a phone near his body, all of our names and numbers were just a few buttons away. So why didn't he call? We'll never know.

My father and mother died in 2013 and 2014, respectively. Victor died in late 2018. So, even though Victor passed away too soon, at least my parents were spared the ultimate tragedy. Burying a son or daughter. I've heard people say that such pain has no equal, no comparison.

Parental Report Card

If I had to grade my parents, I would give them an S—satisfactory. They weren't to blame for our shortcomings, and they don't deserve much credit for any of our accomplishments. However, they did enough to give us a fighting chance. And in life that's all you can ask for. While none of us lived up to our full potential—and here I can only speak for myself—it's been a pretty good life.

How would Mom and Dad grade themselves? I hope that they wouldn't beat themselves up too much. They gave us what we needed to move up the ladder of life. Sure, they lacked in several key categories, but they did their best with what they had.

It's easy to say that my wife and I have done better than my parents. We have a stronger marriage and more stable finances, and we worked hard to raise our daughter in a loving home. But we started at different places than my parents. Comparing our lives would be like pitting an apple against a 1,500-pound state fair pumpkin.

When I met my wife, we were both in our mid-twenties. We had a lifetime of experiences compared to when my parents first got together. I was a homeowner, and my future wife was living on her own, already paying her own way. We had steady employment, dependable transportation, and common goals and dreams.

Once we got married, we started our own version of winging it. We lived paycheck to paycheck, had no clear career paths, and were basically having a good time. That didn't last long.

Our lack of planning and preparation led to a late summer surprise.

Almost a year to the day we married, we found out we were multiplying. Outside, I was smiling. Inside, I was crapping my stonewashed denim shorts. I still had much to learn about being a decent husband. Now I'm gonna be a father, too?

That was twenty years ago. Today, I can confidently give my wife a big high five. Our daughter was in the school band for seven years. She is more mature in her late teens than I am now. She doesn't use profanity. She has strong faith and direction. She lives a clean life. And she has a level of compassion and consideration that would make any parent proud.

My nephew is a pretty good egg too. My sister, Denise, raised him right and kept him involved with everything and anything. He plays baseball at the rec center and softball for the church league. He's in the church youth group and helps with Bible camp in the summer. He plays in his school band, is liked by everyone he meets, and has a heart rivaled only in size by his typical teenage boy ego.

If William and Elaine were alive today, they would smile with pride at their two grandchildren. They wouldn't be able to help themselves. Seeing the next generation would give them some satisfaction. Maybe it would help them go easy on themselves.

My three remaining siblings and I have been blessed to see and do things that seemed unattainable twenty or thirty years ago. And for the four of us, life goes on. In my case, life is exceptional considering my lack of direction and checkered past.

Hopefully, Victor is in a better place also, perhaps at peace for the first time. I hope to see him again, just not too soon. When I do, I'll hug him and smile. Love you, bro. Missed you too. And we will talk about the good ole days as if he had never left.

Still Learning

The things that I've learned while writing this book are priceless. I've learned some family history and some things about myself. As I put together the last few paragraphs of this chapter, something hit me like a left hook.

Being the youngest by seven years and having better health than I deserve, I will likely say goodbye to my three remaining siblings before I die. I hope and pray those days don't come around soon.

To the youngest go the spoils, the memories, and all remaining tears. I will never forget my parents or any of my siblings. For how they all had a hand in raising me and for everything they did for me over the years, I will always remember them. I will always *Remember When*.

All seven Simpsons at a picnic table in front of the swimming pond at Camp Luther Vista. As dysfunctional as our family was, we had our moments. This picture was one of them.

EPILOGUE

While my mother and father did an adequate job raising us, I wish they did something other parents (including TV parents) do. I wish they encouraged us. What difference would their encouragement have had on our lives? I'll never know.

Throughout childhood, the adolescent years, and our twenties and thirties, my siblings and I were never pushed. Our parents taught us about hard work, but they never encouraged us to be all we could be. We were shown how to meet expectations, not exceed them. We were never told we could do anything we wanted. We never considered becoming extraordinary. Instead, we settled for ordinary. Our parents never expected anything more.

On occasions when we dreamed of more from life, Mom and Dad acted like the parental fire department. "Fire Marshall Bill here. I heard you had a dream that was getting you hot and excited. Let me put out that fire!" With Dad, it was an ego and jealousy thing. None of his dreams came true, so he wasn't about to sit around and encourage his kids to reach their full potential.

Even when it came to something not so dreamy, Dad was less than supportive. A leap up the ladder of life by a couple of rungs was met with a slow golf clap. When I literally doubled my income in two months time, Dad seemed uninterested. His ego wouldn't let him celebrate my victory.

Mom put out dreams to keep us safe and protect us from getting hurt. She literally once said to my sister, "If you don't set your expectations too high, they will never let you down."

We were never pushed. We were taught to always limit risk or eliminate it all together. Don't take chances or stick your head out there for anything or anybody, as it will just get chopped off. We were never inspired to go after something that was out of reach.

Instead of being pushed into difficult situations, we were pulled out of them. Every time life got tough, Mom's tow truck rescued us. It became a way of life for Tom, Vic, and me. No matter how much we screwed up, Mom bailed us out. *Hook up the chain!*

The same chain that repeatedly saved us from ourselves also prevented us from learning from our mistakes. It was a personal growth stopper. If there are no consequences from poor judgment, then there is no accountability. Nothing was learned and we continued making the same mistakes over and over again.

We were never pushed, and we were never taught to go after things we really wanted. We always took the easy road, the road less scary and most traveled. We were never instructed how to take the ball and score. Simpsons feared taking action. We were always on defense. That's why it was such a big deal for Mom to go back to school when she did. It was one of the few times she went after something she truly wanted. Even then, desperation played a bigger role than desire.

Football is the rare sport that allows a team to score on defense. It's my favorite game and offers many great lessons. But life is not football. In life you need to be on offense. In life, you need the ball to score. Mom and Dad never encouraged us to go on offense and attack life.

For years, I thought about what could have been. But I can't go back in time. I can't guarantee that pushing us to be better and teaching us to expect more out of life would have made any difference. Maybe we would have achieved more. Or maybe we would have pointed at Dad's win-loss record in life, laughed, and said, "No thanks. I don't believe in myself or my gene pool. Why add pain to my life while confirming what I suspect to be true?"

That said, I would have liked the chance to overachieve. That's what this book is—my attempt to do more than just get by and meet expectations. My moment to shine, to turn a dream into a reality.

Failure is a possibility. Getting kicked in the face and having my kneecaps bitten off feels scary. Despite this, selling a few copies of this book and launching a new, successful endeavor sounds invigorating! Whatever the result, I only have one regret. I should have gotten my head out of my ass and done it sooner.

Too many people treat life like an exhibition game. Do you long for a better you? Do you want to do more? Do you want to fulfill a dream or two before the end of practice? Does meeting expectations have you stuck in a rut?

If you want change, you have to be honest. Look into a mirror and come clean with who you are and who you want to become. Self-evaluation is the beginning of any new journey, and it starts with a full acknowledgment of your current reality. Where are you now, how did you get there, and where do you want to go?

Personally, I'm sick of getting pulled around. I want to be pushed. I want to push myself. I want to push through to a better life. I want to push so hard that I never again get pulled into that powerful, destructive, life-sucking state of regret. It's one of the worst places any person can be. Nothing kills more time and squashes more dreams.

So, get up and get going. Put in the extra effort. Ask forgiveness when you mess up. Respect yourself and serve people. Find purpose and practice the art of consistent discipline. Do this day after day, week after week, year after year, and you'll outrun regret. You may even make the world a better place in the process.

ACKNOWLEDGMENT

A few words of thanks from a grateful first-time author.

I need to take a few lines to thank everyone who helped and inspired me throughout the years and all the people who helped make this book a reality.

First, thank you, God. You gave me this life, and I'm thankful for every moment.

A big shout-out and thank-you to all my childhood friends who added adventure to my life and saved my ass a few times along the way. To Matt, Chuck, and Jason for all the times we spent goofing off around Euler Road and Sylvan Glen. To my good friend Dean for getting me to drivers' education, bailing me out of more than a few tight spots, and all the good times we shared.

Thank you, Jessica, for the wonderful cover art that captured a common Simpson moment in pencil.

To neighborhood friends, thanks for opening your homes to Heather and I and allowing us to escape the trials of life with some cold beer, good music, and laughter. To Scott and Brook, thanks for all those games of pool. To Kent and Becky, thanks for the fireworks and four-wheel adventures at your freedom-loving estate. To Charlie, thanks for showing Victor and me around Lake Lanier and saving our bacon out there. Thanks to Sheri for introducing me to the love of my life.

Thanks to Scott and the rest of the fellas and gals at MTT. You all made that challenging job much more tolerable. Without you people looking out for me, I would have quit years ago.

To Mike, thanks for providing inspiration with your new castle on the hill and some classic moments in our youth and recently too.

To my good friend Josh—you definitely saved my ass more than a few times. But you also taught me to stick up for myself. So many fun times. I've forgotten more than I can remember. Here is to never again sleeping on the steps of Rick's American Cafe. Some of the family vacation moments from the last twenty years are truly legendary. I am a big, fat jerk.

To the wise couples that inspired and guided my wife and I over the course of our marriage: Nick and Marilyn, Greg and Sue. Thanks for leading by example. Thanks to Mel and Alice for some fun conversation about the good ole days.

Thanks to Pastor Andy for doing so much for our family over the years and providing so much calming wisdom. Thank you everyone at CLC for always giving us a warm welcome.

A big thank-you to my editor, Daniel, or as we call him around my house, The Slasher. Your wisdom and patience is appreciated. Thanks for showing this first-time author how it's done.

Thank you, Uncle Bill and Aunt Sandy for the summer adventures you treated us to and all your hospitality.

A special thanks to my cousin Billy for reading rough drafts of several chapters and making me believe I could actually do this writing thing. You make me laugh and think simultaneously. Thanks to my extended family for all the memorable moments over the last half century. Thanks to Carrie and Al for stopping by and giving us some positive energy regarding our risk-taking venture.

Some thanks go out to a couple of in-laws. Thanks, Dad, for tolerating me all these years and for giving me this beautiful desk on which I wrote almost every word of this book. Thank you, Chris, for helping me consider the other side of things and for giving me the book that has changed my life.

Thank you to grill master Paul for helping raise my nephew and everything else you have done for our family and my sister. Thank you, Janet for getting my brother back to the Mitten, his true home.

A gigantic thank-you to my family. To my siblings—without you this book never would have happened. Victor, we love and miss you. To Denise, Rick, and Tommy, thank you for keeping me alive and making my childhood so much better than it ever should have been. To Mom and Dad, thanks for bringing me into this world and giving me a fighting chance.

To my nephew Ricky—I'm a better man today because of you. I strive to be a good role model for you, and I am driven daily by that desire. Call me anytime. You are the last Simpson man. No pressure. Just do better than we did. I know you will.

To my daughter, Stephanie. You are the main reason I wrote this. If I don't leave you another thing in this world, at least you will have this book. Learn from our mistakes and laugh at our misfortunes. Our afternoon chats inspired me to be a better father, more than you'll ever know.

To my wife, Heather. I would need to author another book to thank you. For everything you do, for the faith you have always had in me. I will never fully understand why you continue to be by my side, but I'm so very glad you are. Without you, none of my dreams would come true. Thank you, Cookie. Your loving husband forever, Stephen McKinley.